Playing with History

Playing with History

American Identities and

Children's Consumer Culture

MOLLY ROSNER

RUTGERS UNIVERSITY PRESS

NEW BRUNSWICK, CAMDEN, AND NEWARK,

NEW JERSEY, AND LONDON

Library of Congress Cataloging-in-Publication Data

Names: Rosner, Molly, 1986- author.
Title: Playing with history : American identities and children's consumer culture /
    Molly Rosner.
Description: New Brunswick, New Jersey : Rutgers University Press, [2021] |
    Revision of author's thesis (doctoral)—Rutgers University, 2017, titled Playing with
    history : American identities and children's consumer culture, 1917–2017. | Includes
    bibliographical references and index.
Identifiers: LCCN 2020035572 | ISBN 9781978822085 (cloth) | ISBN 9781978822078
    (paperback) | ISBN 9781978822092 (epub) | ISBN 9781978822108 (mobi) |
    ISBN 9781978822115 (pdf)
Subjects: LCSH: Toys—Social aspects—United States—History—20th century. | Toy
    industry—United States—Marketing. | Child consumers—United States—History. |
    Material culture—United States. | Children—United States—Social conditions—
    20th century. | National characteristics, American—History.
Classification: LCC HQ784.T68 R67 2021 | DDC 306.4/60973—dc23
LC record available at https://lccn.loc.gov/2020035572

A British Cataloging-in-Publication record for this book is available from the British Library.

♾ The paper used in this publication meets the requirements of the American National
Standard for Information Sciences—Permanence of Paper for Printed Library Materials,
ANSI Z39.48-1992.

www.rutgersuniversitypress.org

Manufactured in the United States of America

For my parents,
David and Kathy

With love and gratitude for going way beyond your job description.

Contents

Playing with History

Introduction

Out of the most diverse threads of information, picked up in the most casual way, from the most unrelated sources . . . there is lodged in [our] mind a mass of unrelated and related information and misinformation [we] fashion a history.   —*Carl Becker, 1931*[1]

When I was a child my grandmother supplied me with wonderful books full of characters of a wide range of races, colors, and ethnic backgrounds. She selected these carefully, passionate about the need for children's literature to represent all children. She was a nursery schoolteacher for thirty years and then worked for nearly a decade at New York City's Head Start program. At the age of fifty-two she returned to graduate school and wrote her dissertation on racism in children's picture books. In it she argued, "Until white adults are sensitized to recognize the insidious and obtrusive manifestations of racism in children's books, even well-meaning authors, artists, publishers, reviewers, librarians, teachers, and parents will continue to perpetuate the institutionalized racism which characterized their own education."[2] Hearing my grandmother talk about this as I got older, I came to appreciate how important it was to pay close attention to what children were being taught through books, dolls, and other childhood entertainments. I came to see that these childhood amusements, even those that were ostensibly about history, told us a great deal more about the world in which they were produced. The books she selected for me in the 1980s also reflected a nationwide shift toward multicultural curricula and progressive schools.

Then, when I was twenty, I heard my father, who is a historian, testify in a trial against the manufacturers of lead paint who were accused of knowingly marketing the toxic substance to children and their parents. The trial exposed previously unseen documents in which company officials discussed the dangers of lead paint and how to keep the public from knowing about them. What caught my attention most were small coloring books that had been distributed to children in the 1920s and 1930s to encourage them to urge their parents to buy lead paint to brighten their toys, walls, and furniture and to make their rooms cheerful, happy places to play. Although these companies used children to promote their products, and weaseled their way into the identities and toy rooms of American children, they blamed and pointed fingers at parents when it came time to hold them responsible for poisoning their consumers. These coloring books, these child's "playthings," when considered in context, make evident that children are conduits for ideology and their playthings are a battleground where companies generate goodwill while disavowing responsibility for causing children harm.

When I began my doctoral program, I encountered the work of Warren Susman, Fredric Jameson, and Arjun Appadurai, who each identified the crucial lessons we can take from examining "cultural artifacts," the objects and sites of everyday life. In his *Culture as History* Susman argues that historians can consult, in addition to written documents, other sources of information, including artifacts, to understand a particular culture at a given time. According to Susman, objects found in homes, stores, or sites of everyday life can all be studied to obtain insight into the cultures and people who created them. Appadurai and Jameson's examinations of consumer patterns, cultural artifacts, and the ambiguous line between history and memory, reinforced for me the idea that children's coloring books, picture books, and storybooks, as well as dolls, toys, and other amusements deserve serious study.

The toys we loved as children introduced each of us to ideas about our nation, in my case, America, and ushered us into the consumer world. My mother's fond memories of playing the board game *Park & Shop* in the 1950s introduced her to the very American activity of driving to a suburban shopping center. My father remembers his toy tiger, Tony, as "probably related" to the mascot on the box of Kellogg's cereal. My brother's Hess truck, the product of a gas company, appeared on our TV screen each Christmas and found its way into our home. My own American Girl dolls first informed my initial understandings of civic engagement. These toys introduced us to what Lizabeth Cohen identifies as our role as citizen consumers.[3]

This book looks at cultural artifacts in the world of children to see what lessons they aim to teach but also what they reveal about the world in which they were produced. No doubt a Raggedy Ann doll tells a different story than a Barbie doll and a plastic toy pistol a different story than a plastic machine gun. Collectively, however, they convey consistent themes: they are artifacts of the American manufacturing system and communicate persistent myths about America. This book asks how these children's toys, dolls, and books—what I am collectively calling didactic amusements—sell a specific version of American history, and use American history as a promotional tool.

Children absorb a wide range of ideas about their country and their place in it from a diverse array of sources. In the more formal setting of school they learn from textbooks, lesson plans, and certain holiday celebrations, which events and people are considered important and what values they represent. But children also learn from the informal activities of childhood—playing with dolls, listening to stories, watching TV and advertisements, even going to an amusement park. These informal sites of learning have received less attention than they deserve, perhaps because they fall distinctly into the messy category of "child's play."

As early as 1897 the noted psychologist G. Stanley Hall suggested that too little attention was being paid to what children learn informally, specifically from dolls. Hall believed dolls were important because they educated "the heart and will even more than the intellect."[4] He noted that "dolls are found buried along with children in the sarcophagi of the ancient Egyptians. A little girl figure was found in one of the buried cities with a doll clasped to her breast."[5] Why then, he wondered, hadn't more attention been paid to dolls by social theorists and psychologists? He argued that their importance was not merely to "keep children young, cheerful, out of bad company," but "to teach geography, history and morals ... in the most objective possible way."[6] He believed "there should be somewhere (a) a doll museum, (b) a doll expert to keep the possibilities of this great educative instinct steadily in view."[7]

Hall recognized that dolls come with signifiers. A doll's physical appearance is often an indicator of moral character. "Psychic qualities are often suggested by looks, dress, or fancied resemblance to someone thought to have good or bad qualities." Hall wrote of the ways boys (presumably white boys) interpreted dolls of different races, stating, "Colored dolls, brownies, German, Chinese, and other dolls are often fancied, especially by boys because they are 'funny' or exceptional."[8] He attributed boys' reactions to nonwhite dolls to their perception that other races are funny and abnormal. Others since Hall have investigated issues of race and childhood toys more deeply and more recently. Most significant was Kenneth and Mamie Clark's famous doll studies published decades after Hall wrote about dolls. Documenting that both Black and white children identified white dolls were superior to Black dolls the study was used to demonstrate the effect of segregation on children's self-esteem and became an important reference in the Brown v. Board Supreme Court decision that legally ended segregation in schools.[9] The way children play with dolls, who is the hero and who is the villain, makes the doll as an object of study particularly revealing.[10]

Children are perceptive and absorb messages from the culture around them, even when those messages are implicit or unconsciously propagated by adults or peers. The study of these cultural artifacts is challenging because of a lack of source material about children's experiences and reactions to their sites of play. For this reason, documentation by people like Tony Schwartz, a legendary documentarian of sound, is helpful. In 1954 he recorded children playing near his home in the Hell's Kitchen neighborhood of Manhattan. From a young age, the

children he recorded could identify where they "belonged" in consumer society—
and where they didn't.

> I won't go to Macy's anymore, more, more
> There's a big fat policeman at the door, door, door
> He'll pull you by the collar
> And make you pay a dollar
> So, I won't go to Macy's anymore, more, more[11]

The rhymes Schwartz recorded demonstrate that children absorb the lessons
imparted to them by the media, toys, and other amusements and that, in the case
of this rhyme, they know certain consumer spaces are off-limits to anyone but
paying customers. This example illustrates that play is a process of making meaning out of the world. Children watch TV, hear the news, overhear adult remarks,
and then replicate, master, and reinterpret what they have heard in their own
play. Throughout this process they also reify and challenge the norms they're
encountering.

This book is composed of an opening chapter on the early years of the toy
industry followed by four case studies from different eras in the twentieth
century, each of which focuses on particular cultural artifacts of childhood—
dolls owned by collectors, early reading chapter books, an amusement park, and
dolls for purchase. Each chapter examines a different aspect of the way these artifacts inform us about what children were being taught about American history
and the culture within which they were produced. Certain questions are considered throughout the book. First, what is the vision of the American nation-
state being offered to children? Second, what does a particular doll, book, or
amusement tell us about the roles race, class, gender, and ethnicity play in the
American project? Third, how do the market, the process of production, and the
methods and venues for selling different toys shape their messaging? And finally,
how do the specific time periods in which these case studies occur shape the
vision of America that they present?

The twentieth century was animated by a search for what it means to be an
American and what values are central to the nation's identity. The story of America changes as the country does, taking on different meanings at different times,
depending on the values and politics of the time. Many stories persist and even
harden into something that looks like a universal truth, exempted from scrutiny.
Often these stories glorify America by celebrating pioneers "taming" the West
and "bringing civilization" to "primitive" tribes, by depicting America as the cru-
cible of democracy, a "melting pot." The project of creating a universal, assimila-
tionist American history inherently excludes those who have suffered in America
or forces them to deny their own story or that of their family in order to gain
entry into American civic discourse. This leaves all people in the nation standing
on a foundation of sand when confronted with America's ills. More recently it has

become clear that there is value and justice in facing and telling the omitted and silenced stories—the story of a nation that drove Native Americans off their land, the stories of the enslaved and the continued ramifications of racism, of a country that interned American citizens of Japanese descent during World War II.

While the definition of America and who is an American changes over time, race, class, and gender serve as the primary criteria for how America is defined throughout. As the first chapter, "Made in America," demonstrates, to be an American in the early part of the twentieth century required that a person assimilate into an imagined American culture reflective of European and white ancestry. But as the final chapter, "Selling Multicultural Girlhood," demonstrates, at the end of the century America's racial, ethnic and cultural diversity had become a selling point of American identity. This new definition of America, one that marketed diversity, included girls (as consumers) as well as boys, even as bias, bigotry and the expectation of assimilation persevered. In the early twenty-first century we see that the globalizing of the American experience downplays differences and emphasizes universality.

Consumerism became a crucial component of civic engagement in late nineteenth century and an aspect of how children engaged as citizens-in-training. Commercial products offered to children, even when intended to educate, aim to turn a profit. While parents want to offer their children toys and books that engage them in the world and teach them intellectual, manual, and technological skills, ultimately they often turn over to toy companies the choice of messages they want to communicate. Although children do have some agency, in that they express their own preferences about toys, the toys they play with are frequently chosen by adults.[12]

The case studies in this book provide a window into struggles over race, class, and gender as they played out during these different periods. It is important to understand that the imagined child for most toys produced in the twentieth century was essentially white and middle class. As Robin Bernstein has pointed out, the innocent child imagined by manufacturers is "part of a 200-year-old history of white supremacy."[13] The manufacturers of consumer items and spaces are largely complicit in promoting a narrow definition of the ideal American child. As the role consumer products play in children's lives has grown throughout the last century, it has become increasingly important to scrutinize the stories they tell, the children they represent, and the messages they impart.

Chapter 1, "Made in America: The Rise of the American Toy Industry," looks closely at the products, advertisements, and ideological arguments put forth by the burgeoning American toy industry to Congress, the public, and the world in the early twentieth century. It lays the groundwork for understanding the ways that children's amusements and activities were part of the ongoing debate about what is America and what it means to be "an American." During this time, consumers were encouraged to buy American-made toys, with the idea that this was a patriotic act of supporting American laborers. Owning manufactured, store-bought toys was an essential part of being an American. Lizabeth Cohen argues that this period saw a "first-wave consumer movement" as people who were "denied access to traditional avenues of power, seized upon the citizen consumer role as a new way of upholding the public interest."[14] It also gave children a sense of belonging to a national club and created a new shared identity among consumers who bought standardized goods. Of course, this meant that those who could not afford manufactured toys were being nudged out of the definition of who was American. The mass market that arose in the twentieth century also played an oversized role in designing gender-specific toys. It is well documented that boys were offered trucks and guns and increasingly sophisticated mechanical toys from which they learned their roles as citizens of the greater world. Girls were offered dolls and kitchen appliances from which they learned their roles as keepers of the home and family. Women, then, became the caretakers of the individual suburban home—the symbol of the American capitalist dream during the Cold War era. African American children were not considered a lucrative market for toys, nor were they always identified as children deserving of leisure and playthings, so little effort was made to represent or cater to them in the world of toys. Small foundries and manufacturers continued to produce racist, stereotyped toys for the amusement of white children. The annual Toy Fair in New York City, sponsored by the Toy Manufacturers of the U.S.A., was the outgrowth of the expanding industry and represented the emergence of America as a modern, industrialized country.

While mass production created an illusion of access to democracy and inclusion, it also standardized narratives and identities in exclusionary ways. Amid the changes wrought by the mass market, pockets of resistance emerged. The second chapter, "Dolling Up History," looks at a Doll Show that took place in Manhattan in 1938 in which a wealthy group of women displayed their doll collections to an enthusiastic public. The Doll Show can be seen to represent a reaction on the part of the upper-class against the changes brought by industrialism and a longing for an old social order where upper-class customs and mores held sway. The collectors were part of a disappearing class of women who displayed dolls modeled largely on aristocratic European women to promote the notion that American culture was an extension of an elite Old World culture. It was at this time that Mamie and Kenneth Clark's famous doll studies, begun in 1938 and continuing through World War II, offered a different critique of American society in the thirties.

Chapter 3, "'Gosh, It's Exciting to Be an American,'" looks at two series of children's historical fiction whose popularity peaked in the 1950s. The first, the Childhoods of Famous Americans, popularly referred to as the "Orange books," was published by Bobbs-Merrill, an Indiana press that consciously sought to glorify and exemplify a "wholesomeness" rooted in a rural, agrarian America.[15]

The second, the Landmark Books series, was produced by Random House, a younger press founded by urbane, college-educated New Yorkers that focused on providing children with serious books about the history of their country. Despite the very different social and regional origins of these presses, these two collections present strikingly similar versions of the country and its history. They both suggest the value of assimilation, ownership, free enterprise, and American expansionism, while they perpetuate fixed racial and gender roles.

Published largely in the fifties, these series can be seen as part of a broad attempt by historians and scholars to reach a consensus about American identity during a particularly fraught period of national anxiety. Many felt it was important to move beyond the tensions that had characterized the thirties and forties and to create a common idea about America that included a shared sense of history and basic shared values. They relied heavily on well-worn myths about the frontier, the idea that colonization was noble and inevitable, about spreading democracy around the world, and about traditional gender roles and white supremacy. The presses relied on these particular, idealized myths of America, perhaps because they feared that any story critical of the United States would attract the attention of the right-wing senator Joseph McCarthy and the House Un-American Activities Committee. This chapter also looks at how Random House succumbed to political pressure to prove its loyalty and patriotism by publishing, for example, watered-down histories of the Civil War and a book extolling the virtues of the FBI.

In addition to books for children, similar Cold War interpretations of American history appear in experiential attractions designed for families. The fourth chapter, "Family Fun for Everyone? Freedomland U.S.A.," looks at a history-themed amusement park in the Bronx in the early 1960s, a time of massive demographic change. Freedomland, spread over acres of previously undeveloped marshland, comprised exhibits, rides, stores, and performances representing different periods and events in American history. It told the history of America in much the same way the children's history books had a few years earlier, emphasizing well-worn myths like that of the pioneers bringing "civilization" to Native Americans. While it was a somewhat successful attraction, today remembered fondly by dedicated fans who visited, its celebratory vision of the American past looks strained today, helping to explain why it unceremoniously collapsed four years later. Just as political activists and historians were critiquing these clichéd stories, the park was ignoring the political climate and its surroundings—the demographically changing Bronx. Freedomland's interpretation of history fell flat and its lifespan was brief. Despite tremendous financial investment, Freedomland filed bankruptcy only five short seasons after it opened.

In the 1960s and 1970s, feminists and other activists articulated the idea that "the personal is political," which undergirded a wide-ranging critique of how popular culture and the ephemera of everyday life had serious consequences for shaping Americans and the society they lived in. The toy industry eventually responded to these critiques, striving in some areas for greater gender and racial diversity. The final chapter, "Selling Multicultural Girlhood: The American Girl Doll," examines what is arguably the most successful example in America of a company's use of history to sell its products. The American Girl Company's dolls, books, and other merchandise became monumentally popular, particularly among white, middle-class girls during the period from the 1980s to the early twenty-first century (in recent years its popularity has been declining). Early on, the company answered the need for a more diverse representation of America in the world of dolls by including the underrepresented stories of American history—those of girls of different ethnicities and socioeconomic classes. Nonetheless, American Girl stories are rooted in commonalities across time and class, and often their experiences reflect those of contemporary middle-class white girls. As a result, the richness of different cultural experiences retreats into the background. Over time, the American Girl Company began to downplay the historical dolls that made it so popular and began to feature dolls that replicated the consumer herself. This accelerated with the purchase of the company by toy giant Mattel in 1998. The changes made by the American Girl Company reflected an effort to train girls to become consumers. The company was masterful at winning the allegiance of girls to the American Girl brand.

This brings me back to my grandmother. In 1995, my Christmas wish list included a miniature nineteenth-century "Tin Pail Lunch," a Victorian "hand muff," and a colonial "bed warmer." These were items from the American Girl catalogue that I'd read about in the books accompanying the expensive dolls. I'd regularly immerse myself in the thick pages of the mail-order catalogue—the only regular piece of mail addressed to me—reviewing the merchandise, reading the descriptions, and writing and reorganizing what I desired the most. When Christmas rolled around I was excited about the possibility of receiving gifts from my list, but what I received from my grandmother instead were five perfectly fitting, hand-sewn dresses for my dolls. The skill and effort put into them were apparent, and today I understand their inherent value.

I politely thanked her and dressed my dolls in the clothes, but really, I was disappointed. My grandmother's logic was sound. She refused to pay for items that she could make inexpensively and expertly on her own. But I had been steeped in the American Girl books and had become desirous of the specifically branded clothing and objects that were often part of the loving exchanges between parents and children in the stories—objects that were illustrated in the margins of the books and available in the catalogues. It took me until adulthood to realize how much more valuable were these unique dresses handmade by my grandmother. While touting the importance of family, tradition, and gift giving,

Figure I.1. Hand-sewn dresses made for the author by her grandmother, Sophie Rosner, in the 1990s. Photograph by Jane Buckhurst.

the American Girl Company had turned me into a loyal consumer devoted to their brand.

This book examines and questions the messages these cultural artifacts of childhood present about who is an American and what values this country holds dear. Taken together, it becomes clear that these sites of play most often reflect their moment of creation far more than the history that they claim to convey. As a whole, they show a stubborn devotion to certain national myths while also revealing consistencies and discrepancies about American identity as it was marketed over time. I join others in declaring that children's toys, books, and amusements provide valuable insights and deserve to be studied in a broader context than childhood education. Given that children learn so much about history through informal activities of play and reading, these often-ignored didactic amusements hold lessons for us all.

CHAPTER 1

Made in America

THE RISE OF THE AMERICAN TOY INDUSTRY

An excellent practice . . . is teaching the child how to make his own toy. . . .
Playthings of great price excite vanity and pride. —Washington Post, 1905[1]

Toy Manufacturers from all over the country . . . will be busy this week arrang-
ing their samples for the big toy fair. . . . The fair will be larger this year than
ever owing to the anticipated shortage in playthings from the German Empire.
—New-York Tribune, 1915[2]

Written a mere ten years apart, the above statements reflect the massive changes
that took place in the U.S. toy industry in the decades around the turn of the
twentieth century. With the expansion of the U.S. industrial sector, the simple
homemade toy gave way to the mechanical, electrified version that could be
mass-produced in new factories. It was a period of enormous excitement about
the possibilities of industrialism not only for those manufacturers seeking
financial gain, but also for the growing numbers of people in cities who were in
need of jobs and were urban consumers seeking convenient access to goods.

As the American toy industry established itself, certain themes emerged that,
through repeated efforts by toy manufacturers, would play out throughout the
twentieth century. First, the toy industry itself would stand as a symbol of the
greatness of America. Its endless commercial possibilities reflected the country's
boundless opportunities. Within only a few decades the American toy industry
convinced adults and children in homes across America to desire manufactured
toys—and, in essence, suggested that toys were essential to an American way of
life. As this chapter illustrates, the toy industry was perceived as so important
to the economy that the government intervened at various points to protect it
from foreign competition—particularly from Germany. Arguing that toys were
educational, the toy industry succeeded in getting the government to pass protective tariffs. The toys produced by the industry would disseminate an ideol-

ogy about America as innovative, powerful, and ever expanding—they became symbols of American industrial capacity.

Second, from the moment of its inception, the toy industry played a signifi-cant role in socializing children into their gender and racial roles in American society, by virtue of both the kinds of toys they produced and the class and racial identities they cultivated through their marketing. In playing with toy guns boys would learn their role in war and industry, while girls would learn their domestic responsibilities through cooking on toy stoves. As manufactured toys became more widespread, so did the messages they carried about the nature of the country and about the place of men, women, and minorities (particularly African Americans) in American society.

Third, the toy industry, with its focus on white, middle-class children and its marketing primarily to them, would reflect and reinforce the segregated nature of American society. Although owning toys became intertwined with being an American and immigrants were quickly indoctrinated into appreciating toys, early in the century clear divisions emerged in terms of who had access to toys, where people shopped, and what they could access. The industry as a whole made little to no effort to create toys that reflected the experience of nonwhite children, instead reinforcing racial stereotypes and catering to whites.

Many changes made the mass production and distribution of toys possible. Advances in manufacturing meant that the toy industry developed the capacity to mass produce mechanical and electric toys. Local dry goods stores were overtaken by department stores like Abraham & Strauss, Filene's and Macy's, which stood ready to sell these mass-produced items directly to the public. Many of today's household-name toy companies either grew significantly or established them-selves during this early part of the century.[3] Parker Brothers, the company that manufactured a host of board games like *Monopoly* and *Sorry!*, was created in 1883. In 1900, the Lionel Corporation began making electric toy trains and that year saw the formation of the Ideal Company, famous for its teddy bear and later for its dolls like Betsy Wetsy and Shirley Temple. Marx Toys, which manu-factured metal cars, buses, and lead soldiers, was organized in 1919. Finally, Has-bro, originally Hassenfeld Brothers, began in 1923 and made children's medical kits.[4] The development of a transcontinental rail and canal system ensured that toys could be advertised and delivered across the country.[5]

Other economic and social forces transforming the country had a profound effect on the lives of children. As the United States shifted from a largely agri-cultural to an industrial economy, the child who once provided an indispens-able pair of hands on rural farms and plantations to milk the cows, feed the animals, maintain the home, pick the cotton, and work the fields, often from dawn to dusk, was no longer essential.[6] Still, this was a time when the experi-ence of childhood was diffuse and changing rapidly—coming under new scru-tiny and regulation and adjusting according to the demands of urban life. While some children did work in factories, this was less and less the case, particularly as turn-of-the-century child labor laws and protective legislation prevented some forms of exploitation of children.[7] The U.S. Children's Bureau was created in 1912 to investigate and report mortality rates and to attend to the well-being of children, becoming the first national agency to expressly focus on youth.[8] Though overturned, the 1916 Keating-Owen Act represented efforts to prohibit the trade of goods made in factories that employed children. Other laws were passed regulating the age at which a child could enter into various trades. Many states also passed laws requiring that children attend school. Immigrants from Europe and African Americans from the South began to replace children in factories in northern cities.[9] Holidays, weekends, and after-school hours became free time for many children to play or read. Idle hands—potentially the "devil's workshop"—presented an opportunity for the newly emerging toy industry to build its reputation selling toys that would educate children and introduce them to the increasingly urban, industrial "American way of life." All of these changes meant children were available to play—at the exact moment the industry was ready to mass produce toys.

The Toy Industry: A Reflection of American Ingenuity

Early in the twentieth century most of the commercially manufactured toys in the United States were imported, largely from Germany, and "were few and costly."[10] These items were sold to wealthy American families living near ports like New York City.[11] But Germany's dominance began to fade as the United States industrialized and as electricity became more widely available. From the start, the U.S. industry promoted its toys as distinctly American and made electricity synonymous with the notion of an ingenious, expanding, dominating America. In 1908 the *New York Times* touted "American ingenuity" as a boon for youngsters and producers alike: "Some clever American mechanic hit upon the scheme of substituting electricity for springs, greatly to the joy of the American boy, and at the same time greatly to the advantage of American toy makers."[12] The *Times* predicted that Americans could combat stiff competition from foreign toy makers by making electric toys: "The coming to the forefront of the electrical toys . . . is a signal for the foreign toy-makers to watch out for American competition. Practically all the devices with motor and dynamo attachments are of domestic make."[13] Like the transcontinental railroad that had been completed forty years earlier, the electric train thundered boldly from American manufacturers into the hands of American children and carried with it its own vision of American supremacy, this time in the toy industry. The *Times* was starry-eyed about the toy railroad, linking the toy version of this mode of transportation that had dramatically altered American life with supposedly American characteristics: "One of the most elaborate of these automatic toys, which appeals directly to the inventive genius inherent in the American, is a railroad, with its equipment of switches, signals, freight houses and stations."[14]

FAO Schwarz, which opened its first toy store in Baltimore before relocating to New York City, prominently displayed in 1900 a "numberless" array of "electric and magnetic toys . . . among the newest [of which were a] mechanical . . . train of cars, with engine and tracks, stations lighted by electricity, signals, guardhouses and every other appendage of a real railroad."[15] By 1909 even Santa Claus had become as "'up to the minute' as any highly enterprising business man. . . . Every year the youngsters find the most up-to-date things in their stockings."[16] The American toy world was young, was not based in traditional craftsmanship, and replicated and reinvented the "march of progress in the mechanical world."[17]

Many of these mass-produced toys that were clever replicas of commodities like the railroad or the automobile appealed particularly to adults.[18] In fact, many accounts omit the experiences of children but focus on the delight of adults.[19] In 1907 it was reported that "there is scarcely a human invention that has not . . . its toy replica. Many of these are so enticing that even an adult feels a half guilty longing for them."[20] The *Times* reported that judges and bankers were purchasing "every new mechanical toy that makes its appearance on the market" and noted that these New Yorkers were secretly indulging "this peculiar passion" by taking "extraordinary pains to conceal the fact that they are buying the toys for themselves and not for their nephews or their little sons."[21]

Mass-produced toys were touted as superior to homemade ones. "The days seem far away when tops and kites and sleds satisfied the Christmas ambition of the American boy," remarked a writer in the *New-York Tribune*. "Now it is toy railroads, telephones, submarine boats and automobiles that fill his Christmas stocking."[22] Furthermore, it was suggested that these mechanical toys would teach and encourage creativity among children. "The trend of design of many of the newer toys adheres closely to that of machines of industry. Trucks, steam shovels . . . highly developed electric train systems . . . are but a few of the mechanical toys that are being offered to encourage the mental development and ingenuity of American childhood."[23] These toys profited American companies, celebrated American technology, and implicitly trained American boys to participate in an American culture of ingenuity and industry. This claim about the educational possibilities of toys is still made by toy manufacturers today.[24]

Although few manufactured toys made direct reference to American history, certain historical events and American heroes inspired toys. In the wake of the War of 1898, which marked the emergence of America as a world imperial power, the teddy bear became a signature product of the emerging toy industry. In 1903, Morris Michtom, the future founder of the Ideal Toy Company, sold "handmade cloth bears from his New York candy store."[25] At the same moment, Margarete Steiff's German toy manufacturing company began producing stuffed bears, which became immensely popular in America as well.[26] They were famously named after Theodore Roosevelt, the country's gun-loving, outdoorsman president who led the famed Rough Riders' charge up San Juan Hill. By 1907, the teddy bear had become the mainstay of the new Ideal Toy Company, which mass produced them at a factory in Brownsville, Brooklyn.[27] The teddy bear was described as "a doll that was acceptable to boys because it was 'masculine.'"[28] Toys that referenced foreign lands often had an imperialist quality to them. A toy produced in 1909 called "Teddy in Africa" showcased the former president performing "remarkable gymnastic feats without losing his pith helmet or his spectacles."[29] This toy equated power with physical fitness and flexibility, all the while holding on to the markers of strength and civilized intelligence—Roosevelt's helmet and, of course, his glasses. It represented America's identity as an imperial, if benevolent, power.

At a time when the nation's foreign policies oscillated between isolationism and imperialism, the popularity of war toys was indisputable. "War toys!" had become "foremost in every toy shop in Atlanta, and in the minds of practically every Atlanta boy," announced the *Atlanta Constitution* in 1909.[30] Military toys— guns, cannons, bayonets—were coming to dominate the industry even before the United States entered World War I. Young boys grew up playing military combat. In many ways this play was a rehearsal for adult life in which patriotism would mean a willingness to go to war.

GENDERED TOYS FOR GIRLS AND BOYS

The toy industry identified and reinforced stereotypes about gender roles and then, by virtue of its distribution and marketing, disseminated these throughout the nation. Toys for boys often conjured up clichés about American history— the bows and arrows, Indian headdresses, cowboy hats, rifles and guns, and leaden soldiers eventually gave way to more technically sophisticated pistols, tanks, and weapons. Boys would be part of American society on both the consuming and producing sides. These toys introduced boys to their roles as citizens of the nation, while toys for girls introduced them to their domestic roles. One article in the *Detroit Free Press* stated that dolls made sure a girl's "instinct for motherhood is roused," while railways and mechanical toys drove boys "wild with delight."[31] The toys suggested that boys would have access to America's future, while girls would be seen as guardians of America's past. While toys for girls harkened back to traditional domestic activities and were less often seen as the medium for ingenuity, the toys for boys pushed the limits of mechanics, science, and engineering.

While American toys marketed to boys celebrated modernity, toys for girls remained pointedly retrograde. It is striking how exhaustively the toy industry continued to produce dolls and kitchen appliances for girls which replicated traditional roles at a time when women were demanding a public role. The New Woman—a modern, independent, educated figure—was taking hold of the public imagination. Suffragists were marching in the streets to demand the right to vote, and political activists like Ida B. Wells, journalists like Nellie Bly, and entrepreneurs like Madam C. J. Walker were becoming household names. In fact, as early as 1908 and in the context of this world where women were assuming more varied roles, there were complaints about the lack of interesting toys for girls. One reporter noted that while everyone "is catering to the American boy, they don't do as much for his Sister." For her, "there is just one new kind of doll, a 'rolypoly.' Adapted from the Japanese, which turns somersaults." Although this reporter bemoans the lack of toys for girls, he himself cannot imagine a role for girls outside the home: "Nobody makes toy washing machines or bread mixers to teach the little girls the business methods of to-day. Nobody tries to appeal to her natural inclinations." He attributes this paucity of toys for girls to the fact that "nearly all dolls come from Germany, where the Emperor preaches 'children, church, and cooking' for the girls."[32] As historian of children's toys Gary Cross explains, "Almost all girls' toys . . . were accessories to doll play. . . . But there were no career toys as there were for boys. The exception was the occasional nurse's outfit."[33]

The industry did gradually expand and improve toy appliances for girls, but these improved toys still conformed to gender roles. "There are toy stoves so alluring that there seems no question about the future generation of women having domestic tastes, provided each little girl can have one of them now," the *New-York Tribune* reported in 1907.[34] Dollhouses were advertised as "including every kitchen contrivance that was ever invented for making housework easier."[35] But, as Cross points out, these advances were made "only in the realm of home appliances. Dollhouse appliances mirrored up-to-date domestic technology."[36] The limited types of toys for girls did not mean that young girls themselves confined their play and behavior to domestic duties, but rather they found creative and rebellious ways to express themselves with the tools they were given.[37] Girls and women were ambivalent about the potential that consumerism held for them during this time. While consumerism could be empowering and provide public female spaces, like Ladies' Mile in New York City, it also had the potential to dictate and circumscribe behavior.

The Marketing and Distribution of Class and Racial Roles

The advent of department stores reconfigured the shopping experience of Americans and helped make it a leisure activity. Department stores began to appear in the mid-to-late nineteenth century: Macy's was founded in 1858, Lord & Taylor in 1860, and Bloomingdale's in 1872.[38] Other department stores followed later in the nineteenth and early twentieth centuries (expanding most rapidly in the 1920s).[39] By 1880 newspapers reported huge crowds in shopping areas in New York City. As Alan Trachtenberg explains, the Gilded Age saw a "changed conception of . . . America itself" and marked a "significant increase in the influence of business in America."[40] Between 1890 and 1930, William Leach writes, a new definition of America as a consumerist society replaced the earlier definition of America as a democracy, concerned with the good of all. "American corporate business . . . began the transformation of American society into a society preoccupied with consumption . . . with more goods this year than last, more next year than this."[41]

At the turn of the century bigger urban populations supported the expansion of the department store. The population of New York jumped from 3.4 million in 1900, after the boroughs consolidated, to just under 8 million in 1950.[42] The department store was a crucial piece of the city's transformation. Richard Longstreth writes, "The rise of a highly centralized pattern of urban growth enabled the department store to emerge as a great, all-inclusive emporium that helped define the character and the purpose of the city."[43] Department stores could operate on a larger scale than a local general store and could offer more lenient return policies and a wide variety of items and services, including delivery. The "toys and dolls" department was one of Macy's earliest, added to the store well before the addition of other now-common departments like rugs, sheets, and wallpaper.[44] As stores like Macy's added merchandise, window displays became increasingly important. It was in 1883 that the annual display of toys and dolls at the Macy's store first "contained moving figures, operated mechanically by steam power."[45]

The toy industry, with its ever-expanding lines of sophisticated toys, needed to advertise and transport their products to consumers. By the mid-nineteenth century the catalogue business was well established. By 1882 Montgomery Ward's catalogue had grown to 240 pages and included 10,000 items. By 1895 the Sears catalogue contained 532 pages, adding dolls in 1896.[46] Through their catalogues these companies could advertise their wares to everyone across the country. At this time the advertising industry was growing as well, with new firms devoted solely to ad services popping up and many newspapers devoting pages to display ads.[47] An expanded postal service and free rural delivery ensured that both ads and toys could be made available to children everywhere.

As the infrastructure of toy production and transportation grew more sophisticated, advertising created new catalysts for shopping. Christmas had become the primary holiday for which parents bought toys for children. In the mid-nineteenth century the tradition shifted from giving to charities and then to servants to giving presents to children within the family.[48] This provided the toy industry with a huge market. Eventually it became imperative that parents purchase store-bought mass-produced toys, especially at regular holiday times. One *New York Times* advertisement from 1910 noted, "The Christmas Store Is Ready! And Toys Are Foremost! . . . Toy Store Twice as Big as a Year Ago."[49]

Christmas and Christmas shopping, as discussed in the press, reflected a basic conflict felt—but not necessarily voiced—about who was truly an American. On the one hand, there were those who welcomed immigrants into the Christmas experience. One *New York Times* article suggested that buying or selling toys for Christmas was a kind of rite of passage for immigrants who were breaking ties with the "Old World" and assimilating into American culture: "Christians and Jews, Italians and Chinamen Share in the Zest of the Holiday Spirit."[50] The *Times* noted the participation of Chinese clerks in Christmas: "The Chinese clerks had imbibed the spirit along with the others of the cast aside. 'Melly Clistmas' was offered to every buyer."[51] Despite labeling their status as "cast aside" and caricaturing their foreign accents, the article celebrated the Chinese clerks' participation in Christmas, which was quickly becoming less a religious and more a secular, consumerist holiday.

At Ellis Island, the literal and metaphorical gateway to America, patriotism mingled with religion as there was a "babel of tongues singing the Star Spangled Banner at [the] Christmas celebration." There, wealthy people could donate to poor immigrants and feel they were signaling that the United States was a welcoming country in which consumerism and gift giving were American acts. "Those at Ellis Island were proud that at last they had reached a country where they could enjoy civil and religious liberty. . . . And then came the Christmas presents." But the presents, while a sign of welcome, were not the elaborate toys wealthier children were receiving but "little things that would serve to cheer the hearts of the new arrivals that would remind them that America would at least be friendly toward them."[52]

Not all children had access to what was becoming the American tradition of Christmas shopping. For one thing, not everyone could afford the toys that were being manufactured and advertised, and for another, consumer spaces demarcated strict class divides. Newly popular glass store windows provided a simple and less confrontational way to "close off access without being condemned as cruel and immoral."[53] Glass windows served as dividers, transparent but solid, literally separating the street population from the customer inside a store. More people could be exposed to the beautiful items on display and were, in fact, "being invited—even baited—to look."[54] But, as William Leach explains, there were more limits on who could access them as a consumer. "The result was a mingling of refusal and desire that must have greatly intensified desire, adding another level of cruelty. Perhaps more than any other medium, glass democratized desire even as it dedemocratized access to goods."[55] The act of looking enabled poorer children to participate vicariously in the desire for goods but physically barred them from the societal custom of shopping. Over the twentieth century, toys came to embody a new way for children to be fluent in American culture, while they simultaneously erected barriers to accessing that identity.

Christmas displays in store windows, particularly electrified moving displays, attracted huge and diverse crowds, but here again class defined who had access. Children would "stand for many minutes watching the strange motions of a doll or a toy soldier," and the police sometimes had to stop the "performance" during the lunch hour because the crowds "impeded pedestrian traffic."[56] Children from the tenement houses were often viewed as interlopers. One article reported, "The only unattended children who were out in the crowd were grimy little ragamuffins of both sexes, who had filtered in from the tenement house districts to gloat on the rare shows in the display windows and exchange in quaint vernacular comment on the eye feasts."[57] Some articles suggested that poor people were happy to just look at the displays. One 1902 piece describes a girl from the "Tenderloin slums" who stood "in rapt, hopeless, fascinated admiration of the delights beyond the plate glass windows" and goes on to suggest that these children, grimy as they were, were "happier than any in the throng."[58] Sometimes poor children's inclusion in the American dream of Christmas came with strings attached. For example, five hundred newsboys received "a regular full course Christmas meal in the clubrooms at 14 New Chambers Street." In exchange for this charity, however, the young boys "prepared a vaudeville entertainment."[59]

Different shopping areas were often ethnically or racially segregated. Newspapers would sometimes tout upper-class shopping areas in New York City as organized, modern, and reputable. Strings "of respectable carriages aligning the curb proclaimed that Miss Fifth Avenue and C. Park West were buying their presents."[60] Wealthy people had their purchases delivered to their homes along the growing Upper East and Upper West sides, a modern service that department stores like Macy's began to offer. By 1891 Macy's was even delivering to people who summered on the Jersey Shore and Long Island.[61] The poor shopped downtown, usually in the evenings after work, at outdoor markets, which the press depicted as fascinating examples of the foreign and exotic. In 1904 the *New-York Tribune* described the scene: "Here pyramids of cheap candy, pickled gherkins and humble 'dollies' alone infused the dash of luxury . . . as good as any expensive toy and would bring joy to a poor child." Articles described the areas as "a sight that combined the features of the Bagdad bazaar, the Nijni fair and Saturday night in the White-chapel High Road in one mammoth aggregation." Descriptions of a chaotic scene in which toys were "whizzing perilously" between ankles and toy monkeys climbing "dexterously from a piece of twine tied to the eyelet of a peddlers shoes up to the level of his chest" emphasized the vast, chaotic, foreign, and mildly threatening shopping scene.[62] One 1908 article dismissed the glamour of indoor department store shopping and praised, or perhaps fetishized, the virtues of the kind of outdoor shopping available to poor people: "There is very little crowding into hot and stuffy stores, for all the wares are to be had at the street stands. . . . There is no waiting seven deep till the haughty saleswoman has finished her analysis of your clothes and general style, of which she apparently disapproves."[63] New York City offered starkly contrasting worlds across a small geographical area: a chaotic old world of immigrants downtown just south of an orderly, gridded American midtown.

RACIALIZED TOYS DURING JIM CROW

Toys, like other consumer goods, reified white supremacy and utilized racist stereotypes in the era of Jim Crow. Overall, early in the century the toy manufacturers made little to no effort to produce toys that represented Black children in positive ways or were designed with them in mind as part of the emerging mass market. Popular catalogues of manufactured toys featured white, middle- and upper-class children. The only widely available toys that did represent Black children were essentially the same racist toys that had been produced before the Civil War in small shops and foundries. They repackaged and perpetuated racist caricatures that could be found across all media, from radio to vaudeville and cartoons. These racist nineteenth-century tropes continued in the twentieth century, as immigrants embraced Blackface and white supremacy as a way to demarcate themselves as Americanized.

In 1882 an "Illustrated Catalog to the Trade" advertising a line of products by Automatic Toy Works was published in New York and marketed to white children.[64] The catalogue contained detailed drawings of pricey (between $2.50 and $4 in 1882, equivalent to $63 to $100 today) wind-up mechanical toys that featured patently racist figures modeled on Black people performing different jobs.[65]

One juxtaposition of a toy with a white character and one with a Black character showcases just how differently they were described and respected. The description of the "Mechanical Sewing-Machine Girl" reads, "The little figure is elegantly dressed in the latest fashion. It combines the attractiveness of a beautiful French doll with the interest of life-like motion."[66] On the page directly opposite is the toy "Old Uncle Tom, the Colored Fiddler," whose name both refers to the character in the novel *Uncle Tom's Cabin* and expressly calls out the character's race. Meanwhile, the fact that the sewing machine girl is white goes unmentioned. The description of Old Uncle Tom reads, "We consider this toy one of the most comically quaint of anything yet made. When seen in motion, laughter is irresistible. . . . Funny as it is, there is something almost pathetic in it, too."[67] The description of the toy as "quaint" speaks to the clear association of this toy with the antebellum period and the enslaved character that lent the toy its name. This archetype endured in the years after the Civil War. While the sewing girl is depicted as skillful, disciplined, and fashionable, the fiddler is described as comical and pathetic.

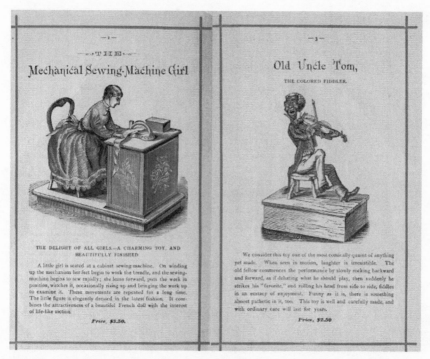

Figure 1.1. Mechanical toys from the 1880s depicting racist stereotypes. "Sewing Machine Girl and Old Uncle Tom," *Automatic Toy Works Catalog* (New York, 1882), 2–3. Library of Congress. https://archive.org/details/automatictoyworkooauto.

The catalogue also featured two toys modeled on African American women that reproduced the idea of "happy slaves," a myth used to deflect attention from the horrors of slavery in the antebellum era and that persisted well into the twentieth century in hugely popular films like *Gone with the Wind*. Later in the catalogue, the toy "Old Aunt Chloe, the Negro Washerwoman" is depicted as contentedly smiling at her role as she does laundry; the text reads, "Old Aunt Chloe demonstrates that happiness may be found in a wash tub as well as in a palace." Noting that she is "faithful in her toil," the description suggests that young ladies (meaning young white ladies who would presumably own this toy) might learn from her the lost art of laundering.[68] "The Old Nurse" on the right, taking care of a white baby, is the materialization of the "Mammy" caretaker—a well-known archetypal character popular from the time of slavery through the twentieth century.[69] "This mechanical toy is made to imitate an old negro nurse playing with a white child." The description reads, "Her motions are as natural as life. She holds the child in her hands and when the mechanism is started, (by being wound) she leans backward and forward tossing the child up and down in a most surprising manner."[70] The nurse is depicted as a natural caregiver (not

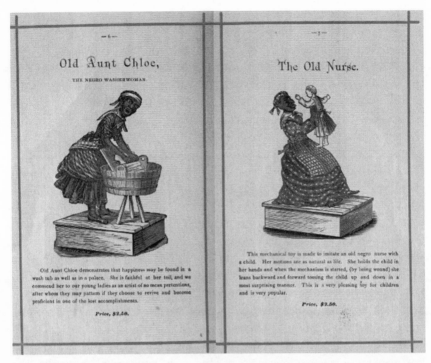

Figure 1.2. Descriptions of the mechanical toys encourage children to laugh at Black characters. "Old Aunt Chloe and the Old Nurse," *Automatic Toy Works Catalog* (New York, 1882), 6–7. Library of Congress. https://archive.org/details/automatictoy workooauto.

considered a skilled laborer) but is not portrayed as a parent. What is created, in the pages of this catalogue, is a situation in which a real-life white child consumer controls this toy figure of a Black adult woman.

The text accompanying an illustration of "The Celebrated Negro Preacher" once again encourages children to laugh at the Black figures. It emphasizes how comical the preacher was: "The motions are so life-like and comical that one almost believes that he is actually speaking. . . . The face and dress alone provoke irresistible laughter."[71] The text under "Our New Clergyman" reads only, "The description on the opposite page applies to this brudder [*sic*] also." No Black people, even those of the clergy, were deserving of anything but derisive comments. These toys encouraged children to typify, objectify, and literally own them.

Racial and ethnic stereotypes in toys evoked a legacy of white supremacy and also shaped children's understanding of contemporary immigration. In this catalogue, the next pages feature two toys designated as Chinese. The figures look alike, each with long braided hair. One is doing laundry, the other ironing. The character on the left is called "Fing Wing, A Melican Man." By labeling the character "A Melican Man" instead of "American Man," the text emphasizes his foreignness and pokes fun at his assumed stereotypical accent. The other character, titled "Ah-Sin, the Heathen Chinese," is depicted ironing. The text states, "The mechanism of these novelties is so perfectly made, that only the greatest abuse can put them out of order." Go ahead, the ad seems to say, treat these heathen foreigners as violently as you can. These toys conveyed to children that certain races and ethnicities were meant to be subservient, disposable, and abusable—not so different from the treatment of Chinese and Black laborers who worked to build America's railroads and labored in cotton and tobacco fields.

Racist toys had long been a staple of American toy culture, but they would reach their zenith in the early twentieth century when Jim Crow laws legitimated segregation and the attendant racism. While large companies largely ignored Blacks in the production of their toys, small foundries continued to produce racist toys rarely sold in the national marketplace. Among these racist toys were cast iron mechanical banks, which were popular at the turn of the century. The toys depicted people with caricatured features resembling those of Blackface actors. These cast iron banks with their racist images normalized racism in the child's playroom.[72] The white child playing with a caricatured Black doll or mechanical figure replayed the power dynamic of owner and slave in the domestic realm of the twentieth-century children's toy.[73]

The dancing jigger, a painted wooden toy that caricatured an African American man, was popular among white children early in the twentieth century. The "jigger," dressed as a bellhop or other low-status service worker, had an exaggerated smile plastered on his face. The child could make the jigger dance. One advertisement touted the "wonderful" quality of the toy, which performed on demand, much as minstrel singers had. "'Mr. Jigger' is a many-jointed, wooden figure which jigs to any tune whistled or sung by merely rapping a board in time."[74] Again, in addition to reinforcing racial stereotypes, this toy allowed the white child who could control the smiling, subservient, dancing Black man to feel racial superiority. Male "sambo" dolls and figurines and "pickaninny" dolls with big eyes, wearing rag dresses and eating watermelons, continued to be produced well into the twentieth century. These staples of racist culture imparted to white children the idea that Black people were laughable, noncontributing members of American society.[75]

One of the most famous characters disseminated early in the century was "Aunt Jemima," a figure used widely in advertising campaigns. Aunt Jemima was modeled on a Black, subservient, caretaking character from minstrel shows and embodied the stereotype of the mammy who took care of white families by making pancakes.[76] The R. T. Davis Company created an advertising campaign with an image modeled on a real person, Nancy Green, who had formerly been enslaved. Green went to the 1893 World's Exposition in Chicago to promote the pancakes.[77] In magazines Aunt Jemima, speaking in dialect, smiled broadly as she served a white family. "Lawsy, me now de Eskimo chillern want my pancakes

Figure 1.3. The character Aunt Jemima, discontinued only in 2020, used antebellum stereotypes to sell pancakes and collector items including dolls. "Pan-Cake 'Mammy' Is Dead," *Chicago Daily News*, August 31, 1923, 4.

so bad dey's got to have a aeroplane bring 'em," she proclaimed in early 1923.[78] The coupons from four purchases of the pancake mix and sixteen cents could buy a "family" of "amusing" rags dolls complete with "Aunt Jemima," "Uncle Moses," and their children, all of whom took great pleasure serving a white family as jovial, happy servants reminiscent of the pre–Civil War plantation South.[79] Aunt Jemima products, including dolls, continued to be lucrative for decades, and in 1937 the Quaker Oats Company bought the company and registered the Aunt Jemima trademark.[80]

These racist dolls and images made up the majority of the nonwhite dolls and toys that were mass-produced. Few less offensive representations of nonwhite characters were available for mass consumption. Awareness of the absence of "attractive" Black dolls free of racism and stereotyping spurred Richard Henry Boyd, a former enslaved person, to establish the National Negro Doll Company in Chicago in 1911 and to advertise in papers around the country.[81] A 1927 article in the *Pittsburgh Courier* reported, perhaps too optimistically, that it was no longer uncommon to see white and Black children playing with Black dolls. "The Negro parents who desire to see their child grow up unashamed of the hair and color with which nature has endowed it, and having pride, affection and loyalty for the people possessing these characteristics, should start very early in instilling this group pride and loyalty. There is no better way to start than by purchasing the child a black doll."[82] Black newspapers had long advertised Black dolls to their readers, implicitly acknowledging that young children should see themselves reflected in the toys with which they play. Another article in the *Pittsburgh Courier* proudly announced that the Standard Company in Harlem "has for the past several years devoted all of its resources to developing the doll trade among Negroes" marketing the "Harriet Tubman" doll, which was dressed in a blue silk dress with silk bows and patent-leather slippers and said "mama" and cried.[83] This doll is an interesting example of how a historical figure could be simultaneously prized and infantilized. Tubman is depicted not as a grown woman who aided in the escape of more than three hundred enslaved people but as a child crying for her mother.

The toy manufacturers, with their spectacular goods, were eyeing a market of white, middle-class children and seemed to see no need to make toys for Black consumers. The market for Black dolls was completely segregated, a fact that reflects the segregationist nature of much of America at that time. In response to this situation, in 1908 the *Baltimore Sun* featured instructions for making a multiracial collection of dolls at home "from discarded dolls of the Anglo-Saxon race." It reasoned, "It is perfectly possible to paint the white dolls black, brown, yellow or copper colored, and to dye, frizz or braid their hair into suitable wigs. Care must be taken, however, to see that the eyes are dark when the dark-eyed nations are to be represented."[84] While this was a solution to the dearth of nonwhite dolls, it was a solution in which whiteness was the default race that consumers had to work around or cover up—the dolls must be drawn on, dyed, and mutilated to represent other races.

That same year, when catalogues still regularly featured racist pickaninny dolls or windup toys that caricatured educated Black men, the Colored National Baptist Association argued that children should have access to dolls specifically reflecting their race. The *Atlanta Constitution*, a white establishment paper, reported that the group, "in solemn conclave at Lexington, Ky., has gone officially on record as favoring negro dolls for negro babies," a conclusion with which this white newspaper heartily agreed.[85] The newspaper editorialized that "The Indian baby wants a doll that looks like an Indian papoose. The Esquimaux child would probably not know what to make of a doll unless it looked like an Esquimaux. The babies of Holland are furnished dolls dressed in queer little bonnets and wooden shoes, just like the grown-ups wear. The Kaffir child would not take the same measure of delight in any doll baby that did not look like itself."[86]

This argument that children should have dolls of their own race, while meant as a sensible alternative to the production of mainly white dolls, reflects the reactionary Jim Crow era notion that it was "natural," and preferable for people of different races to stay within their group—a theme that persists in contemporary lines of dolls. It was a way of denying that the existing patterns of social segregation and race relations at the time were harmful social constructs. The solution, according to the paper, "in the future the negro baby must have a doll at Christmas that looks like itself and must not be deformed in feature until it looks like something else."[87] In effect, the newspaper was taking solace in the idea that nature—as well as the Colored National Baptist Association—seemed so in line with the social custom of segregation.

Outside the Black community the impulse to produce an attractive Black doll was picked up in white southern papers, but these efforts were still tinged with racism. The *Nashville Tennessean* reported that a woman "widely known for her kindliness and philanthropic work" in Nashville was advocating for "pretty black dolls." Mrs. Foxhall Daingerfield, it was reported, "has written a card advocating the manufacture of 'pretty' negro dolls for the use of negro children, holding that negro dolls of handsome appearance would go a long way toward instilling in pickaninny minds a regard for the beautiful, and resulting in an ultimate benefit of the entire negro race through the medium of these dolls."[88] While arguing, however condescendingly, for pretty Black dolls, Mrs. Daingerfield uses the word "pickaninny" to describe young Black children themselves, conflating the derogatory popular image with the children themselves. Holding two seemingly opposed ideas in her head at once, she saw the need for more human and pretty Black dolls while using dehumanizing language to describe Black children. The history of slavery and of racist stereotypes was strikingly present in the toy and doll industry from its inception, teaching children an affiliation with white supremacy.

GOVERNMENT PROTECTION OF THE TOY INDUSTRY

The repeated interventions of the U.S. government on behalf of the toy industry are a striking sign of the centrality of the American toy industry to the U.S. economy. In January 1913, eight months before the outbreak of World War I in Europe, the U.S. Congress was poised to reduce the tariff on imported toys. Because the tariff gave them an edge in the market, the new American toy manufacturers were alarmed and began vigorously opposing this reduction. They wrote to the House Ways and Means Committee to object. Without this protective tariff, one manufacturer noted, the "budding doll industry in America would be crushed at once, since we could not hope to overcome by special machinery in this line the advantage Germany holds by its cheap labor."[89] The company spokesman pleaded, "Under the circumstances, we trust your committee will not disturb the tariff on toys, and stand by the people and the good industries of the United States, who are endeavoring to make the United States the most prosperous and leading nation in the world."[90]

In addition to arguing that its survival depended on the tariff, the toy industry gave other, seemingly more high-minded reasons to support their businesses, suggesting that playing with toys would be practice for participating in American culture. They argued that during a time of war, not only could toys be used to build morale through the promotion of militarism, jingoism, and manliness, but promoting the industry would train men and women, workers and consumers, and families in their new "American way of life."[91] The toy manufacturers argued that it was essential to protect the industry because toys were educational. One company spokesman said, "You will note by looking through our catalogue that we make a large variety of accessories and equipment, all of which go to make a complete railway and we feel that these items, when handled by a small boy, act more or less as an educational feature."[92] Remarkably, these arguments about the educational role of toys proved convincing enough for the government to again pass protective legislation in 1913. The industry won government support for a tariff on imported toys, even when it did not necessarily make economic sense—the tariff would not necessarily preserve long-held jobs since the industry was young, nor would it guarantee that the industry would become successful. Although the government encouraged other sectors of American manufacturing to focus on war production, it was unusual that an industry that provided no benefit to the war was given government support.[93]

Around the same time these tariffs were being debated, the outbreak of the First World War in Europe halted imports from Germany. In 1914 the *Washington Post* announced, "Toy Shops Are Silent, Germans at War, and Famine Is Feared at Christmas. All Imports Ceased."[94] The article warned, "Germany, where 95 percent of all the dollies in the world come from, is at war. Who is going to bother with shipping dolls and lead soldiers and Noah's arks when clanking troops have to be transported?"[95] This halt in German imports and the passage of the protective tariff allowed American manufacturers to move in and secure their place in both the domestic and world toy markets. The industry promoted its products as made in America, by Americans, and for Americans. During the war, journalists pointed out that manufacturers could take advantage of the lack of imports and encourage Americans to buy American and they did. Many magazines called for people to buy items made in the United States.[96] The 1915 Made in U.S.A. exposition was held to "foster and encourage the demand for goods made in the United States."[97] In a short time American toy makers claimed to "revolutionize" the industry. As the European war continued, demand for American toys grew both domestically and overseas. By 1916 the *New-York Tribune* reported, the "World Looks to America for Its Toys."[98] The *Tribune* gleefully predicted that American-made toys "will not only find their way into the homes of nearly every family in the United States next Christmas, but the youngsters in nearly every foreign country with the exception of Germany and Austria will be made merry with the products of American toy factories."[99] The *New York Times* reported in 1917, "Among the many American exports which have increased tremendously during the last two years is the American made toy.... In the toy trade, Germany's loss is America's gain."[100]

The influence of toys on children's understanding of America cannot be overstated. As Europe entered into war and as the United States prepared for it, the toy industry prepared in its own way, producing "patriotic" toy soldiers, shotguns, and war games. As the *Times* reported, through toys "soldiering [was] made familiar in the nursery."[101] By 1917, just as the United States was about to enter the European war, the disparate manufacturers of toys had organized themselves into the Toy Manufacturers of the U.S.A. for "the purpose [of helping] the toy merchants . . . exchange ideas . . . relating to manufacturing problems" and to "push the sale of American-made toys not only in this country but throughout the world as well."[102] In 1918, they created an advertising limerick that appeared in the *New-York Tribune* linking commercial, factory-made toys, the war effort, and patriotism. To buy American toys was to support American workers and thereby support America. It was a patriotic duty.

> The pennies spent on Yankee toys
> For Uncle Sam's own girls and boys.
> In turn, of course, go back again,
> To our native workingmen.
> American—the workman's hand,
> American—'twas built and planned,
> American—in spirit, too,
> America's toy gift to you.[103]

Figure 1.4. American Made Toy Brigade pin, ca. 1920s. Shows Uncle Sam cradling a young boy and girl in his arms as they look at toys spilling over his upturned top hat. The club was sponsored by Toy Manufacturers of the U.S.A.

The industry continued to appeal to patriotism and war in promoting its toys. To win the loyalty of citizen-consumers, domestic toy manufacturers developed various gimmicks to give children a feeling of inclusion in a patriotic activity. The Toy Manufacturers of the U.S.A. even created the "American-made Toy Brigade," through which they symbolically militarized groups of young consumers. Children received a button indicating that "they have expressed a sincere desire to stick to and ask for American-made toys. The expression of this intention is the only fee there is for membership in the brigade."[104] A loyalty oath gained them admission into the group, but even more so children were learning to vote with their pocketbooks. It was through their consuming habits that children could show they were active participants in American democracy and supporters of the war effort.

In 1921, despite the end of hostilities, the trade group once again went to the government for continued protection, petitioning the Senate Finance Committee to maintain the high tariff on imported toys from Germany and other foreign countries in order to protect American interests. Spokesmen for the manufacturers "piled high the committee table with toys, ranging all the way from wooden letter blocks to electric trains, to support their argument that they had revolutionized the industry by coupling the educational with the amusement feature for the children." The argument shifted from the underdog battling the long-established German craftsmen to the industry arguing that new production techniques improved the quality of the toys available for Americans. They "had turned from the 'flimsy, namby-pamby' things imported before the war to substantial toys that laid the groundwork for the child's education."[105] Toys became part of a moral crusade against poor craftsmanship, a weak foreign work ethic, and unproductive leisure time. In addition, the industry continued to promote its goods as superior to Germany's and even stooped so low as to suggest that German toys were made through the exploitation of child labor.[106]

Toy production itself was a celebration of the American assembly line. In 1920, the Ford Motor Company produced a film called *Playthings of Childhood*, intended to familiarize Americans with the wonders of their new factory system and convince them of the value of mass-produced toys.[107] The famous Ford Motor Company had entered into the business of making toys, dolls, and other playthings and this film was one of many that Ford made (covering a wide range of topics about American life) between 1914 and 1954.[108] It could be said that early in the century appreciating the wonders of industrialism had come to be the same as appreciating America. This 1921 film attempted to bridge the gap between the magical world of handmade toys and the ingenuity of mass production. It refuted the notion that mass-produced items were impersonal by emphasizing the human touch over the mechanical one. The film opens with a text extolling childhood play: "The Joys of Childhood; that Fairyland of memories that hangs forever in our thoughts. An old rag doll or tin train played wonders with the imagination, and everything else was forgotten in—Toyland."[109] The wistful tone of words like "fairyland," "imagination," and "wonders" primes the viewer to recall the magic and fantasy of childhood. It is notable that this industry-sponsored film begins with a reference to handmade toys from the past, positioning the modern mass-produced toy as a continuation of this tradition. The next frame looks to ancient history to legitimize the modern toy industry by steeping it in tradition: "Joint dolls and crocodiles with movable jaws were found in the tombs of Egypt." The film suggests that toys were a crucial part of both timeless childhood and advanced civilizations.

The film then cuts to factory workers on an assembly line making toys. Individual workers—all white men and women—assemble, paint, sand, sew, and braid a different part of a few different toys. The film focuses primarily on the people themselves, some of whom are smiling at the camera while showing off their work, suggesting not the monotony and boredom of repetitive work on an assembly line but the pleasure of work in a factory creating toys that would make children happy. The assembly line process is deemphasized as individual, intricate work is highlighted: a woman sews wigs for doll heads; another worker fine-tunes the keys on the toy piano, screwing them on individually and then testing them. This presentation of American factory laborers as artisans suggests to the public not only that great care was taken in the production of Ford toys but also that the factory was integrally connected with the American playroom.

The film concludes with a bizarre stop-motion scene, set entirely outside of the factory, where the toys come to life: A little blond girl is shown sleeping in her bedroom. The scene cuts to a toy chest out of which comes the doll we saw being assembled earlier, and then two baby dolls. The two baby dolls go and share a bed while the "mother" doll primps in front of a mirror before tucking them in and leaving the scene. In the next scene the two baby dolls (the action is still created by stop-motion) get in and out of a bath after being washed by a third doll. Then a small clown and clay elephant perform miniature circus tricks. Finally, the little blond girl wakes up, rubs her eyes, and looks around, indicating that this was all a dream—a dream in which mass-produced toys entered the homey space of her bedroom.[110]

This film touches on many themes that this book explores. It shows how industry attempted to blur the distinction between lovingly handcrafted items and the affordable, mass-produced toys of modern industry. It places mass-produced toys within a longer history of individually crafted homemade childhood toys. It attempts to minimize the alienation of the factory and humanize the deskilled factory work that goes into producing Ford products by showing the connection of the work to the children themselves. The mass-produced doll enters the child's bedroom, bringing joy and excitement, just as surely as the homemade rag doll of an earlier era, made by a parent, brought joy to their child. From this Ford propaganda film we also learn who will count as a viable consumer and American citizen. The white, blond, and female child is the quintessential sentimentalized child whose dreams come true through mass production and consumerism. *She* doesn't work in the factory; the factory works for *her*.[111] As mass production entered the child's bedroom, children's toys gained a foothold in the business world.

THE TOY FAIR

The toy industry's annual Toy Fair was squarely situated in the world of business— not even accessible by the public—and oriented around innovation, profit, modernity, and large-scale production. By the 1930s the annual Toy Fair, begun at the turn of the century by toy manufacturers, was held in a building on a fashionable stretch of Manhattan's Fifth Avenue at Twenty-Third Street, near the Metropolitan Life Insurance tower and the famous Flatiron Building.[112] While early in the century mass-produced toys were marketed nationally through ads in newspapers and catalogues and sold in stores, over time toy companies needed to make a greater appeal to the international market. The Toy Fair in New York City, representing all that was new and modern, provided the Toy Manufacturers of the U.S.A. an opportunity to sell their newest toys directly to buyers from around the world. In many ways the 1937 fair represents the toy industry's entrance onto the international stage: "More than 3,000 buyers from every State in the Union, as well as Canada, England, France, Holland, South Africa, Australia and South America, are expected to attend the fair."[113] For those who visited the fair it was a shining example of all that was modern and ingenious, like the United States itself.

The fair displayed thousands of the most innovative and exciting mass-produced toys then pouring out of the modern factories owned by companies like Louis Marx and Company and the Ideal Toy Company. A photograph of an exhibit at a toy show that took place a year earlier shows a boy given the opportunity to "direct" the marvelous planes of the future. The toy show promoted a "futuristic atmosphere."[114]

A FUTURISTIC ATMOSPHERE AT THE TOY SHOW HERE

Figure 1.5. A young boy plays with futuristic toys at the annual Toy Fair in New York City. "Gates of Toyland Crashed by Adults," *New York Times*, April 21, 1936, 25.

The annual Toy Fair offered toys that replicated objects of everyday life like household appliances or trucks and cars. The replicas were generally very sophisticated and mechanized, displaying cutting-edge technology, and they were promoted as innovative, modern, streamlined, and "product-tested" by children. The *New York Sun* marveled, "Every new streamlined train, automobile or airplane design has its toy counterpart. . . . Plump baby dolls are drinking from bottles."[115] This fair aimed to promote its vision of a futuristic world even as the country was emerging from the worst economic depression in its history. One reporter marveled at the rising popularity of toys in 1937 despite the depressed economy and the fact that the population of children was shrinking. He pointed out that the industry was doing better than it had since the economic collapse of 1929: "The Fair of this year will top the records of the fair of [pre-Depression] 1929 by 10 per cent."[116]

Reviews of the Toy Fair centered on the progress-oriented and modern educational qualities of the toys. As the *New York Times* reported, "The seven acres of exhibits included countless practical playthings designed to teach youngsters up-to-the-minute developments in building construction, scientific experiment, transportation, metal working, fashion and art." Included were "miniature trailers, equipped to the last detail," which would "roll behind the latest in streamlined bicycles and express wagons." There were also models of "sleeper transcontinental airplanes and clipper ships."[117]

In contrast to the action toys for boys, the toys for girls, like those produced earlier in the century, reinforced traditional feminine roles but were now more mechanized. The *New York Sun* noted that "dolls have been taught a number of new tricks. Doll voices are clearer and proof against laryngitis. A new style walking doll has no windup machinery, but raises her feet gracefully when propelled from behind." This new technology allowed the girls to see "smiling and pouting dolls, dolls that cry and dolls with fingernails," which provided "a new thrill for the juvenile mothers." The newspaper noted that the new dolls could "have their diapers changed" as well.[118] These dolls scripted girls' actions to take place mainly in the home.[119]

While the toys at the Depression-era fair would have provided a diversion for New Yorkers, the event was open not to the public but only to buyers who intended to advertise and market the toys to children. The decision not to invite the "consuming public" reflects the industry's goal of marketing to suppliers of large stores. The Toy Fair still happens today, and its customers continue to be major buyers and industry insiders. The *Times* reported in 2008 that "the International Toy Center always sounded like just about any child's definition of heaven. But very few children—and not that many more grown-ups—ever got inside the two great fortresslike showroom buildings on the west side of Madison Square Park."[120]

Still, the ultimate goal of the fair was to get the toys to as many children as possible. The mass manufacturing of these toys transformed them from luxuries that only wealthy children could own to commodities available to almost everyone. A *New York Times* article announced that toys had become part of life for the richest and the poorest alike. "From the overstuffed nursery of a Hollywood baby star to the hovel of the Southern tenant farmer, toys have taken on a new quality and a new importance in the design for living."[121] By the 1930s the toy industry's health was often cited as a signal of the country's recovering economy.[122] The people in charge of the fair were mostly men from the industry interested in selling American toys around the world. Four hundred manufacturers participated, primarily led by men who remained rather anonymous. Industrial toys were seen as consumer products relegated to the realm of economics, business, and industry, and no emphasis was placed on who created and produced the toys; in that way the human element was removed.

Part of what the American toy manufacturers wanted to display was the abundance made possible by modern manufacturing techniques. As the managing director of the Toy Manufacturers of the U.S.A., James L. Fri, announced, "Every aspect of the more abundant American life has been reproduced in realistic miniature at low prices."[123] By 1937 the pure quantity of toys had grown a staggering amount: "Fifteen thousand new toys that will delight youngsters next Christmas morning were put on display."[124] As part of this display of abundance the dolls at the fair came with their own extensive wardrobes and accessories. "One really stylish doll has twenty pairs of shoes, clothing to match them all and luggage made to scale." Clearly neither the dolls nor the children needed all these accessories, but the industry was invested in convincing consumers they wanted more and better toys.

In its advertising, the toy industry touted their products as "tested." According to a *Times* article, "All the new toys being introduced this year had been tried out by youngsters before they were put into production to check their age suitability, fun appeal and educational value."[125] The *Christian Science Monitor* reported Fri as saying, "The 1937 toys, tested for age suitability, safety and educational value, illustrate dramatically the 20 years of evolution of modern toys from holiday novelties to everyday necessities."[126] In fact, testing had become a requirement for companies: "Very few makers have offered new playthings this Christmas without testing and retesting them with real children in real play."[127] Involving the children in testing did give them some personal agency in that they determined what toys were most interesting, but not until the 1970s would safety testing become a mainstay of the industry.

The toy as a cultural artifact tells us a great deal about the United States in the early decades of the twentieth century. The early years of the American toy industry set out themes that play out in the case studies examined throughout this book. As the country emerged as an international economic, military, and industrial power, toys played a role in identifying who was and who was not an American, who had and who did not have power, who would be included as the managers of the new industrial state and who would take care of the home. In the midst of a booming economy and a changing toy industry, people's roles were being defined by gender, race, and class. Decisions by the toy companies both reflected and reinforced these roles. Meanwhile, the paucity of adequate toys for Black children reflected the nation's continued failure at confronting a racist past. It was clear that the men running the toy industry did not think of African Americans and other minority groups as an integral part of the nation's identity or even as potential consumers. It would be a long time before minorities would be even modestly more adequately represented in the world of toys. At the same time, as part of a culture of abundance, the industry benefitted from an increasingly widespread feeling on the part of the American public that more was better. Nonetheless, enthusiasm about industrialism as a reflection of a growing, powerful country would take a hit during the Depression years, when the drawbacks of industrialism would become clear.

CHAPTER 2

Dolling Up History

1930S ANTIQUE DOLLS AND THE
CLARK DOLL STUDY

Dolls have so long been one of the chief toys for children, and are now so nearly universal among both savage and civilized peoples, that it is singular that no serious attempt has ever been made to study them.
—G. Stanley Hall and A. Caswell Ellis, A Study of Dolls[1]

While the toy industry early in the twentieth century reflected enormous excitement about the United States as an industrial, increasingly mechanized nation, there was evidence of dissatisfaction with the culture that had grown up around industrialism. In 1938 a group of blue-blood ladies from New York, Boston, Chicago, and elsewhere gathered in New York to display their antique dolls for the public. Taking place in the midst of the Depression, the Doll Show represented an effort to promote the mores and customs of an imagined American past of aristocratic privilege. At the same time as these elite, often wealthy, women were displaying primarily white dolls, African American communities were making known their dissatisfaction with the toy industry's continued failure to create Black dolls. Most significantly, Mamie and Kenneth Clark, two young psychologists finishing graduate school at Columbia University, were conducting their famous doll studies, which would demonstrate how both Black and white children had absorbed the notion reinforced by segregation that Blacks were inferior to whites. While the Doll Show represented a longing for the hierarchical preindustrial past, and the Clarks pointed to how segregation affected children's self-esteem, both examples took seriously the way dolls reflected cultural values.

By the 1930s evidence of industrialism was everywhere. As we have seen, the toy industry was a part, albeit a small part, of this larger transformation. From a home and craft-based industry often associated with skilled workers in woodworking and furniture manufacturing a number of national toy companies emerged. Some celebrated the mechanized, electrified toys being produced by the many new companies, while others extolled the virtues of the simple, home-made toy. This conflict reflected a broader discussion about industrialism. As Warren Susman notes in *Culture as History*, "The culture that grew up around this Machine Age gave rise to a great deal of opposition expressed in debates being held in magazines, journals, books, and even newspapers."[2] As examples of this conflict, Susman points out that, on the one hand, in April 1935 an Industrial Arts Exhibition in the new Rockefeller Center displayed and celebrated the latest in manufactured products. On the other hand, the developers of Williamsburg in Virginia were restoring the old colonial capital to its nineteenth-century form in what was a glorification of an earlier preindustrial era, complete with displays of handmade crafts. Similarly, in two different exhibits at the Museum of Modern Art one could see these competing views of American culture. One 1934 exhibit displayed toasters and electrified household items as machine art, highlighting a culture of modern abundance. The other, in 1932, called "The Art of the Common Man In America," celebrated folk art as an American tradition to be displayed as fine art. Notably, the exhibit covered art up until 1900.[3]

The annual Toy Fair examined in the previous chapter was a celebration of all that was modern, sophisticated, and innovative. Meanwhile, there were those, among them the doll collectors, who were nostalgic for an idealized feminine past with strict social hierarchies. Although modern, mass-produced toys for girls were still situated squarely in the realm of the domestic, dolls that cried, crawled, and peed were considered by the collectors to be crass and cheap and not up to their standards of femininity. Consciously or not, they were unhappy with the changes happening around them and wanted to reassert the traditions of a preindustrial age.

Discontent with industrialism was rooted in the very real events of the twenties and thirties. With the collapse of the stock market in 1929 and the Depression that followed, America's diminishing national income accounted for more than half the world's decline in industrial production. Between thirteen and sixteen million Americans were out of work by 1933.[4] The Depression revealed a world in the midst of financial and political chaos. It was a period of fierce reckoning, a time when the limitations of the great industrial and market forces of the previous century were coming into full view to millions of Americans from all walks of life. The cultural and social tensions that had been largely suppressed during the "good times" of the 1920s emerged full-blown.

Some older elites and wealthy Americans experienced the social disruption of the Depression as particularly dangerous and threatening to their status and wealth. Labor strikes by unions like the radical Congress of Industrial Organizations (the CIO) and the newly invigorated Communist Party were disrupting major industries like automobiles and steel. Franklin Roosevelt and the federal government appeared to be empowering the "dangerous" classes through New Deal programs like the Works Progress Administration and acts like the

National Industrial Recovery Act and the National Labor Relations Act.[5] Meanwhile, immigrants from Ireland and southern and eastern Europe were moving into urban centers and even into positions in city government, threatening the power of traditional elites.

Likely in reaction to the rapid industrialization of the nation, there were efforts among the upper class to identify who had the right to control the culture of this rapidly changing country. Those who claimed to be descendants of the white English and Dutch settlers had, in their minds, established the country and therefore had a claim to it and its future. They established their own clubs and organizations. Founded in 1890, the Daughters of the American Revolution, for example, claimed descent from the original framers of the Declaration of Independence.[6] In 1891 the Colonial Dames, an organization of white Protestant women who claimed descent from colonial settlers, was also established.[7] The Mayflower Society was founded in 1897 by those who could trace their ancestry back to the original Pilgrims who landed at Plymouth Rock.[8] These groups all shared a common belief that the country's spiritual, political, and moral well-being rested or should rest on their shoulders. By glorifying the past as a less confusing time, they implicitly and explicitly critiqued the changes wrought by industrialization, mass immigration, and urbanization, which they felt threatened to destroy the America they believed in.

While these groups represented some of the broadest opposition to the quickening pace of industrial life, individuals, columnists, and collectors expressed their fears and opinions through other outlets. For example, Alice Hughes, a part-time columnist, wrote an advice column called "A Woman's New York" for the *Washington Post* and the *New York Herald Tribune*. In 1938, after reviewing the toys available for Christmas, she wrote, "A hard day spent previewing the 1938 Christmas toys, I am forced to sigh for the days of simple, curly—haired plaster dolls, and mere toy wagons for the little boys." She recalled her own childhood and the "romance that we wove about our trifling playthings" and bemoaned "the toys of this graceless age" as "strictly streamlined and functional." The very qualities that the toy industry enthusiastically celebrated at their Toy Fair were the subject of her scorn. The fact that "the dolls of '38 talk, blow soap bubbles and carry on in superhuman style" in no way pleased her and, in fact, she mocked the modern girl who might like these toys. "Your daughters will no doubt sneer at a playhouse kitchen cabinet which lacks a percolator that perks not, or a grinder that doesn't grind." Hughes had no more patience for modern toys for boys. Again, the qualities that the toy industry celebrated were those that she found ridiculous. "Chemical and electrical sets are now so elaborate that I'd want a B.S. before I'd even touch 'em." She objected to those toys that sought to prepare children for the practical world of work and she longed for a time of "romance" characterized by less utilitarian playthings. She saw the mechanical firearms not as a wonderful sign of American military might but rather as a representation of a country ready to go to war: "Pacifism has gone out of style in America today and rearmament is the word."[9]

It was within this conflicted social context about the merits and pitfalls of the changes happening in American society, that a group of doll collectors displayed their collections of rare and antique dolls. While children were being treated in the mass market as proto-adults and offered toys mimicking adult tools and weapons, their collections can be seen as a defense of a childhood away from the mechanized world but also as a space to offer lessons in the etiquette of a fading, upper-class culture.

The Doll Collectors' Show

In the summer of 1938 more than 40,000 people visited the Doll Collectors' Show taking place in the Spear Auditorium in a building at 22 West 34th Street, right next door to the eight-year-old art deco Empire State Building (where the 1939 World's Fair Corporation was in the midst of their own planning). It was just thirteen blocks north of the International Toy Center, the massive building at the intersection of Fifth Avenue and Broadway where the Toy Fair had just displayed ingenious, factory-made toys. Unlike the manufacturers at the dazzling Toy Fair, the collectors at the Doll Show were not interested in selling anything. They were displaying their handmade and antique dolls from all over the world to remind modern viewers of a world that once was. The show was their opportunity to teach the public about the customs and behaviors of what they considered a better time.

Ironically, the building that housed the Doll Show was itself the picture of the crassness of modernity, according to the preeminent architectural critic Lewis Mumford. He not only found the building's design offensive but felt that the entirety of Thirty-Fourth Street was "architecturally the one really comic street in New York. Here you will find all the latest fashions promptly embodied and caricatured, sometimes by the best architects."[10] In 1938 he called the Spear Building the "perfect example of the fake functional." He argued that "its sturdily severe façade, with banks of windows, slightly projecting beyond the brick, looks like the German work of the mid-nineteen-twenties," leading the observer to "believe that it was real but for the fact that a huge vertical sign covers the bank of windows that faces Sixth Avenue." He had only disdain for "the yellow neon lights on a blue foreground and the simple entrance portico" that pitted the functional against the artistic and might "make sense to a furniture dealer, but it's the sort of thing that drives an architectural critic crazy."[11]

The exhibit of dolls inside this garish building, however, was decidedly not modern. Thousands of them, mostly antique or rare figures, were on display, having been loaned by the members of the National Doll and Toy Collectors' Club, a loosely knit collaboration of doll collectors from Boston, Baltimore, New York,

Figure 2.1. The Spear & Company store, which housed the doll show in 1938.
Black-and-white photo of Spear & Company store ca. 1939, Museum of the City of New
York, acetate negative.

Chicago, and elsewhere. Brooklynite Mary E. Lewis, the club's president and
founder, "not only showed her own collection," but also coordinated this exhibit
"of more than 2,000 dolls, dating from the 16th century to the present day,
dressed in costumes of the world."[12] The dolls were described in the newspapers
as elegant and informational and were repeatedly credited as examples of the
fashions, habits, and details of life in the past.[13] On display were "dolls from
Greece, Algeria, Brazil, Russia, France, Switzerland, the United Sates, Great
Britain; dolls made of paper, wax, china, wood, silk stockings, tin, yarn, straw,
nuts, fruit and rubber; pretty dolls, ugly dolls; dolls representing actual person-
ages; antique dolls and modern dolls, dolls made by amateurs and dolls made by
professionals."[14] Dolls highlighting specific geographical areas and particular
regional customs appealed to the 1930s audience. One *Brooklyn Daily Eagle*
article described a collection this way: "Every doll . . . is authentic. There is

Figure 2.2. Spear Building in 2013. Photo by author.

Mr. and Mrs. Arabia, for instance, a couple of pretty rag dolls that represent modern Arabs."[15] Counterintuitively, the doll collectors, while wanting to preserve the world as it was, were also participating in a growing, modern interest in the world beyond the provincial. As international trade and national economic involvements broke down local boundaries, Americans became interested in other countries and cultures. The dolls were presented as curiosities, as a way for the public to learn about the world, to become more cosmopolitan.[16]

It was not only the doll collectors themselves who were interested in the relics of a bygone era. The public attended in huge numbers. The show that opened on July 11, 1938, was intended to close on August 6, but its life was extended for two weeks to accommodate the high number of men, women, and children interested in the first installment of what would become an annual show.[17] The *Christian Science Monitor* wrote, "Clearly, there is something about dolls, since the National Doll and Toy Collectors' Club is able to report that of the 40,000 persons who have visited its first show . . . which opened two weeks ago, only 18 percent were children." Many adults came not as chaperones to children but out of a genuine interest in these relics from the past. The show was so popular with adults that time had to be set aside for youngsters to visit and see the dolls for themselves.[18] The show appealed not only to women and children, newspapers reported that "the history-ranging, world-wide character of the exhibition [brought] plenty of men observers."[19] An article from the *New York Times* noted that "men have flocked in."[20] Unlike the Toy Fair, meant for business men and wholesalers and closed to the public, this show did not have a consumerist goal. Although the show's location within a furniture store did require the public to walk past merchandise in order to view the dolls, no entrance fee was charged and no dolls were for sale.

What was it about these dolls that made the show so popular? For one thing they were a diversion from the everyday reality of life at the time. New York, in particular, was a city of extreme discrepancies in wealth in the 1930s. "Shanty-towns" were scattered across the city and occupied by people who had lost everything in the Depression. From "an encampment of squatters lin[ing] the shore of the Hudson from 72nd Street to 110th Street," to Red Hook's city dump filled with "sheds made from wrecked cars and barrels," the Depression's effects showed on the city's landscape.[21] Although not all wealth disappeared in the 1930s—mansions still lined Fifth Avenue and other avenues of the city—even the upper classes found their social position undercut.[22]

For another thing, beginning in the 1920s, there was an increased awareness of the importance of defining "America as a culture, and . . . by the 1930s this awareness had become a crusade."[23] As part of that crusade, "All-American" events that were so popular in the extravagant 1920s transformed in the 1930s to "a national mythmaking machine that communities could harness, for their own purposes, on a smaller scale."[24] The Doll Show can be seen as part of this phenomenon—a public event whose purpose was to define American culture.

Between 1928 and 1940 collecting as a pastime broadened enormously and became, along with fine art collecting, an acceptable middle-class hobby.[25] While collecting dolls from other countries introduced people to other cultures, the art of collecting was also a way to keep control and reframe a changing world. The concern for realism, authenticity, and "Old World traditions" and the "search for the 'real' America" coincided with a conservative trend in 1930s pastimes that "would become a new kind of nationalism," meant to "reinforce conformity."[26] Authenticity also found a home in the world of folk art, where in the 1930s it "fulfilled many longings for an imagined bygone America of ethnic and cultural homogeneity and social stability."[27] Folk culture felt to many "rooted in the American past and culture" and fostered a "national aesthetic tradition."[28]

Collecting miniatures like the antique dolls of the Doll Show was a particularly evocative way to create the sense of a different era and curate an imagined past. "The miniature," theorist Susan Stewart writes, has the "capacity . . . to create an 'other' time, a type of transcendent time which negates change and the flux of reality."[29] The Doll Show's miniature dolls, patterned after adult women, offered visitors the myth of a past, aristocratic time of order and good manners.

At the same time, by displaying and collecting dolls, women like Mrs. Lewis were able to travel vicariously to other countries by importing foreign goods and incorporating them into their homes and social worlds.[30] And, paradoxically, despite their celebration of a past that was emblematic of traditional values, these women were engaging in a modern, inherently feminist activity. By educating people about the customs and behaviors of people from other countries they were acting as experts and transforming what had been a hobby into an area of expertise. They involved themselves in public life—arranging shows, giving talks, and advocating for museums to house historical dolls. Ironically, despite their longing for a past time when women had little public authority, they entered the public arena where they gained some power and influence.

The Doll Show merits attention for a number of reasons. First, it represents a rejection of the culture of industrialism with its mass-produced dolls and toys. It embodies the wish for a return not only to handmade, high-quality dolls but to a traditional model of feminine behavior, with an emphasis of demure, polite, strictly regulated behavior. The flapper, the professional woman, even the suffragist make no appearance in this record. Second, the show's major focus on European dolls and the consistent celebration of royalty suggested that, for these collectors, Europe, with its aristocracy and hierarchal structure, was somehow superior to the more hardscrabble, democratic United States, at least in terms of fashion and manners. Third, the distortion of historical facts and the exclusion and omission of dolls that represented anyone other than white aristocrats or their colonial subordinates resulted in a sanitized and false presentation of American history. While emphasizing certain Old World nations lent collections a global identity, the notable absence of Black dolls resulted in a show that excluded nonwhite groups of people from its definition of citizenship and erased them from American history.

Mary Lewis, who organized the show, resided with her many dolls on Ocean Parkway in Brooklyn. Her collection grew each year, and by 1951 she lived in a "10-room house . . . with her husband and 3,000 dolls."[31] In 1947, Mrs. Lewis published *The Marriage of Diamonds and Dolls*, a book meant to highlight for the world the enormous collection she had gathered and shown in 1938.[32] Published by H. L. Lindquist, a member of an organization called the Collectors Club, the book offered descriptions, illustrations, and photos of her dolls. The book serves to highlight the themes and ideas that the Doll Show had likely promoted while Lewis wrote it. Mrs. Lewis's book combined advice, historical research, nostalgia, material culture, and a chronological narrative of bridal traditions. It served as another way for Mrs. Lewis to display her dolls—this time with descriptions that shed more light on what she was trying to communicate in the 1938 Doll Show.

Lewis herself sought to replicate a lifestyle of the rich and famous of old by organizing charity events for children both in the city and abroad, educating the poor, and serving as the hostess for distinguished guests who visited Brooklyn. The *Knickerbocker News*, itself a paper whose name harkened back to the Dutch settlers of an earlier era, reported, "The history of what Brooklyn women are doing, world-wide, in philanthropic work is most inspiring. . . . Mrs. Mary E. Lewis of 798 Ocean Ave., is co-ordinator of a pageant-benefit for tubercular children in Greece."[33] When Lewis wasn't traveling, she hosted parties for both foreign and New York elites where she could show her collection. These events were often coordinated with visits to institutions like the Brooklyn Children's Museum, which also housed a display of dolls. Mrs. Lewis entertained "members of the National Doll and Toy Collectors' Club at her home . . . the guests will visit the Brooklyn Children's Museum, where there is a permanent display of international dolls, and will return to Miss Lewis's home for supper."[34]

The doll collectors exemplify old models of feminine leadership by hosting and educating in accordance with a "moral suasion" model, attempting to teach children their values. In the 1930s these doll collectors began to sponsor events to introduce people to cultures beyond the borders of the United States. The youngest "member" of the Doll Collectors' Club, Mabelle Cremer, age seven, was said to have "hosted" an international festival of children, with "dolls on every hand representing all races and most of the periods of world history. . . . There were New York City children and some visiting from other places, and then there were those from the New York consulates, wearing costumes of Bulgaria, Czechoslovakia, Estonia, Finland, Greece, Guatemala, Hungary, Latvia, Mexico."[35] The irony was lost that these collectors were celebrating diverse people from around the world by displaying a collection that valued whiteness above all else, in a city where each day people arrived from around the world.

The dolls in the New York show were seen as representatives of their cities. The *Boston Globe* announced, "Antique dolls dating back more than a century are to leave the Children's Museum in Boston for New York today to participate in the first national show." The article went on, "Dressed in old-fashioned gowns which attendants have pressed up and restored for the showing, the dolls will make the trip in an ancient horsehair trunk." The dolls were emissaries, according to the article, with "a 'mission' to perform. They are intended to make doll collecting so popular that New York will support a doll and toy collectors group, just as Boston women" had.[36] The dolls were treated as diplomats, bringing New England tradition to the possibly more "modern" world of Manhattan. Sometimes the press, in a tongue-in-cheek way, referred to the dolls as real women. One article noted that "great preparations are under way at the Children's Museum in Jamaica Plain to restore coiffeurs and the dignity of ruffles and bustles so that the delegates will do credit to Boston."[37] The same article in the *Christian Science Monitor* referred to the dolls' ages: "Life is beginning at 140 [years old], at 100, and at 75 for a dozen ladies out of Boston's past who are busily preparing to leave town tomorrow for a month's visit to New York City. . . . To many New Englanders a trip to Manhattan may be a casual affair, but for these twelve—all beloved dolls—it is the most exciting experience since the Civil War when they were in their prime."[38] The dolls are described as giddy children, unused to any type of travel, who are finally leaving behind Boston, and their bland New England lives, for the metropolis of Manhattan.

The Doll Show reflected a growing movement in the 1930s to establish doll museums for all major U.S. cities.[39] According to the *New York Times*, the National Doll and Toy Collectors' Club "announced plans yesterday for the establishment of a national museum, exclusively for dolls of all ages and nationalities."[40] They approached members of the New York City government with a view toward arranging for museum space in some existing municipal museum or other building. The *Times* announced that "municipal officers . . . are in wholehearted agreement that a comprehensive national doll and toy collection would serve a useful educational and cultural good, not only for children but for their elders as well."[41] In 1938, just one year after its formation, the National Doll and Toy Collectors' Club lobbied the city government for a permanent home for a doll museum. The Museum of the City of New York was open by this time, having amassed an extensive array of toys and dolls for what would be one of their cornerstone collections. It was later noted that Mrs. Lewis and Anna Billings Gallup, who founded the Brooklyn Children's Museum, attempted but failed to establish a permanent home for doll collections, emphasizing the educational and cultural promise of such a site.[42]

Mrs. Lewis continued to be fascinated by royalty, even priding herself on a fantastical personal connection to Princess Elizabeth. In 1947 the *Brooklyn Daily Eagle* reported that Mrs. Lewis was invited to a tea party with Princess Elizabeth. Unable to attend because of distance and commitments, she sent a copy of her book to the young princess in honor of her wedding. In excited tones the *Eagle* held Mrs. Lewis responsible for making sure "Brooklyn wasn't forgotten, when the invitations to the marriage of Elizabeth and Phillip went out around the world."[43]

Despite this fascination with wealth and aristocracy, the United States, never a country with a formal aristocracy, was moving further away from having the kind of elite upper class that the doll collectors longed for. In fact, the 1930s was an era focused on the common man, on industrial workers and the plights of their families. As Michael Denning points out in *The Cultural Front*, radical politics and celebrations of the average man were central to both politics and popular culture at the time. The plays of Clifford Odets, the music of Earl Robinson and Paul Robeson, and the photography of Dorothea Lange were all focused on the plight of the poor and working-class people, as were books of John Steinbeck, John Dos Passos, and Zora Neale Hurston.[44] The national government's efforts to lift the country out of economic depression focused on employing struggling artists like Grant Wood, Edward Hopper, and Jacob Lawrence through the Federal Arts Project. These artists depicted displaced victims of the Dust Bowl, the struggles of the industrial worker, the mass migration of African Americans, and even the loneliness of a late-night cup of coffee. Post office murals across the country showcased the lives of Americans struggling to build— or rebuild—the country. Even Henry Ford and the Rockefeller family hired radical artists like Diego Rivera to paint murals of the worlds of work and struggle.[45] The 1930s was a decade of contrasts, united at times around popular culture and celebrities like Shirley Temple—herself repeatedly imitated in doll form—whose performance of girlhood seemed to comfort people amid the chaos of an economy in collapse.[46] Americans of all kinds, whether antique collectors or industrial workers of the Popular Front, all loved this plucky American girl who exuded youth, vitality, and accessibility.

Yet the doll collectors persisted in extolling the traditions of an upper-class, aristocratic world that had never really been America, except perhaps in the Antebellum South.

Susan Stewart, writing about miniatures, points out that a dollhouse "has two dominant motifs: wealth and nostalgia."[47] Many of the dolls in Lewis's collection, and their descriptions, operated around these very motifs, commenting on the quality of their materials, their societal status (as brides or as belonging to royalty), and their wealthy owners, all undergirded by a wistful tone for a bygone time.

One of Mrs. Lewis's favorite European dolls, as reported in her book, was her "Pretty Parlor Doll: Edythe," from 1870. A "little Victorian 'parlor doll,'" "Edythe," reminded her "of the wedding dolls that . . . commemorate[d] the nuptials of members of the Royal families." "My doll is not a representation of any famous person nor a doll that any little girl ever played with," she reminded the reader. "Dressed in the manner of a bride of 1870," she "stands sedately and safely under her glass bell on a little wooden platform."[48] Like the ideal Victorian woman, this doll stands apart and isolated from the dangers and contaminations of the world. She sits in the parlor, frozen in time, which, amid the chaos of the increasingly mechanized, modern, Depression-era New York, must have held special appeal. As Stewart writes, a doll behind glass remained in a "miniature world," which was "perfect and uncontaminated by the grotesque so long as its absolute boundaries were maintained." This boundary isolated the doll, keeping it out of reach from the viewer and other forces of nature. "The glass eliminates the possibility of contagion, indeed of lived experience, at the same time that it maximizes the possibilities of transcendent vision."[49]

Another Victorian doll, introduced as "To the Queen's Taste: Victoria, 1830," represented Harriet, the Duchess of Parma. This doll actually belonged to Queen Victoria when she was a child. Interestingly, Mrs. Lewis does not seem to idealize this doll as she did the Victorian parlor doll. Instead she describes her as "a lonesome little girl without brothers or sisters." Although this was one of Lewis's prized dolls, likely because of its provenance, Lewis was less enthusiastic about the commonness of the doll's material. "Basically, she is just a painted

Figure 2.3. One of Mary E. Lewis's dolls sits protected under a glass bell jar. Mary E. Lewis, *The Marriage of Diamonds and Dolls* (New York: H. L. Lindquist, 1947), 7.

wooden figure and not half so pretty. . . . The doll seems to have been made of a turned piece of wood with a funny little nose put on afterwards. This was the way furniture pieces were made, and it is quite possible that one of the palace cabinet-makers also supplied the Princess with her dolls."[50]

In imitation of a European custom whereby miniature doll versions of royalty were created, Mrs. Lewis had a replica of herself in her own wedding dress made for one of her dolls. "Having no daughter to wear my dress and veil and gloves," she explained, "I thought one way to preserve them would be to create a miniature Mrs. Mary E. Lewis. So, I got out my wedding pictures and had Lulu Kriger copy my dress and veil for the doll."[51]

Although Mrs. Lewis claimed to pay great attention to historical accuracy, that accuracy had more to do with the changing styles of and materials used for the dolls than with any historical period. As one review of the Doll Show states, it was the dolls' value as historical artifacts and the history of "the customs and costumes of an era" that mattered to collectors. "To the connoisseur these play-things are more than sentimental mementos of another day; they are valuable records of period influences."[52] While the article headline, "Antique Dolls Tell a Story Today," suggests that the value of these dolls lay in their historical narra-tives, in fact, their value lay in the way they evoked the history of fashion and craft. The collectors were considered experts who could "tell you when the painted wood doll went out of fashion, when bisque and wax heads came in."[53] Lewis's dolls ranged from "hand carved Swiss dolls made about 1750" to "colo-nial dolls still dressed in the faded textiles of the time, with the characteristic voluminous skirts. Some, attired in costly embroidered silks, come from wealthy households; others, more simply dressed, once belonged to some little girl of humbler family."[54]

Mrs. Lewis presented the history surrounding her dolls as though they were in a clear chronology, telling a progressive story. Her search for order elides the disarray of history and glosses over times when, say, modern materials were used to mend her dolls. One doll, which she called "A Little Bride: Yvonne, 1750," is described as one of Mrs. Lewis's most valuable. And while Mrs. Lewis admitted that various parts of the doll's body often dated from different time periods, she valued it for its rarity. These inconsistencies highlight Mrs. Lewis's attempt to reconfigure history into a more orderly arrangement. In fact, her decision to overlook the inconsistencies seems to have reflected her approach in general—to offer an orderly history of doll fashion in the face of a messy present.

The only contemporary mass-produced doll Lewis features in her book is the Kewpie doll (pronounced Cu-Pee, playing off the word "Cupid"), which was explicitly recognizable as commercially available. Kewpie dolls were one of the more popular character dolls in U.S. doll history and Mrs. Lewis's was a gift from the artist and creator of the doll, Rose O'Neill. It is ironic that Mrs. Lewis included them as traditional brides, and emblems of refined femininity, given that they were modeled on babies and designed to appear androgynous.[55] The photo's caption in Mrs. Lewis's book reads, "Coy little Kewpie bride dressed in net and ribbons by a child, about 1912." Her chapter on "Kewpies and Other Characters: 1912" acknowledges that these dolls were not meant for display but were meant to be played with. "Kewpie dolls were toys, prizes, favors, table dec-orations and statuettes. Millions of them were sold."[56]

By reconfiguring the Kewpie doll as a grown woman and transforming this androgynous, mass-produced doll into a traditional bride, Mrs. Lewis undid all of the original ambiguity of the Kewpie doll in order to make it a model of femininity. She used the chapter on the Kewpie doll to discuss only tangentially related topics, including other famous doll collections and exhibits, paper dolls, and Parisienne fashion dolls. To further her vision, Mrs. Lewis placed this commercial doll of America in the company of ancient civilizations and elevated the doll by giving it a history. She wrote, "While all authorities agree that the doll was first associated with religious services, they also believe that children played with toy dolls from early times. In Egypt and Greece little girls played with their dolls until marriage and then placed them at the feet of the Goddess Venus."[57]

The 1920s' speakeasy dolls, named after the hidden bars that sprung up during Prohibition, appear to have been particularly offensive to Mrs. Lewis's aesthetic and moral sense. The world of the 1920s, or at least the popular image Mrs. Lewis would have had about the decade, was quite different from the world the collectors sought to display. The 1920s would have conjured up images of Prohibition, flappers, and the Charleston, as well as short-haired women wearing pants, drinking, smoking, and having promiscuous sex. A pair of speakeasy dolls dressed in clothes made of linen and "stiff white paper" could not have been more different from the dolls dressed in silks and satins.[58] Part of Mrs. Lewis's distaste for these dolls probably related to their connection to the world of commerce. "Composed of celluloid and wire, they were a shade grotesque and foreshadowed that whole generation of exaggerated, long-necked characters which appeared in store windows, advertisements and fashion illustrations following the exposition of 'art moderne' in Paris in 1925."[59]

While uncritical of the luxury of royalty whom she admired and wished to emulate, Mrs. Lewis described the decade of the 1920s as "a time of extravagance and irresponsibility." Calling the dolls "exaggerated" and "grotesque," she indicated her disapproval of the particular type of femininity this speakeasy doll conveyed. "The bride is too thin, too dead-white, her bobbed hair too brassy-red, her cigarette too obvious. She symbolizes a strange, hard type of femininity that we called the flapper. . . . This was a 'low brow' era in more ways than one."[60] How different from the stately, distinguished, and elite femininity that Mrs. Lewis prized in her other dolls.

As part of a reaction to industrialism, the Doll Show represented a rejection not only of the mass-produced toys being offered by toy companies but of the overall culture of the period. By presenting a seemingly more stable past, the doll collectors attempted to hold on to a world that was fading fast as industrialism continued to change the nation. The world the doll collectors presented was not the world of 1930s America. The collectors paid little attention to dolls representative of working- or middle-class women or nonwhite women. This is not par-

Figure 2.4. Mr. and Mrs. Speakeasy. A pair of dolls from the Prohibition era described as crass and cheap by their owner, Mary E. Lewis.

ticularly surprising given that in the 1930s the United States was still segregated by law or practice.

One particular and famous incident illustrates how out of touch many upper-class elite women were with the changes that were happening in America when it came to race. In 1938, the same year as the Doll Show, the Daughters of the American Revolution (DAR) refused to allow Marian Anderson, one of the country's most prominent opera singers, to perform in Constitution Hall in Washington, D.C. Dedicated to the memory of "men and women who achieved American independence," DAR's stated purpose was to "cherish, maintain, and extend the institutions of American freedom. To foster patriotism and love of country," DAR quickly became a powerful voice for upper-class white Protestant women who could trace their ancestries back to the Revolution. By the end of the Depression it claimed a membership of 143,000, among them the wives of presidents, cabinet officials, and merchant capitalists. By the 1930s, it considered itself "one of the most powerful women's organizations in the world," with 2,550 chapters.[61]

However powerful the organization imagined itself to be, it was about to learn of its eroding position in late 1938 when it was proposed that Marian Anderson sing at Constitution Hall for an integrated audience. DAR, which owned the hall where Anderson was scheduled to sing, quickly nixed the plan, claiming that local customs and Jim Crow laws of the era forbade an African American, no matter what her international reputation, from singing on their stage. This created an uproar in the press and within the White House. The *Afro-American*, among the country's most important Black newspapers of the era, noted that Constitution Hall "stands almost in the shadow of the Lincoln Memorial, but the sentiments of the Great Emancipator are not shared by the DAR's."[62] In protest against the decision to bar Anderson, Eleanor Roosevelt resigned from the organization. Marian Anderson "instead gave a free and much publicized outdoor concert at the Lincoln Memorial," making well-known DAR's discrimination.[63]

The white, ancestry-oriented collection of Mrs. Lewis that she featured in her book included only two non-Anglo-Saxon dolls, and the descriptions of these dolls reflected certain prejudices and imperial attitudes. Lewis valued her California mission doll, Dolores, from 1835, not for being American but for her connection to the Spanish aristocracy. Mrs. Lewis noted the attire of peasant brides who "wore black for marriage" and "who wore strand after strand of silver beads and long chains of reliquaries, medals, charms, and amulets pinned from the shoulders." She announced that her doll, "a bride of wealthy and aristocratic class would wear white with a white lace mantilla."[64] In case it was still unclear, she wrote, "My little California bride is an aristocrat with nothing about her to suggest the peon or the Indian."[65] All of her finery "would have come hundreds of miles overland from Mexico or direct from Spain." Mrs. Lewis, while loving this doll, referred to her condescendingly as "my little Spanish Bride-doll," denoting ownership of this miniature foreign royal.[66]

The conspicuous absence of any Black dolls, who, one can guess, did not fit Mrs. Lewis's ideal, seems to point not simply to a perceived deficit in well-made Black dolls but to their exclusion from the story of America. Included in her collection was "A Little Island Bride: Maria, 1940." This Puerto Rican doll was among the only exceptions to the generic whiteness that characterized other dolls. Dressed in the style of 1940s Puerto Rico, Maria was supposed to "repre-

Figure 2.5. "Little California Bride." A "Spanish Bride" doll, one of only two non-Anglo-Saxon dolls featured in Mary E. Lewis's book.

sent all native brides in the islands under Uncle Sam's protection."[67] For Mrs. Lewis this doll represented America's role as a colonial power. She treated this doll as Uncle Sam treated his protectorates. She acknowledged it was different from others in her collection in that she was "a modern doll of the kind that children really love to play with. She has a soft, plump, unbreakable body of flesh-pink cotton and her little head is also cloth. The head represents a new process in American doll manufacture."[68] This doll was manufactured, not hand-made, and compared with the white dolls included in this collection, the Puerto Rican doll was described as appropriate for throwing, touching, and playing as opposed to observing or preserving behind glass. This is the only time this kind of treatment of a doll is prescribed in the book.

When viewed overall, Mrs. Lewis's collection can be seen as part of a culture that excluded African Americans and, in the world of toys, suggested to Black children that they were not part of the story of America.[69] The doll collectors' preoccupation with white, upper-class life stood in stark contrast to the concerns of the Black community. Although Black dolls were being produced, they were segregated into two distinct sets of stores and distribution systems. For the most part, dolls were either low-brow racist caricatures or antique, often high-value dolls that were exclusively white. The department stores of white America sometimes sold racist "Sambo" dolls for white children, while some stores that focused on African American communities sold more respectful dolls generally produced by African American–owned companies for African American children.[70] Although some of the most pernicious forms of segregation began to break down especially in cities like Chicago and New York and in other north-ern industrial communities, the United States in the 1930s remained largely seg-regated and prejudice against Black people was woven into the culture. Children learned from observing the world around them who was valued, who the lead-ers were, and who was considered beautiful.

Mamie and Kenneth Clark's Doll Studies

Mamie Clark was among those concerned with the real-life consequences that the absence of mainstream images, at least positive images, of African Ameri-cans had on children. As a social psychologist she was following in the footsteps of others who had turned their attention to children and how culture impacts the development of personality. G. Stanley Hall's understanding of the cultural importance of children's playthings reflected a broader movement in American social psychology and educational thought during the early twentieth century. In 1922, John Dewey wrote *Human Nature and Conduct: An Introduction of Social Psychology* in which he argued that "the environment in which a person lived would determine, in many ways, what the person thought and how that person acted." He noted that personality was a product of the "interactions of elements contributed by the make-up of an individual with elements supplied by the out—door world."[71] Other early twentieth-century personality theorists and develop-mental psychologists like Piaget and Freud continued to explore the question of how the environment influenced children's character, and some turned their attention to the construction of racial identity in Black children.

Ruth Horowitz, a professor of educational psychology at Columbia's Teachers College, published one of the earliest social psychological studies of the way race shaped children's identity. In "The Racial Aspects of Self-Identification in Nursery School Children," Horowitz used both photographs and line drawings of people of different races and asked twenty-one white and Black children to nod, point, or use language to identify the representation that was like them.[72] She then tabulated the "correct" and "incorrect" choices and observed that as the children got older their identification with "white" or "Black" became more "accurate." For Horowitz this meant that racial identification was a stage in the development of personality rather than considering that the children might have focused on height, weight, expression, or clothing rather than race in identifying the characteristics "most like them."[73] Here, adult preoccupations with race occluded the insight that children do not unanimously prioritize race as a defining physical attribute.

Nonetheless, Horowitz's studies were timely and provoked interest among other social and developmental psychologists on the question of racial identity. Mamie Clark was a graduate student writing her master's thesis at Howard University when she began a study of racial identification of African American children utilizing some of the same techniques that Horowitz pioneered. But, unlike Horowitz, who saw racial identification as an inborn developmental process, Clark identified a child's social surroundings as critical. As she related in the paper she coauthored with her husband, Kenneth Clark, in 1939, she employed "a modification of the Horowitz picture technique," testing "150 Negro children in segregated Washington, D.C. schools." A year later she again joined with her husband to write a much more direct critique of developmental psychologists titled "Skin Color as a Factor in Racial Identification of Negro Preschool Children."[74] Questioning Horowitz's conclusion that racial identification was a phase in the development of consciousness itself, they instead posited that race is a social concept that children learn from their environment.

By the 1940s the Clarks had turned to dolls as a better proxy than drawings for "self-identification" among children, both white and Black. Dolls offered a three-dimensional, more lifelike appearance than did line drawings or even photographs. The tests generally presented children with dolls identical in all respects other than color, asking them to identify the one that they believed was prettier, more interesting, and more intelligent. The results were troubling. African American children as young as five years old showed a preference for the white doll and generally identified it as prettier and better. The results of the doll test "tend to support previous results, although the trend was seen more definitely with the Dolls test."[75] The questions that they used in their famous doll studies focused more on the children's explanations for their preferences, subjective statements about the ugliness or prettiness of the dolls.[76]

Mamie Clark's master's thesis appeared in article form in the *Journal of Social Psychology*, and the Clarks published a second "Preliminary Report" titled "Segregation as a Factor in the Racial Identification of Negro Pre-school Children" in 1939.[77] This study specifically identified segregation as the variable the authors wanted to study. They explained that "some Negro children from mixed New York nursery schools were compared with the main group of Negro children from segregated Washington, D. C., nursery schools." The Clarks hypothesized that "such a comparison would give an indication of the possible effects of segregation as a factor affecting the problem investigated."[78] They concluded, "It appears that where the child brings up the subject of race at all, his expressions are indicative of negative attitudes toward the Negro race."

Some of the data were used to quantify the responses of Black and white children who picked out "pretty" white dolls over "ugly" Black dolls. But some of the most damning information came from the listings of responses that both Black and white five-year-olds had when asked to explain their preferences: Why was the brown doll rejected by the child? "Cause him black—cause his cheeks are colored—it's ugly," "looks bad all over," responded children from a southern state. Children from the North were not more subtle or progressive: when asked why they rejected the brown doll, they simply said, "I don't like brown" or "cause it looks like a Negro." Drawing out broader implications of their study, the Clarks concluded that "it is clear that the Negro child, by the age of five is aware of the fact that to be colored in contemporary American society is a mark of inferior status."[79]

The Clarks's conclusions were also geographically and socially specific. The children in the segregated Washington, D.C., schools had rigid distinctions between "white" and "Negro," "pretty" and "ugly." But the children from New York, where white and Black children more often attended school together, showed a much lower tendency to identify themselves by associating the color in the pictures with themselves. They were more likely to focus on a variety of characteristics and subtleties in skin shading in their identification of "white" and "Negro." "In the segregated group racial identifications were made for the most part upon the basis of the skin color of the subjects." But, the Clarks observed, "there was no tendency whatsoever toward this trend in the mixed group."[80] They began to shape the argument that would prove so critical in the Supreme Court's 1954 decision striking down racial segregation.

In 1951, right before *Brown v. Board* was argued in the Supreme Court, a reporter for the *Baltimore Afro-American* outlined the dire implications for children of the Clarks's doll studies: the children, he reported, were "told to choose the 'good' doll," and the overwhelming majority of them chose the white doll. "Thus by the age of six, American children of all races, discovered to be colored must mean to be 'bad' and that happiness and freedom is reserved for the lights." The reporter noted that "Thurgood Marshall, the NAACP lawyer, [is using] the doll experiment as an illustration of the idea that segregation is immoral." He paraphrased Marshall as saying "that it is time we recognize discrimination for what it is."[81] Ultimately, the doll studies were crucial in the Supreme Court's *Brown v. Board* decision, which overturned *Plessy v. Ferguson*, the infamous 1896 Supreme Court ruling that had established the "separate but equal" justification for legal segregation. American history was forever changed by dolls.

In 1938 the Doll Show represented an attempt and echoed other attempts by elites to hold on to a vision of America that was dominated by white, upper-class, wealthy Protestants. At about the same time, Mamie Clark demonstrated the consequences this view of America would have on children. Her work with Kenneth Clark demonstrated that the absence of positive depictions of African Americans in American culture was negatively impacting Black children's self-esteem. The vision of a white world that the doll collectors were trying to hold on to was not only inadequate but harmful at a time when the country was becoming increasingly diverse. The Doll Show and the Clarks's doll study demonstrate how particular cultural artifacts, in this case the doll, can provide a window into the culture that produced them. Although they were the focus of attention at roughly the same time, the dolls in these two cases represent two very different views of 1930s America and who belonged as Americans.

CHAPTER 3

"Gosh, It's Exciting to Be an American"

THE "ORANGE" AND LANDMARK HISTORY BOOKS DURING THE COLD WAR

Will you please tell me what matters more than what children read? What other books [than children's books] are as much lived in, acted out, and, if they are remembered at all, remembered for as long?
—*Anne Parrish, "Writing for Children"*[1]

In an interview about her attempt to reprint the Childhood of Famous Americans series, popularly known as the Orange books (for their distinctive orange covers), Florrie Binford Kichler recalls that when she was eight years old and confined to bed her aunt bought her "an orange biography of Mary Todd Lincoln. That was it. I was hooked."[2] Similarly, an early reviewer of Random House's Landmark series identified the important change the books represented: "I remember my own study of American history at the age of ten," wrote Katherine Shippen, who would eventually write two Landmark books herself. "Then the voyages of Columbus were simply three black lines drawn on a map. The causes of the American Revolution were a list to be learned."[3] But the new literature for children emerging in the 1940s and 1950s was significantly different—relating fictionalized stories to young readers in ways that grabbed their attention and taught them important, if selective, civic lessons. "The writing of history for young people," Shippen noted, "has certainly come a long way since we first studied it. The publication of this series of books is in itself a landmark in that progress."[4]

The Orange and Landmark books played a significant role in the lives of children in the years following World War II. The books focused on notable characters in American history, and the covers, language, and packaging were oriented toward a young audience. Both series were immensely successful, together reaching and influencing millions of children. Bobbs-Merrill (originally Bowen-Merrill) started the Orange series in 1932 with its first book, *Abe Lincoln: Frontier Boy*, by Augusta Stevenson. Only two others were published between then and the outbreak of World War II, one about Thomas Jefferson (1939) and another about Robert E. Lee (1937). But with the outbreak of war, publishing accelerated. By 1943 Bobbs-Merrill had sold a hundred thousand copies of the Lincoln book.[5] By 1952 there were more than sixty Orange books in print, and by 1960 another seventy. By 1970, the number reached 218.[6] Random House began publishing its Landmark series in 1950 and had published ninety books by 1960 and another thirty-two between then and 1970.[7] The immense popularity of these books meant that children across the country were all learning a particular version of American history, developing a consensus about American heroes and training to be conversant with it. This chapter explores the particular history that emerged from these series during the postwar years as well as the factors that contributed to that history, including efforts to produce a unifying national story as well as decisions made in response to the repressive political climate of the time.

Published by Bobbs-Merrill, the Orange books were designed for boys and girls aged eight to twelve and became "familiar to baby boomers across the country" who fondly remember "their bright colored jackets, their neat binding and numerous illustrations," which were a "tempting display for [any child] to look through."[8] The books were originally geared toward boys, and intended to be called "Boyhoods of Famous Americans."[9] The authors of the books imagined how famous Americans, primarily white men but including a few women, came to possess the traits that led to their becoming great American leaders. For example, according to a *Chicago Daily Tribune* reviewer in 1949, the author of the book about Myles Standish, the leader of the original *Mayflower* settlers, having scant evidence about Standish's childhood, "brings him to life as a strong-willed, independent youngster who didn't like fancy clothes." Similarly, the story about Harriet Beecher Stowe's childhood "revealed the generosity and the sense of justice that were later to result in her writing 'Uncle Tom's Cabin.'" As a child, Abigail Adams, who would become the wife and confidant of John Adams, is described as a humble child, a keen observer of people and events, who probably never would have guessed that her writings "would one day be collected into a book." Oliver Perry, also of humble origins, lived in sight of the Atlantic Ocean and had a seafaring father who prepared him to be adventurous and brave, qualities that would give him the courage to take on the British on Lake Erie.[10] Through tales of social mobility and humble beginnings, books in the series accentuate the idea that America is a land where you do not need to be born into wealth in order to achieve greatness.

The Landmark books were geared toward slightly older children and also to boys, aged ten to twelve, as evidenced by their focus on subjects assumed to be of interest to boys and by the fact that Random House tested some material in *Boys Life*, the magazine of the Boy Scouts of America.[11] The books featured not only American heroes but also what the press deemed "landmark" events both within and outside the United States. Presenting history as adventure, different from the (dull) way history was often taught in schools, the Random House books purported to be nonfiction. Nancy Wilson Ross, the author of the 1960 Landmark book *Heroines of the Early West*, explained that her stories were, in fact, "history" because they were based on actual diaries and letters. "These diarists, letter writers and autobiographers of the Far West, in the years between the 1830s and the early 1900s, were, though perhaps unaware of it, serving History as ably as any trained historian."[12] Nonetheless, Wilson Ross imagined the lives of her heroines in ways that many would say earn the designation fiction, with contrived anecdotes to fill in the historical record.

The authors of the Orange and Landmark books were generally not professional historians but Random House, in particular, recruited experienced writers, many of whom were winners of prestigious prizes for children's literature, to write the Landmark books. They enlisted Armstrong Sperry, an illustrator and Newbery Prize–winning author of adventure books for children, to write *Voyages of Christopher Columbus*. James Daugherty, winner of the Newbery and Caldecott prizes for children's literature, was chosen to write *The Landing of the Pilgrims* and *Trappers and Traders of the Far West*, ostensibly using original sources, including William Bradford's diaries. Robert Penn Warren, author of the Pulitzer Prize–winning novel *All the King's Men*, wrote the Landmark book *Remember the Alamo!* in 1958. Some authors brought their expertise from other professional areas. Bobbs-Merrill recruited Augusta Stevenson, initially a librarian in Indianapolis, to open their series in 1932 with *Abe Lincoln: Frontier Boy*.[13] Both series promised to deliver exciting historical narratives—a common trope in the advertising of history-themed commodities. The promotion of these generally fictionalized stories as history gave them a certain gravitas.

Reading these books today one can see why they were so popular. They are full of adventures, information, and incidents of interest to children.[14] The illustrations are detailed and evocative. Yet despite the significant impression they made on children, they have been studied little outside the world of children's literature.[15] This chapter views these books as cultural artifacts that shed light on the historical period in which they were written, particularly the Cold War period between 1945 and 1960. These series offered a generation of children a particular story about U.S. history—that of white men exploring, battling, inventing, and conquering in the name of freedom and democracy; of people improving their social status by pulling themselves up by their bootstraps; of women and minorities as primarily minor, supporting actors, or vehicles to support a consensus view of history as predestined, celebratory, and just; and of conflicts "resolved" and in the past. While these books presented an appealing story, they downplayed or ignored the tensions of American history—tensions between men and women, rich and poor, Black and white; between a view of the United States as a beacon of democracy and a view of the United States as an international military power. More complex and troubling aspects of American history were sometimes noted but rarely interrogated in any depth. Written largely in the shadow of the Cold War, as Joseph McCarthy, HUAC, and the FBI searched for Communist "traitors," even in the world of publishing, these books presented action-filled but anodyne histories of the country's past.

Bobbs-Merrill got its start in Indianapolis in the nineteenth century, almost two decades before Random House was founded. It "would gradually evolve from an organization mainly concerned with local and regional wholesale and retail sales of books and stationery into a trade and specialties publishing house of national stature."[16] The heyday of the company was in the late 1800s, and although it continues to publish books today, it "ceased to be among the country's leading publishing houses" by the late 1950s. Its Orange book series was significant as one of the few available to "introduce young readers to history and biography," and its success helped "bring into focus the market potential for children's nonfiction series."[17]

Although it had an office in New York and was itself a major press, Bobbs-Merrill considered itself a product of the Midwest, with an identity as a wholesome publishing house somehow different from its East Coast peers. The Indiana publisher's identity was deeply affiliated with the frontier myth of the Midwest. In 1916, the company published a children's book commemorating the centennial of Indiana's statehood, called *Once Upon a Time in Indiana*. It featured more than 200 pages of stories intended to help young readers "come to appreciate the high purpose of the brave men and women who have made of the wilderness the sunlit garden of opportunity and happiness which we enjoy."[18] Its books were largely conservative in language and story and offered "good, clean fiction and corking good tales."[19] Its writers strove for a midwestern sensibility, emphasizing the values of agriculture, family, and Christianity, and hoped to appeal to a broad, national audience without being "too alien to their readers," and the press sought "clean, wholesome, and spirited manuscripts."[20] David Lawrence Chambers, the editor of the Orange series, "had no use for the rough language and realism of younger writers such as Ernest Hemingway, James T. Farrell, and John Dos Passos" who would become literary icons of American publishing and many of whom, including Dos Passos and Hemingway, would be published by Random House. He preferred to work with female authors because he found them to be more "compliant than men."[21]

The books of Augusta Stevenson, who wrote 30 of the 215 in the Orange series, reflected their patriotic American focus. Stevenson said she disliked children's books that "glamorized foreign children and plac[ed] a halo on distant lands."[22] Some reviewers saw books like hers that "glorified American boys and girls of the past" as a needed antidote to earlier biographies that focused on the "for-eign and . . . un-American leanings of other writers of the era." George Crane, a widely syndicated newspaper columnist in the 1950s and early 1960s, critiqued what he called a "modern trend to disdain Americanism!" and lauded Steven-son, for her work taught "loyalty and devotion to ideals, plus patriotism," thereby inoculating children against "communist influences."[23]

The formula for the Orange series was clear.[24] Present the story of America as one of normalcy where "the dominant virtues" of Middle America reigned— "intelligence, courage, loyalty, generosity, faith, independence, honor." The children in these stories grew up with the same, average, upstanding parents as did their readers from rural American towns and villages.[25] One writer, Jessica Mannon, a social conservative, believed the books were so successful because they were about children who "were inordinately good."[26]

Some reviewers, however, found this simple representation inadequate. "In the 'childhood' biographies, life is always too neat, and too stereotyped," com-plained Douglass Adair, a professor of English literature from William and Mary and the New York Times reviewer of the new children's literature appearing in the early 1950s. While he embraced the recent surge of engrossing children's his-tory books, he found the formulaic depictions misleading. "Here Washington, Wild Bill Hickok, Grant, Boone, Franklin, Lincoln and Lee all appear as 'nor-mal' happy boys, with good average parents, playing the right kind of pranks and dreaming only respectable adolescent dreams. And inevitably they all look very much alike as personalities, no matter what clothes they wear, what age they lived in." He argued that these books "exclude[d] the mystery, the shades and varieties, the heights and depths of personality—those very qualities that make biography an introduction to life and a substitute for experience." They failed both to communicate that it was the struggles and strains of youth that could lead to greatness and to confront the persistent stream of conflict that ran through American history. The "mystical, almost morbid strain in Lincoln's personality reflected a tragic view of life, not unrelated to the compassion and humility which set him above all our statesmen." Similarly, "Grant's shyness, isolation and ter-rible loneliness . . . were not unrelated to his military talent."[27]

Random House, in contrast to Bobbs-Merrill, was a liberal, New York–based publishing house at the center of the intellectual ferment of the middle decades of the twentieth century.[28] In 1925 Bennett Cerf, a young Columbia College graduate, proposed to college friends that they publish "random" books, often classics in the public domain and therefore not subject to royalty payments to long-dead authors. With their early efforts to reproduce cheap editions of "mod-ern classics," Cerf and his friends began to build one of the great publishing houses of the twentieth century.[29]

Over the course of the next half century Random House would publish a huge number of America's most influential authors, playwrights, and poets, including Saul Bellow, Truman Capote, Sinclair Lewis, Gertrude Stein, Thornton Wilder, W. H. Auden, Allen Ginsberg, Robert Lowell, Lillian Hellman, Eugene O'Neill, Tennessee Williams, and Toni Morrison.[30] The press also published the work of many of the leading political scientists, economists, and historians of the time who were central to creating the intellectual agenda of the nation, including John Kenneth Galbraith, Richard Hofstadter, C. Vann Woodward, Arthur Schlesinger, and Arthur Schlesinger Jr. Random House editors regularly corresponded with public figures like Eleanor and Franklin Roosevelt, Jackie Robinson, and J. Edgar Hoover. Books on virtually every conceivable historical subject and time period appeared under Random House's imprint.[31]

Random House almost immediately established itself as a more urbane, sophisticated press than Bobbs-Merrill by defining itself as a defender of literary free speech. The press challenged censorship laws that had banned the publication of James Joyce's *Ulysses* in the United States because of its "obscene" language. In 1933, ten years after *Ulysses* was first published in Europe, Cerf arranged to have an edition of the book seized by U.S. customs officials when he returned from Europe on an ocean liner. Following its seizure as an obscene, banned book, Random House sued the U.S. government, challenging its obscenity statutes in court on First Amendment grounds and won a "monumental decision" in District Court overturning the ban. Cerf then published "a beautifully made" American edition of *Ulysses*, and the press became known as a defender of the First Amendment.[32]

Having founded Random House, Cerf continued as editor and later envisioned his own concept of an American history series for children, the Landmark series. In his oral history he tells the origin story of the series: While on vacation with his family in Cape Cod in 1946, Cerf and his ten-year-old son argued about whether the Pilgrims landed in Provincetown or in Plymouth, Massachusetts, the site of the famous rock. Finding no books about the Pilgrims at the local bookstore or beyond, Cerf realized there were none of any substance and certainly none for ten-year-olds. As Cerf recounts, he set out to produce "serious" books about history that would be accessible and interesting for kids. "I began thinking about this, and then the idea suddenly struck me about this series of books . . . on some great episode in American history." He continues, "By the time we left Provincetown, I had a list of the first ten titles and the name of the series, Landmark Books. My thought was not to get juvenile authors for this. I was going to get the most important authors in the country."[33] Undoubtedly, Cerf did his homework and was aware of Bobbs-Merrill's Childhoods of Famous Americans series, which by that time was a decade old and had garnered blockbuster sales. Landmark books, which published its first edition in 1950 and whose heyday ended in the early 1960s, represented the press's most sustained and important long-term effort to attract younger readers to serious intellectual and historical issues.[34]

Cerf established the series' liberal credentials by first approaching Dorothy Canfield Fisher, a feminist social reformer and author of novels that centered on independent young girls and women overcoming societal limitations.[35] She agreed to write two of the first Landmark books, notably not about girls or women, one on the Constitution and the other on Paul Revere.[36] In succeeding months Cerf corralled John Mason Brown, a well-respected Broadway and literary critic for the *Saturday Review* and author of eight books, to write the Landmark *Daniel Boone: The Opening of the Wilderness* in 1952.[37] According to Cerf, this book alone sold in the "hundred thousands."[38] Despite its liberal ideals, and in contrast to the Orange series, only 18 percent of Random House's Landmark authors were women.[39]

Both presses published books about many of the same heroes. Understandably, their lists included books about the country's founders—Washington and Jefferson—and sometimes their wives, as well as books about Betsy Ross. But strikingly, both also included stories about the same lesser-known actors and events including Sacagawea, a Native American woman who served as scout for Lewis and Clark, and Narcissa Whitman, known as the first pioneer woman to cross the country. Each press also published a book about George Washington Carver but no other book about an African American until much later.[40]

While the two presses differed markedly in their social and regional origins, the stories they told about the country were remarkably similar. Both celebrated the pioneering spirit of those who conquered the West, subdued Native Americans, and civilized a wild country. Their heroes and heroines were generally independent, fiercely focused young men who were brought up with strong values. By and large, women played a supporting role to the men who made the country, and African Americans were generally absent or depicted as (happy) slaves and servants. When mentioned at all, slavery was a mistake that had been corrected, racism a by-product of slavery that could be overcome by the personal efforts of the former slaves and their descendants. Domestic or foreign conflicts were seen to be forced upon Americans by aggressive foes who attacked their peaceful wagon trains, sank their battleships, or bombed their naval ports.

How is it that these two very different presses published books not only about the same famous Americans but with a very similar interpretation of U.S. history? How did such a uniformly positive and noncritical view of American history cohere at a time when the country was feeling the damage and disruption from the Depression and the war? For one thing, despite the economic and social upheaval of these years, the country had managed to unite around a common cause during the war years—the defeat of fascism. A massive propaganda campaign had been undertaken to explain why the country was going to war and what principles and ideals united such a geographically, ethnically, and politically diverse population. Films, posters, and educational campaigns encouraged men to join the army, women to take jobs as welders in the airplane and shipbuilding industries, and children to join in collection drives for scrap metal, paper, and string.[41] African Americans in the South were encouraged to come to Detroit, Chicago, and other northern cities to fill recently vacated positions in heavy industries. America was fighting for what Franklin Roosevelt called "the Four Freedoms"—freedoms of speech and religion and freedom from want and fear. Frank Capra's seven-part series of *Why We Fight* films, shown to troops and in theaters throughout the country, explained why "our boys" from every region, ethnic group, and social class should join to fight the goose-stepping Nazis to save the "free world."[42]

It took no small effort to find the commonalities that defined such a diverse country. Nonetheless, the rallying cry about the need to defeat fascism helped join together previously antagonistic groups. Blacks and whites, radicals and conservatives suppressed their differences to forge an alliance with a common mission of defending democracy that all could agree on.

After the war this unity of purpose began to fray. Tensions that had been held in check reemerged. Returning Black veterans faced a resurgent Ku Klux Klan. White southerners worried that "uppity Negroes returning from the war would destroy their way of life" and "big business found [union demands] positively subversive."[43] And there was much concern about the stability of the family. Psychologists, social workers, and criminologists fretted that "the family would fall apart" if women "abandoned their domestic role as homemaker and mother" for the more public roles they had assumed in the industrial labor force during the war.[44]

One of the main sites for this postwar conflict about the stability of the family was the behavior of children. Juvenile delinquency rates appeared to be rising and became a national preoccupation, along with nuclear war and racial integration that people claimed was happening "too fast," of 1950s America. In New York, "an upsurge in crime is an after-cost of all wars," declared a committee identifying what was expected in future years. "All wars threaten family life, but this war has blasted many of our families in every direction."[45] In 1943 the *Washington Post* ran an interview with J. Edgar Hoover, who argued that this seeming upsurge in juvenile crime was due to the absence of fathers who were at war and mothers working away from home. Hoover stated, "Crime prevention must start in the home. It is the weighty responsibility of fathers and mothers to inculcate in the hearts and minds of their children a real appreciation of the personal and property rights of their fellowmen."[46]

A *New York Times* article titled "Bad Boy: A Portrait and a Prescription" argued that "juvenile delinquency has its roots deep in our slums, in the economic inequities of our system, in the vast, subterranean human and social dislocations produced by war."[47] The federal government called conferences to address the "juvenile crime" crisis. In July 1946, five hundred civic, educational, academic, and philanthropic leaders from around the country came to Washington to address the findings of a report by Hoover on the "alarming" rise of juvenile crime whose "roots," President Truman said, "lie in the home, the schools, and churches of our nation."[48] Those involved with children knew that they had to be part of an effort to provide stability and moral values to the next generation. Bobbs-Merrill and Random House can be seen as part of that effort to provide children with a vision of a stable country where the rules and values were clear and where its heroes exemplified model behavior.

Professional historians were also part of this effort to shape an inspiring and conflict-free, positive national story. In the decades before the 1950s, which were fraught with social and political turmoil, many known as "progressive" historians including Charles Beard, Frederick Turner, and Vernon Parrington had presented American history as characterized by class and social conflict. But after the war academics who came to be known as consensus historians rejected the earlier scholarly work and argued that such a tension-filled history accentuated divisions in the country. Instead, these consensus historians centered on a story of America as held together by a belief in democracy and economic and religious freedom and touted the idea that America was perfectible. They maintained that Americans on every side of every political divide shared in the "sanctity of property," the "right of the individual to dispose and invest," "the value of opportunity," and the "natural evolution of self-interest . . . into a beneficent social order." These qualities celebrated America as fundamentally good, and that goodness was rooted in free enterprise. There was the notion that these American characteristics would lift all boats. They then, as many do, projected these values onto the past, viewing significant events in American history through this lens.[49]

The development of this consensus interpretation of American history coincided with the rising political repression of the McCarthy era, the postwar decades between the end of World War II and the early 1960s. Given the widespread fear of the communist infiltration of American institutions, any critique of America by writers, journalists, antiwar activists, or leftists could be perceived as un-American—like Pete Seeger, who was studious of American history but blacklisted during this period. In this climate some of those historians who still saw class or social conflict as central to the American story were labeled as dangerous radicals, even as communists who threatened the country.[50] Some lost their university jobs or found themselves sidelined by the larger intellectual community. Daniel Boorstin, a professor at the University of Chicago who would be recruited to write a two-volume Landmark U.S. History textbook in the late 1960s and who then became the librarian of Congress, was a particularly partisan warrior in the attempt to purge the profession of those he perceived as critical of America. Called before the House Un-American Activities Committee (HUAC) in 1953, he named "many members of the historical profession whom he suspected of being communists."[51]

It is striking but not surprising to note, given the pressure to conform to a conservative, conflict-free view of American history, that Random House chose to tell the story of America as one of noble deeds and to deemphasize more troublesome aspects of American history. At least twenty-eight Landmark books celebrate westward expansion, with titles like the *Lewis and Clark Expedition* and *Trappers and Traders of the Far West*, while other books glorified the California Gold Rush or contained hagiographies of Daniel Boone, Davy Crockett, and Kit Carson. The books about Colonial America and the establishment of democracy focused on Benjamin Franklin, George Washington, and Thomas Jefferson. Forty-two books were specifically about war, including twenty-four about World War II, with titles like *The Battle of Britain*, *The Commandos of World War II*, *From Pearl Harbor to Okinawa*, *The Story of D-Day, June 6, 1944*, and *Midway: Battle for the Pacific*. The appeal of books about the war that had just ended would reach both parents, who had experienced and even fought in it, and children, who could relish in the glory of America's military might and the contributions of their family members.

Overall, both series omitted significant events in American history. Despite the many stories about westward expansion, Andrew Jackson's forced migration of Native Americans in the Trail of Tears did not merit attention from the publishers. No book in either series is devoted primarily to slavery, although it had persisted in the United States for 250 years. The books about World War II include nothing about of the internment of the Japanese or the testing of nuclear bombs. Although there are descriptions of "Indians" scalping people, there is no mention of lynchings and other actions by the Ku Klux Klan. Nor is there mention of the denial of women's right to vote through much of American history. And the list goes on.

NATIVE AMERICANS AND THE WILD WEST

The frontier story, so central to each series, was a perfect vehicle for consensus history. As Richard Slotkin points out, the 1950s were the heyday for Western films, "sustaining ideological consensus from its seedtime in 1948–54 . . . to its disruption by the failure of the war in Vietnam."[52] In written stories of the frontier, white American pioneers brought civilization and Christianity to a primitive people. In *The End of Victory Culture* Tom Engelhardt argues that the country came to embrace the frontier story as foundational because it "deflected attention from the racial horror story most central to the country's development— that of the African American." He goes on to explain the presentation of history in the 1950s. "If occasional wrongs were committed, or mistakes made, these were correctable; if unfreedom existed within America's borders, it was only so that— as with slavery—it might be wiped out forever." This triumphant American story became the lens through which major events—particularly wars—could be viewed: the nineteenth-century Indian wars were necessary to bring civilization to a barbarous people; the American Revolution and the Civil War were periods when "whites had fought each other reluctantly, with great heroism, and for the highest principles, whether in rebellion against a British king or in a civil war of 'brother against brother.'"[53] Pearl Harbor came to be described in this way: "At the country's periphery, a savage, nonwhite enemy had launched a barbaric attack on Americans going about their lives early one Sunday morning, and that enemy would be repaid in brutal combat on distant jungle islands in a modern version of 'Indian fighting.'"[54] This ideology holds true in the Landmark and Orange books' descriptions of Indians and the battles white Americans like Daniel Boone fought on the frontier.

Engelhardt explains how the narrative of the massacre of the Pequots in 1737 transformed into a story of English settlers' self-defense.[55] Over time, the story of the settlers' slaughter of the Native Americans was justified by the Indians' "treacherous ambushes, their torture of captives, their savage use of fire and other hellish modes of killing."[56]

American children in the 1950s came to see three primary types of Native Americans in popular culture: those who were vicious killers; those who were anonymous, hidden enemies; and those who were allies with an overall loyalty to the expansionist white American hero. But the popular depiction of Native Americans as savages seems to have the strongest grip on the American imagination. Even nineteenth-century schoolbooks contained graphic descriptions of Native Americans with "tomahawks raised, about to murder and presumably scalp a helpless white mother holding an infant in her arms."[57] By the 1950s, numerous TV shows about cowboys and Indians—*Gunsmoke, The Lone Ranger, Have Gun—Will Travel, The Deputy,* and *Hop Along Cassidy*—featured white male cowboys, settlers in wagon trains, vigilantes, gunslingers, and card sharks who were all part of the "settlement" story of the country, the broad uneven effort to bring civilization to untamed lands. The exceptions to this rule, Native Americans depicted as allies and sidekicks, like Pocahontas, Sacagawea, and Tonto, were important in lending legitimacy to the stories of white frontiersmen like Davy Crockett, explorers like Lewis and Clark, and cowboy characters like Roy Rogers.

In both the Orange and Landmark series Native Americans are most often depicted as dangerous and uncivilized or, when helpful to the pioneers, as naïve or clueless. The Landmark book *The Witchcraft of Salem Village* depicts indigenous people as predators, stating that "the Indians were a constant danger" and "a man working alone in a field was easy prey for them." The farmers had "to keep weapons by them always" for "there had been killings by Indians around many of the small villages nearly every year, and as late as 1691 it had been necessary for the county of Essex to establish a corps of twenty-four scouts for protection."[58] Being killed by an Indian was considered a threat that came with—and was part of—the terrain, no different from the possibility of starvation or freezing to death. According to the Landmark book *The Pony Express,*

"Every trip was an adventure. . . . The course was marked with grim reminders. Here and there were rough boards marked with the sad words: 'Died of Arrow Wound July 8,' 'Perished Here of Thirst,' 'Buried Where Found Frozen.'"[59] The first pages of *Heroines of the Early West* list Native Americans as one of the "natural dangers" lurking in the West, even for the most courageous pioneer women. "Nothing could seem to hold the women back—not even terrifying stories about cannibal Indians, fever-ridden swamps, strange wild beasts, poisonous snakes, mountains too high to climb, rivers too deep to ford, forests that were trackless jungles."[60]

Both series include a story about Narcissa Whitman, remembered as the "first white woman across the Rockies," who married Dr. Marcus Whitman, a missionary from upstate New York.[61] Together the Whitmans set out west to civilize "unknown Indians." Even though Indian women taught Narcissa how to bake bread and use various roots, the book reverts to a depiction of Indians as uncivilized, untrustworthy, even vicious. The Whitmans felt that they had to "teach the Indians, against quickly growing opposition, the simplest fundamentals of cleanliness and morality—white style."[62] There is a recognition in the story that the Indians longed for their old life, but this longing is seen to reflect ignorance and laziness. Narcissa surmised that the Indians would have chosen a life in which they did nothing but "hunt, eat, drink and sleep" over the "better" life she and her husband offered.[63]

At the end of the story Narcissa is "brutally murdered, along with Marcus, by the very Indians they had hoped to 'save.'"[64] The accompanying illustration (next page) is a vividly detailed description of the Indians' vicious killing of Narcissa: "A number of bullets entered her body as the settee dropped to the ground. An Indian rushed up, overturned it, and thrust her down into the thick November mud. . . . Another Indian lifted her head by its long pale golden hair and struck her face viciously with his leather quirt. No one knows how long it took her to die."[65] These graphic descriptions make it clear that violence was not the reason that the titles in these series excluded and omitted the histories of slavery, massacre, or internment.

Even in death, the work of the pioneer is not conveyed as futile. After the Whitmans' deaths, fifty angry settlers retaliated by killing a great many Indians and bringing five of them to face "white" justice. In response to the massacre, something "good" came out of it: President James K. Polk provided government protection "for the Far Western settlers and for the admission of Oregon as a Territory." The Whitmans' deaths became justification for the conquest of the West. "Thus the martyrdom of Narcissa and Marcus Whitman beyond all doubt helped decide the fate of this portion of the American West."[66]

The book about Narcissa Whitman as a child in the Orange series offers a slightly less brutal version of Native Americans but still depicts them as dangerous or ignorant. One missionary visiting Narcissa's family declares that "the

Figure 3.1. A graphic
Landmark book
illustration of a Native
American character
whipping and killing
the pioneer woman
Narcissa Whitman in
*Heroines of the Early
West* (New York:
Random House, 1960), 87.

threat of danger is never over—no matter how long we live with them." The other
visiting missionary suggests, patronizingly, that the Indians are ignorant for not
trusting settlers. "In times of trouble they forget that we do much to help them."
He goes on, "They need doctors. They need schools. They must learn how to farm.
They can't always be killing off the game and then moving onto fresh hunting
grounds."[67]

When not viewed as dangerous, Native Americans are treated like bother-
some pests or children. "At the end of their patience these [pioneer] women would
suddenly chase Indians from their kitchens with brooms." Nothing frightened
them. They would "slap their uninvited guests' hands as they would naughty
children's when they were caught greedily reaching for a freshly baked pie: or
they would scold them soundly for not going home to help their own squaws
with the hard labor."[68] Even the curiosity of the Native Americans was described
as an unhygienic nuisance. "They enjoyed poking their unwashed fingers into
the strange white balloons [baking bread]."[69] Ultimately the author offers children

a degrading vision of Native Americans. "Even when friendly, their grotesquely painted faces, their half-naked bodies, their wild war whoops, their rough, husky, unintelligible speech must have been a nightmare to timid young girls and anxious mothers."[70]

Each press published a story about Sacagawea, who acts as a conciliatory figure in both series. The Landmark book celebrates her skill in saving supplies, giving directions, and calming hostile Indians who threatened the expedition. Sacagawea is never seen as a person in her own right but rather as a supporting character in the American story of the conquest of the West by white explorers. The book even ends by suggesting that later in life Sacagawea is rewarded for all her work by seeing her son "become a guide and interpreter" for "rich European noblemen who came all the way by slow boat across the Atlantic . . . to see . . . the strange aboriginal natives before civilization had altered the picture."[71]

THE "GOOD" WOMEN: PIONEERS IN DOMESTICITY

When it came to publishing stories about women, both presses engaged with the past to convey messages to modern children. Few books had a woman as the hero (heroine) of the story, even though many of the authors were women. Of the 218 Orange books, only 39 books focused on girls or women even though fully 93 percent were written by women.[72] In 1943 Bobbs-Merrill did publish a book about Louisa May Alcott and between 1947 and 1954 books about Martha Washington, Abigail Adams, Dolly Madison, and Mary Todd Lincoln. Many of these stories depicted these women as important for their relationship to men rather than of importance in their own right. Of the 122 Landmark books, only 24 percent were written by women and only 10 had girls or women as their subjects.[73] The books that were devoted to particular women or had women as minor characters focused primarily on their traditional roles as mother and housekeeper.

Some of the stories verge on the comic in their description of hardy pioneer women who continue to cook and clean no matter what was going on. Nancy Wilson Ross describes Mrs. David Blaine who, "during an Indian uprising . . . was hoisted aboard [a gunboat] with her newborn babe in her arms." When things quieted down "she insisted on being rowed back and forth several times to her abandoned log cabin . . . to 'wash and iron and some other work.'" She was so committed to her housework that she would "cope with any Indian she met" along the way.[74] Elsewhere in the introduction Wilson Ross wrote that "one of the things that maddened women most on the western trip was the endless dust and dirt. Some men complained that women in the wagon trains gave a lot of trouble because they were forever wanting to 'stop and wash up.'" Wilson Ross even quotes a pioneer woman, Mrs. Van Dusen, who later recalled that "many times she sat in her cosy little kitchen on wheels and cleaned and cooked a bird while the wagon moved along."[75]

In Landmark's *Abe Lincoln: Log Cabin to White House* Sterling North wrote with similar admiration about Lincoln's stepmother's housekeeping skills. "With good-natured efficiency . . . she scrubbed the cabin, . . . emptied the old ticks, washed them, filled them with fresh cornhusks and over these put her feather beds and clean bedding. . . . Lime was purchased, and the walls and ceilings were whitewashed." And, the narrator comments, all of these efforts were meant to "encourage Abe in all his ambitions."[76] In Quentin Reynolds's 1964 Landmark book about General Custer, his mother's strength lies in her ability to withhold her tears and to submit to her husband. "She was a pioneer woman, and pioneer women always swallowed their tears. Besides, she knew that her big husband was always right."[77] In the book about Narcissa Whitman in the Orange book series, Narcissa knew as a young girl what her role would be, even if she presented it resentfully. "'I know all about ladies. They stay home and take little street stitches. They brush and brush their hair. They keep neat. They're forever washing their hands.'"[78] In the Childhood of Famous Americans story about Martha Washington (nicknamed Patsy in the book), Patsy's Aunt Mary worries that her niece won't grow out of her adventurousness. She is later comforted by "how quietly Patsy worked at home—how stiff and straight she sat. 'She may turn out to be a lady yet,' she thought."[79] Overall, the female characters in these books are not so different from those depicted in the popular TV sitcoms of the time. *Father Knows Best, The Adventures of Ozzie and Harriet*, and *Leave It to Beaver* all featured female protagonists who, while sometimes spunky, essentially stayed at home, made dinner, watched the kids, and supported their husbands.

The limited portrayal of women was noticed by one young female reader of Landmark books, although at the late date of 1965. She wrote to Robert Loomis, the author of *The Story of the U.S. Air Force*, in 1965, "I have found your book . . . very good and factual, but there is one complaint. I have not found anything on what part a woman has played, do they not fly?" She goes on, "I think that something should have been said on the woman's place in the Air Force. For you see I would very much like to make the Air Force a career (and fly). I hope you will take me seriously on a woman's place in the Air Force is important. Sincerely yours, Dorothy Johnson."[80] Though the evidence is scant in the archival documents, one can only guess that other girls felt equally dissatisfied with women's roles in these stories.

On the one hand, this limited portrayal of women can be explained in part by the fact that the series focused on military and political landmark events whose heroes were traditionally male. On the other hand, it is surprising that women were depicted so narrowly given that they had so recently taken up work in factories and some had gone to war themselves. One Landmark book does actually capture the tension between women's conflicting roles. The cover of the 1960 *Heroines of the Early West* features a woman dressed in an apron while holding a rifle. At the time, this image might have appeared to parallel the moment—

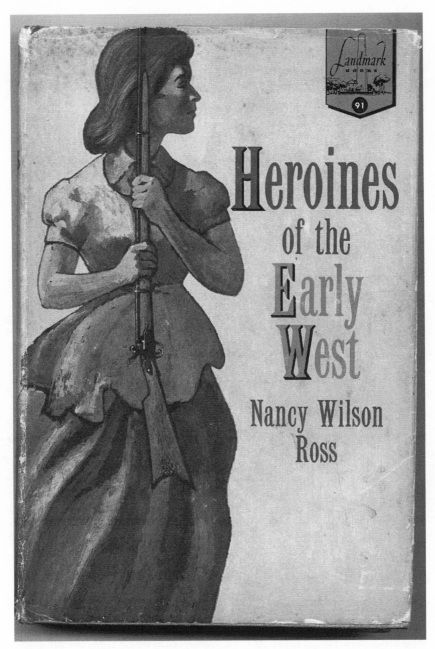

Figure 3.2. Cover of *Heroines of the Early West* (New York: Random House, 1960). The material for this book first appeared in *Westward the Woman* in 1944, long before the start of the Landmark series. (New York: Alfred A. Knopf, 1944.)

when women were taking on new roles to defend the home front while men were at war overseas.

The cultural tension about women's roles after World War II was reflected in advertisements of the time. One 1950 twenty-eight-minute promotional film for Whirlpool washing machines demonstrates this tension. Titled *Mother Takes a Holiday*, the drama shows three young women working on a homework assignment about—as the commercial put it—"women's liberation, et cetera." After rejecting the "old-fashioned" idea of writing about the struggle of women for the right to vote, they decide on a more modern issue, "freedom in our own home . . . emancipation from home chores. . . . That's the kind of emancipation any woman can understand."[81] Whirlpool's line of "Imperial" kitchen appliances, in this case refrigerators, was appealing because its appliances were "independent" and "free-standing."[82] The plot of the infomercial revolves around getting their fathers to realize that "women's liberation" was a new washing machine, one that reflected the American values of consumerism, individualism, and private home ownership.

The Happy Slave and the Benign Past

Throughout these books, Black and white women are described very differently, even when they share in their primary roles related to domestic work and child rearing. African Americans rarely appear in these series and generally as stereotyped minor characters. In 1947 Jean Brown Wagoner wrote *Martha Washington: Girl of Old Virginia*, which essentially depicts a plantation filled with happy slaves where the young Martha is in training to become the plantation mistress. The competence of the slave character, Mammy Tuck, who looks after the children and keeps house, is viewed not as a reflection of her own abilities but as a sign of the good training she received from Martha's mother, who, in fact, performs little labor herself. "There were slaves who did the hard work, but her mother told the slaves what to do and showed them how to do it."[83] Martha's mother talks about the slaves as children who are afraid of many things because they "haven't been in this country long." (The first African Americans were sold into slavery in the colonies in 1619, almost forty years before George Washington's family immigrated from England to the American colonies in 1657. Regardless of whether or not they were recently enslaved, the description elides any details that may hint at the inhumanity of their capture and enslavement). There is no mention in most, if not all, of these books about where the slaves came from, the moral and political failure slavery represented, or how the slaves were brutalized by the plantation system.[84]

Much like the Native American characters, the African American characters are described as ignorant and uncivilized. For instance, Patsy's mother explains that because Mammy came to her "straight from the jungle" (not from the auction block), Patsy needed to teach her how "to clean kettles, to clean her kitchen, to clean the food, even before she taught her to cook." She goes on, "'Mammy had never known before how to wash her hands. She just licked her fingers and wiped them on her waist.'"[85] In a back-handed compliment to Mammy, the mother still manages to take credit. "'Mammy was smarter than most slaves, and she loved me so dearly that she learned quickly. You won't find a cleaner, better cook anywhere.'"[86] There is hardly any suggestion in these books that this enslaved woman might be unhappy with his or her bondage.[87] When Martha's parents return from a visit to Williamsburg, they bring gifts for everyone including the field slaves. "'It's almost as good as Christmas!' they all said."[88] The depiction of slavery as benign at worst and largely benevolent is reproduced throughout many of the books.

Before 1965 the Orange series included only two books featuring an African American protagonist, both by Augusta Stevenson: *George Carver: Boy Scientist*, published in 1944, and *Booker T. Washington: Ambitious Boy*, published in 1950. Meanwhile Random House produced only one Landmark book before 1960 that featured an African American protagonist: Anne Terry White's *George Washington Carver: The Story of a Great American.*[89]

Augusta Stevenson's book about Carver stands out for its acknowledgment of the harsh realities of racism in the South during Reconstruction and Jim Crow but ultimately concludes that there is nothing to be done about the situation. Stevenson depicts George as having little agency but goes to great lengths to depict enlightened white characters who come to George's aid over and over again. The Carvers try to rescue George's mother, their slave girl, from kidnappers and teach George to read and write and do math. Mr. Carver reprimands his nephew for calling George a slave and explains that the war is over and Negroes have been freed. The cooper defends George when he is being verbally abused, and George's boss reassures George that he can go to school. "We believe in everyone going to school, black, red, white and yellow." Nonetheless, despite the fact that characters call out racism when they see it, George is urged to accept racism as a fact of life. When George learns he can't go to school his brother, Jim, tells him, "You've got to get used to that."[90] In response to a boy whose parents told him that they needn't pay attention to the emancipation of African Americans in Missouri, Mrs. Carver replies with a legal rationale rather than a moral imperative that they recognize the freedom of formerly enslaved people. "Your folks are wrong. We do have to pay attention: it's the law. George and Jim are as free as you are."[91]

It is significant that these presses offered such a limited portrayal of African Americans during the forties and fifties, when there was plenty of controversy about the limited and often racist depiction of African Americans in textbooks and, to some extent, in children's literature. As early as 1944 African American leaders pointed out to school officials in New York City that their textbooks still referred to happy slaves and applauded the Klan for keeping "'foolish Negroes'" out of government. They critiqued the many distortions in texts in all subject areas.[92] Racism was a staple in children's bedtime stories. The *Washington Post* told of little white boys who would "not go to sleep without 'Little Black Sambo' and a little girl whose night was lost without Joel Chandler Harris's 'Tar Baby.'"[93]

Meanwhile, conservative white school administrators and state officials in the South were vigorously resisting attempts by Black leaders to get textbooks revised. They turned on its head the argument taken up by Black leaders and developed in the 1954 *Brown v. Board* Supreme Court decision that segregation damaged the self-esteem of Black children. White lawyers argued "that any negative material about their own past would harm" the delicate psyches of the white child.[94] The pleas of Black leaders for book revisions were generally ignored, even by the seemingly liberal New York publishing houses. In fact, after the 1954 court decision, some editors, fearful of losing the southern textbook market, tried to delete any mention of African Americans in their textbooks. Some insisted that research showed these texts did not contribute to prejudice. Others accused Black people of being overly sensitive. The *Washington Post* referred to efforts to remove *Little Black Sambo* from a school curriculum as "humorless touchiness."[95]

Some college textbooks contained phrases that were shocking even at the time they were written. Henry Steele Commager and Samuel Eliot Morison's popular textbook, *Growth of the American Republic*, referred to the stock character Sambo as "adequately fed, well cared for, and apparently happy." Morison privately mocked complaints from African Americans and refused to remove the term "pickaninnies" or other racist terms like "Sambo" from new editions of the textbook. "I'll be damned if I'll take them out for . . . anybody," he commented.[96] Notably the History Department faculty at Queens College in New York, even though their colleagues at City College of New York had been fired ten years earlier for "subversive" teachings, boldly refused to use the textbook because of its racist imagery and distortions. The faculty informed the college president and representatives of the college's chapter of the NAACP that instead they would use John Hicks's textbook, *The Federal Union*, which was first published in 1937.[97]

In 1952 a group of southern segregationists who had found even Commager and Morrison's original textbook too friendly to Black people, stepped up their resistance to change and blocked any sympathetic depiction of African Americans in the textbooks they would use. They demanded the removal of a textbook chapter titled "Minority Groups Should Share Equally with All Others in the American Way of Life." The governor of Alabama declared the text an "insult to Southern traditions."[98] In response, the publisher altered and ultimately dropped the chapter to please southern critics and ensure that the schools continued to buy their textbook.

The failure of Bobbs-Merrill and Random House to better address the representation of African Americans in their series at a time when there were demands to do so speaks to the timidity of publishing houses during the McCarthy era as they faced the scrutiny of school and library systems with power to ban their books and, even more, the scrutiny of the government. The presses seemed to fear publishing books about even the most famous African Americans. With the exception of the Carver biographies, the stories of Frederick Douglass, Jesse Owens, and even Harriet Tubman would have to wait for publication until the late 1960s or later.[99] While Gary Schmidt argues, persuasively, that the publication of any books about African Americans in the forties and fifties was significant for depicting characters outside "mainstream white experience," he acknowledges that not until *Crispus Attucks: Boy of Valor*, first published in 1965, did the Orange series address the injustice of slavery.[100] It was followed by *Harriet Tubman: Freedom Girl* by Gertrude Hecker Winders in 1969 and *Frederick Douglass* by Elizabeth Myers in 1970.

One could argue that the stereotypical and often racist portrayal of African Americans simply reflected the prevailing stereotypes so embedded in American culture at the time. On TV African Americans were depicted not as equal to the white characters but as servants or comic foils for stand-up comedians. Jack Benny had his Black "valet," Rochester.[101] *Amos 'n' Andy*, the 1950s adaptation of a vaudeville and wildly popular radio act, featured white actors wearing Blackface and acting out demeaning and stereotypical versions of urban Black life.[102] The Landmark chapter on Sacagawea in *Heroines of the Early West* contains a depiction of the explorers and Indians celebrating Sacagawea's reunion with her brother. The accompanying illustration is reminiscent of popular racist depictions of African Americans as entertainers. "York, the Negro," the only African American in the expedition, danced "cakewalks, clogs and shuffles."[103]

In many cases the authors of these children's books absorbed the prevalent ideology, which then became part of their stories. Robert Sutherland describes

Figure 3.3. An illustration of "York, the Negro" entertaining Lewis and Clark and Native peoples during the expedition, from *Heroines of the Early West* (New York: Random House, 1960), 46–47.

what is called the politics of assent as an author's "passive, unquestioning accep-
tance and internalization of an established ideology, [that was] transmitted in
the author's writing in an unconscious manner" and that not only "affirms the
status quo but continually reinforces it."[104] This is apparent in the books about
pioneers, Native Americans, and African Americans where the prevailing
stereotypes dominate the stories.[105]

Writers of children's books were not only reflecting the rosy and often segregated vision of America shown in popular culture but also reacting to the political pressure of the time to present an upbeat, conflict-free history of the country.
As the Cold War gathered steam, Joseph McCarthy, the junior senator from Wisconsin, joined with HUAC to search for domestic communists in government,
the army and beyond. It was a period of repression and fear that affected even
the authors of children's books.[106]

On the one hand the world of children's books provided a haven for many
progressive writers during the Cold War. As left-wing writers found their options
in mainstream media contract, many turned to the less-noticed world of children's
books. Julia Mickenberg points out that because "a large segment of society prefers
to believe that children's books are naïve, simple, and non-ideological," authors
might well encounter fewer censors publishing children's books.[107] On the other
hand, it became clear that even the authors of children's books needed to exercise
some self-censorship if they were to continue earning a livelihood. All would
have been aware of the threat from McCarthyism and the right. They would have
seen left-wing authors suffer financially as newspapers called them out as communists writing "pink-tinged pages."[108] They would have read headlines denounc-
ing the appearance of left-wing authors at schools, universities, bookstores, and
libraries and have known of writers forced to find new outlets for their writing,
albeit not very lucrative ones, outside of the big publishing houses.

The way writers responded to this threat varied. Augusta Stevenson, in her
book about George Washington Carver, showed some courage by including
numerous examples of the racist treatment of Carver. Yet probably aware of the
danger of being labeled a communist, she made clear in a questionnaire to Bobbs-
Merrill that she stood on the "right side." She explained that she "saw the neces-
sity of developing patriotism in children" in order to counter "the communistic
plan of treating our American heroes with ridicule and contempt."[109] Some writers, conscious of the peril they faced, found the choices they had to make
wrenching. As one writer put it, "How can we write honestly . . . when at this
time the forces of destruction are in the saddle, and sell what we write?"[110]

Authors of these series were continually faced with choices about how to present the past while knowing their choices would have deep implications for
their careers. Was Robert E. Lee a hero or a traitor? Was Andrew Carnegie a "rob-
ber baron" or a "captain of industry"? Was Teddy Roosevelt an imperialist figure who sought to expand the American empire into the Caribbean and the

Philippines or a hero who led the struggle to repel Spanish colonialism (the author ultimately settled on "all-round boy" to describe him)? Would their answers to these questions make them sound like leftists to McCarthy and his followers? The decisions these writers made affected not only their future careers but also what books were published, sold in stores, or bought by libraries.[111]

Academic historians were similarly faced with these kinds of choices about how to depict figures in American history. Even Abraham Lincoln, once presented as a revolutionary figure who embodied egalitarian values and worked for the abolition of slavery, was recast during the McCarthy period as a pragmatist trying to hold the Union together at any cost. In his 1948 essay, "Abraham Lincoln and the Self-Made Myth," Richard Hofstadter played down Lincoln's radicalism and antislavery views and wrote that Lincoln's inconsistent thinking regarding slavery was "incidental to his main concern," which, he wrote, was "free republicanism and its bearing on the common white man with whom he identified himself."[112]

Despite the pressure of the times, Landmark authors appear to have had fairly wide latitude in terms of how they addressed their assignments. Some books were surprisingly radical. Anne Terry White, the author of Landmark's 1953 *George Washington Carver: The Story of a Great American*, would be blacklisted during the 1950s by many presses because of her left-wing views on race, capitalism, and social injustice.[113] In her books she offered a graphic description of the moral bankruptcy and hypocrisy of Jim Crow racism during the period between the end of the Civil War and Carver's death in the 1940s. Like the Orange book about Carver, hers began with a nod to the generosity of the Carvers, the benevolent white Mississippi farming family. But the tone of the book is very different. White is quite direct about the horrors African Americans experienced in the South. She explains that, even as a prominent and recognized scientist George continued to experience racism and humiliation. On trains he was required to "ride all day in the uncomfortable, dirty cars set aside for Negroes" before going to lecture at night. "Always there was the problem of where he could eat, where he could sleep." When George would arrive in a town and be confronted with signs warning him, "Nigger don't let the sun set on you in this town," he would wonder, "Is it worth it?"[114]

Teddy Roosevelt and the Rough Riders, published in 1954 and written by Henry Castor, was also radical in its depiction of the War of 1898 as little more than an effort to expropriate the remnants of the Spanish colonies in the waning days of Spanish colonial power. Although much of the book describes military efforts like the Battle of San Juan Hill, Castor does turn a critical eye to the corruption that lay behind much of the bloodshed of the war. He views the invasion of Cuba as a "newspaper war" spurred by the likes of William Randolph Hearst, who wanted to sell newspapers, and moneyed interests eager to profit from government contracts for war materials or from direct control over Cuba's resources.[115]

Castor even considers it a point of pride that America had few colonial holdings. He agrees with President McKinley who said "'forcible annexation (of Cuba) would be criminal aggression.'" Castor even worried that the takeover of Spanish colonies had undermined the country's moral authority. He points out that "even during the Spanish-American War there were many good, respectable people who were ashamed of it," and he lists former presidents Grover Cleveland and Benjamin Harrison, Mark Twain, Andrew Carnegie, and the "presidents of Harvard University . . . and Stanford University."[116]

Some authors wrote mostly uncontroversial books but occasionally slipped a critical comment into the text. For example, in *Heroines of the Early West* Nancy Wilson Ross points out that there were those who opposed westward expansion. "Mr. Daniel Webster was just one of many famous statesmen who was convinced Americans should not even bother their heads about the vast unknown territory that lay beyond the Rocky Mountains."[117] Similarly, in *Andrew Carnegie and the Age of Steel* Katherine Shippen hints at the oppressive nature of nineteenth-century steel work by noting the unfairness of the use of armed guards during the Homestead Strike of 1892. Yet she describes this not as a systemic problem but as an unfortunate act of betrayal by Carnegie's partner Henry Frick.[118]

In contrast to these examples, many other books, particularly those about the Civil War, are striking in their whitewashing of American history. Mackinlay Kantor's *Gettysburg*, written in 1952 for the Landmark series, describes the Civil War as a conflict between North and South unrelated to slavery. The reader learns little to nothing about the social and political origins of the war but learns of the valor and heroism on both sides of the conflict. According to Kantor, there was a moral relativism that balanced the story: "It is an old truth that warfare brings out the very best and the very worst in human beings."[119] Even Lincoln's Gettysburg Address, perhaps the singular event that shapes our collective memory, is an addendum to the book. Not until the very final pages of the book is there acknowledgment of its significance as the foundational document of the kind of country Lincoln imagined, one "conceived in liberty, and dedicated to the proposition that all men are created equal."[120] Similarly, Sterling North's 1956 *Abe Lincoln: Log Cabin to White House* offers an equally inadequate history. For much of the book we learn only that Lincoln came from a pioneering family that confronted Native Americans and "settled" the wild frontier. The first serious reference to African Americans ("Negroes") comes two-thirds of the way through the book when North mentions one of the first bills that Lincoln introduces into Congress.[121] Not until the last pages of the book do we learn anything about the words for which we remember Lincoln: the Emancipation Proclamation, the Gettysburg Address, his second inaugural address. The Civil War was simply "the tragic and bloody four-year struggle," which is described in morally neutral terms as a war between brothers: "The volunteers of these two armies differed little in idealism and courage; average weight and height; color of hair, skin, eyes;

love of family and country. They left behind them weeping mothers and proud fathers, women with whom they were in love. With an ardor that might better have been spent on binding North and South together, these bearded . . . striplings threw themselves at each other with fratricidal fury. At times they even cheered the bravery of those who came on against them."[122] Even more, North, while having expressed little feeling for African Americans, expresses his concern for the South's loss. "When at last the gallant Robert E. Lee and his weary troops— lacking food, medical supplies, and ammunition—were forced to surrender . . . the Union had been saved, but at what a terrible cost!"[123]

A few other books virtually lionize Robert E. Lee. Hodding Carter's Landmark book *Robert E. Lee and the Road of Honor* opens with an epigram about Lee's honor and heroism. "This book is about a great American who was guided by something he believed to be the most precious quality in life. It is called a sense of honor, a force inside us which not only tells us what the right thing for us to do is but also impels us to do it."[124] Similarly, MacKinlay Kantor's *Lee and Grant at Appomattox* "explains" the South's rationale for maintaining slavery. "Southerners, however, believed that it was important to own slaves. . . . They felt that their way of life would be harmed without slavery [and] the Federal government had no right to dictate whether they would own slaves in their states."[125] African Americans, in Kantor's writing, were not included as southerners.

To publish these versions of the Civil War almost required that the authors put blinders on. These books appeared at exactly the moment when the civil rights movement was bringing the nation's attention to the gross inequalities stemming from slavery and Jim Crow through boycotts, protests, and school integration.[126] And yet these authors continued to write accounts of the Civil War with little to no acknowledgment of the horrors of slavery.

The publishers' concerns about drawing the attention of McCarthy and HUAC were well-founded. By 1951, attacks on authors from New York publishing houses were reported daily in local newspapers, and the publishing houses had to be aware of them. John Gunther, well known for his various *Inside* books and author of the Landmark book *Alexander the Great*, was attacked by the right-wing outlet *Counterattack* because his book, *The Riddle of MacArthur*, was "being serialized in *The Compass*, a newspaper which fails to meet the test of being anti-communist."[127] Publishers themselves came under withering criticism for hiring writers considered of dubious loyalty. In the course of a few months in 1951, right-wing groups attacked the *Atlantic Monthly*, Little, Brown and Company, and editors from the *New York Herald Tribune*, *New York Times*, and *Saturday Review of Literature*. The editors of the right-wing magazine *The Freeman* argued that New York presses wanted to publish only procommunist books. "Anyone who has had detailed experience with New York publishing circles," he argued, "knows how difficult it has been to get . . . anti-Communist . . . books published during the past two decades." Other papers reported that

"some otherwise respectable firms are being infiltrated not only by Soviet sympathizers, but by actual Communist party members."[128] The right was reinforced
in their suspicions about communism in the press by the revelation that Angus
Cameron, the editor in chief at Little, Brown, a Boston house, had resigned after
"*Counterattack*'s revelation of his [former] Communist party affiliation."[129]

Throughout the country local watchdog groups screened books in libraries
and schools and, in some towns, removed books from shelves or segregated them
in a special part of their library, requiring readers to sign in and explain why
they wanted to read them. In Illinois, a bill was introduced into the state legis-
lature in 1951 "to establish an elaborate machinery for the censorship of all
teaching materials used in the public schools" to ensure that they were "'con-
structive, friendly to democracy and non-subversive'" and not "'antagonistic to
or incompatible with the ideals and principles of the American constitutional
form of government.'"[130]

The fear at Random House in particular was palpable. In the fall of 1951 its
editors joined the staffs at the various presses to consider how to respond. Theodore Waller of the American Book Publishers Council, the trade association for
many of the big publishers, began to collect articles about "the various attacks on
intellectual freedom" with the intention of distributing them to members and
publishing them in newspapers and magazines around the country. Donald
Klopfer, Bennett Cerf's longtime partner at Random House, organized a committee of publishers to protest and counteract censorship. In the records of the
Random House archive at Columbia are numerous letters to virtually every publisher in New York and Boston inviting them to meet, sign petitions, and con-
tact congressmen to stop the censorship efforts of state and local governments
as well as local watchdog committees in libraries and schools.[131]

But some publishers were very cautious about joining the opposition, worry-
ing that they might be pulled into league with actual communists whom they
opposed as much as they opposed the right. So they chose to police themselves
by identifying and keeping their distance from any communists or fellow travelers among their various friends.[132] Waller argued that "more issues are gray
than are black and white." Perhaps, he maintained, the industry should "retain
two or three consultants . . . to advise publishers on how they may maintain a
maximum degree of freedom without serving subversive interests."[133]

HUAC had clearly decided to search for communists in the world of children's
education when in 1948 it created a series of pamphlets to warn the public of the
danger of communism lurking in their schools. One such pamphlet, "100 Things
You Should Know about Communism and Education," included a long list of
questions and answers to teach people about communism. It begins "What is
Communism?" and explains that it is "a conspiracy to conquer and rule the world
by any means, legal or illegal, in peace or in war." It asks what communists want
and answers, "To rule your mind and your body from the cradle to the grave."[134]

The pamphlet claims that communists teach "such courses as history, economics, public speaking, art, drama, and music" and that "every course is just so much window dressing for Soviet theory and propaganda." With the pamphlets came a list of particular schools that were identified as communist, including the Walt Whitman School of Social Science in Newark, New Jersey, and the School of Jewish Studies in Philadelphia.[135]

While children's book publishers generally did not draw the attention of HUAC, Random House did. Its list included some books by political radicals, particularly Edgar Snow's *Red Star over China* (1937), *People on Our Side* (1944), *Stalin Must Have Peace* (1947), *Red China Today* (1963), and *The Long Revolution* (1972). Given Random House's publication of these books, it is not surprising that the press was viewed with no small amount of suspicion by the FBI during the 1950s.

In Bennett Cerf's oral history, he recounts how he was directly pressured to demonstrate the press's anticommunist credentials. In the 1950s George Sokolsky, whom Cerf had befriended in college when George was a "wild-eyed revolutionary," reappeared in Cerf's life. Sokolsky had become rabidly right wing and had developed close relationships with some of the most hard-line people in McCarthy's entourage. Although Sokolsky had called Cerf "the pinko publisher" at various times over the years, Cerf recalled one memorable lunch at the Stork Club when Sokolsky berated him for being a liberal and a communist sympathizer. "If you lean over, you never lean over to the right side. You always lean over to the left side." Cerf objected and pointed out that the press "had printed a lot of books that some people might call me a fascist for publishing." Not buying that argument, Sokolsky challenged Cerf by saying, "if I ever come to you with a book on the right side, if it's good enough, will you publish it?" Cerf responded, "You're damn right I will."[136]

In what almost looks like a response to Sokolsky's challenge, in 1954 Random House published a book called *The F.B.I.*, the forty-sixth title in the Landmark series. It was authored by Quentin Reynolds, a prolific journalist who had covered battles in France and England during World War II and had written 383 articles in only six years. Reynolds had been accused of being communist and in fact won a libel suit against Westbrook Pegler, the conservative columnist who had accused him. Reynolds's authoring of the FBI book served two objectives. First, produced with the approval and cooperation of the FBI, the book cleared up any doubts about Reynolds's loyalty. Second, it ingratiated Random House to J. Edgar Hoover, director of the FBI, who, according to letters in the Columbia archive, became Reynolds's personal friend. What greater act of patriotism could Sokolsky and the FBI have asked for than an homage to the very organization that was terrorizing the left?

The FBI book is explicitly propagandistic in its positive portrayal of the Bureau.[137] Agents track down criminals and traitors in all areas of American life.

Using new laboratory technologies including fingerprint and blood analyzers, the G-men protect Americans from dangers they didn't even know existed. Full of the adventures of agents chasing robbers, it describes how important good early behavior is in becoming an FBI agent and holds out an invitation: "J. Edgar Hoover is always looking for bright young men to join his department." When Hoover considers an applicant he investigates their past, going "way back to his records and behavior at school." Hoover's experience "tells him that ninety-nine times out of a hundred a decent, healthy boy with a fairly good school record will grow up into a decent, healthy adult."[138] Children are encouraged to be suspicious and fearful since communists can hide behind a show of patriotism. The book even conflates Nazis and communists, arguing that both used the same tactics to undermine the country. "The Bund members always carried American flags in their parades, just as the Communists do today. This practice was good camouflage." It warns children that efforts to promote dialogue with the Soviet Union are akin to the efforts by Nazis during the war whose pleas for dialogue "fooled a lot of well-meaning German-Americans who thought that the organization was trying to promote friendship between this country and Germany."[139]

Since Landmark books had focused overwhelmingly on people and events from the past, the FBI book that chronicled a contemporary event was an anomaly. Additionally, it was the only book in the series to include photographs rather than illustrations, removing it from the historical past and placing it in the realistic present. While it read like a history book, in fact it was an ideological effort to inculcate in children a fear of communism. Its message to readers is explicit and ideological: communists, like bank robbers, murderers, and kidnappers, are the enemy and must be hunted down wherever they are hiding. By including this book in its series, Random House placed the contemporary FBI in the company of books that were seen as authoritative, indisputable American history. With no pretense of journalistic objectivity, Random House included a preface written by none other than J. Edgar Hoover. In it, he explained what the agency looks for in future recruits: "We want to know if he respects his parents, reveres God, honors his flag and loves his country."[140]

The success of *The F.B.I.* led Random House to consider publishing more books on the subject. In an undated letter, Fred Rosenau, an editor at Random House, wrote to Paul Lapolla, another editor, and explained that Random House had tested the popularity of a new FBI story for children in the magazine *Boys' Life* but acknowledged that there was already a Landmark book on the same subject. He wrote, "If the test does well in *Boys' Life*, we will want to make a cheaper edition (For Young Readers), but I don't want to invest in new plates or a rewrite." Rosenau concluded, "It would make sense if we didn't have the Reynolds Landmark already, of course." But another audience—slightly younger boys, six to eight years old—was certainly a promising market.[141]

Ultimately Random House published two books about the FBI—Reynolds's 1954 book aimed at children between eight and twelve and Donald Whitehead's 1956 book for adults, *The FBI Story: A Report to the People*, both with forewords by Hoover. Whitehead, recommended to the press by the FBI itself, was a Pulitzer Prize–winning reporter with the Associated Press. He was given editorial feedback by Hoover, who deemed the book the FBI's "certified" history. Random House continued republishing these books extolling the FBI for almost another decade.[142] Both books were given a guaranteed market, with the FBI itself purchasing hundreds of copies of each. And other organizations further promoted the books. The American Jewish League Against Communism, organized during the 1940s, disseminated the FBI book and paid to have the book sent to over fifteen hundred of its members.[143] Executive Director Rabbi Benjamin Schultz requested that "in each book you are to insert a suitable slip of paper reading: 'In the cause of human rights, this book is sent to you with the compliments of the American Jewish League Against Communism.'"[144]

Hoover's involvement with these books was not a trivial episode in his anticommunist career. He went about autographing copies of the Whitehead book, and when it won an award from the American Booksellers Association, he sent congratulatory messages to Random House's editor Paul Lapolla. "Mr. Nichols has called to my attention the award which Random House received for its handling of The FBI Story. This is most attractive, and I am sure it is one which your associates and you were most happy to receive." He goes on, "The fact that you want to share it with the Bureau is most thoughtful, and we are happy, indeed, to have it. With best wishes and kind regards. Sincerely yours, J. Edgar Hoover."[145]

As late as 1968 Random House published under the Landmark series two volumes on American history authored by Daniel Boorstin, an aforementioned consensus historian. By this time a new generation of social historians had begun writing a new version of "history from the bottom up." They wrote histories of women, labor, immigrants, and other groups that had been left out of works by many consensus historians and implicitly critiqued the United States for its treatment of women, Native Americans, and African Americans. Boorstin, in these two volumes, responded to these new critical versions of American history, going so far as to suggest that abolitionists and the North escalated the conflicts that led to the Civil War while people in the South merely responded to this aggression: "As northern propagandists became more and more violent, more and more unreasonable, Southerners too became more and more unreasonable."[146]

The Landmark books present a clear example of how politics and ideology infiltrated the child's world. To sell books, Random House went out of its way to appear politically unbiased, or even conservative, to the extent of involving the director of the FBI. Children were encouraged to accept what they were reading as factual, particularly in books that were designated as historical. Yet this example from the Landmark series demonstrates that interpretations of historical events merely reflect the particular moment in which they are being offered. In the case of the Landmark book about the FBI, children were reading not about historical events but about a contemporary institution. Random House's wish to prove its anticommunist credentials led to the publication of a book that was more contemporary propaganda than history.

In her review of the Landmark books Shippen asked, "Will a youngster reading these volumes find in them matters that he has not understood before? Will he be able to see beyond the world of the immediate present, into a world whose existence he did not fully realize? Will he gain sympathy with people who have long since died and, having it, will he better understand the people who are around him?"[147] She answers that the books will do all of these things, but the answer is more complicated. As the Landmark and Orange series demonstrate, historical accounts often reveal as much about the time in which they were written as about the past that they describe.

Bobbs-Merrill and Random House made a serious attempt to teach children about American history. Yet the history they told was reflective of the dominant, triumphalist narrative popular at the time. In their history Native Americans were threatening, women were homemakers, and African Americans were invisible or servants. In the fifties, as the fear of a McCarthyism grew, the books, particularly those about the Civil War, downplayed or nearly ignored historical conflict, particularly about slavery. And ultimately, with Random House's publication of the FBI books, the ideological underpinnings of this historical fiction were no longer invisible. The prevailing, politically conservative ideology of the time was made explicit—communism was evil, spies were everywhere, and all Americans should be on the lookout for radicals who were threatening our history and therefore the country. These conservative ideological strains can be traced back in time, to the doll collectors of the 1930s, as well as forward, to the 1960s and today.

CHAPTER 4

Family Fun for Everyone?

FREEDOMLAND U.S.A., 1960–1964

Now this may be Indian Territory and it may look like the Old West but the time is today and the place is Freedomland! . . . Here they built the places and the buildings representing 200 years of American history. . . .
—Freedomland Promotional Video, 1963[1]

The Bronx is cheering. This is unusual, for there is very little to cheer about in the Bronx. . . . Why are they cheering? Freedomland is open. In case you hadn't heard, this is one of those artificial islands of escape. No, it is not surrounded by water. Just the Bronx. —Los Angeles Times, 1962[2]

In the spring of 1960, nestled between the Hutchinson River Parkway and Pelham Bay Park, a strange spectacle arose, "an animated history book in which cowboys will soon fret, stagecoaches will be robbed, and Chicago will burn— every twenty minutes."[3] This was Freedomland U.S.A., an eighty-five-acre amusement park in the Bronx.[4] If you were to fly over the area before 1960, you would have seen only empty marshland; between 1960 and 1964 you would have seen a space filled with rides and buffered by a 120-acre parking lot; today you would see the massive buildings of Co-op City. Freedomland was ostensibly an East Coast answer to California's Disneyland, though it would only be open during the summer months. Touted as an amusement park constructed around the history of the United States, Freedomland promised to give its visitors a tour of the landmarks of American history.

Freedomland attempted two things. By creating a literal miniature nation, which required the purchase of tickets for entry, it made consumer citizenship the primary mode of engagement with U.S. history for both children and adults; and, by re-creating and miniaturizing the past for spectacle, it attempted to make the tumultuous, violent, and conflicted past controllable and simpler to digest. Yet ultimately the combination of historical exhibits and amusements proved

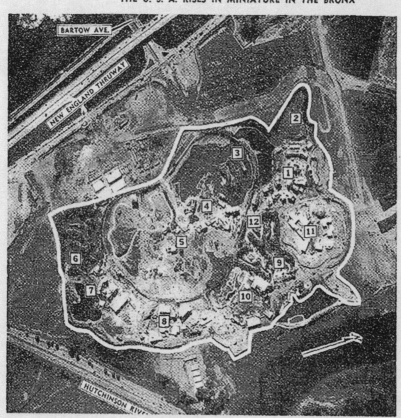

Figure 4.1. An aerial photograph of Freedomland, with the outline drawn around it, mimicking the shape of the continental United States. "The U.S.A. Rises in Miniature in the Bronx," *New York Times,* June 12, 1960.

unsuccessful. Freedomland closed its doors forever in 1964. People have offered a variety of reasons for the failure of the park—financial mismanagement, the changing demographics of the Bronx, competition from the World's Fair, the rise of social movements, and a changing political climate. There is general agreement today that the theme park was a placeholder for Co-op City and wasn't intended to exist in perpetuity.[5] But this chapter suggests that regardless of the reason for its demise, Freedomland was a failure in its approach to history and entertainment, which resulted not in a more in-depth or appealing experience but in a watered down, indeed irrelevant, version of each. The ideology behind its planning and execution deserves scrutiny within the larger context of how children were presented with American history. By the early 1960s, the nostal-

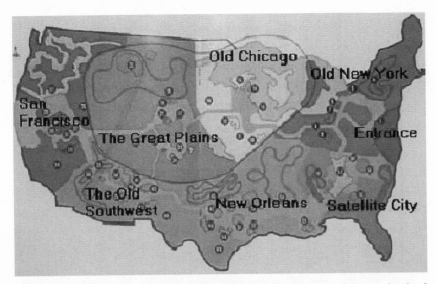

Figure 4.2. A color-coded brochure map showing the different areas of the Freedomland amusement park.

gic, romanticized vision of the country that had been promoted in books, movies, and television began to fray. Given the rise of the political and social movements of the 1960s and the questioning of consensus history among historians, it was difficult to buy a history that completely ignored, and actively erased, the country's more despicable actions like the massacre of Native Americans, imperialism, and slavery.

For the creators of Freedomland, history was an entertaining and alluring gimmick; they never intended to offer any serious exposition of history. Instead, the park relied on superficial depictions of landmark events, well-trodden myths, and stereotypical displays of famous characters from American history. The designers of Freedomland took "exciting" elements of U.S. history and stripped them down to their most basic for the purpose of creating amusements. From its inception to its demise, the park was about money, but its creators attempted to elevate its appeal through the idea that the space was educational. While it is clear that Freedomland's closing was due largely to insurmountable financial problems, it was also due to the failure of its historical narrative to capture the city's and nation's imagination. The park's clever displays proved insufficient for drawing an audience that had abundant other options for thrill rides on the one hand or history museums on the other. Its attempt to walk the line between a believable-but-mythic world and authentic history simply failed. Ultimately, Freedomland relied entirely on a narrative about American history that had become irrelevant.

The Development of Freedomland

The primary inspiration for Freedomland was Disneyland, whose popularity and financial success stood as an appealing model to the designers. In fact, the original pitch and design for Freedomland came from C. V. Wood, the former general manager and vice president of Disneyland who fell out with Walt Disney before moving back to the East Coast. Sued for representing himself as Disneyland's master planner, Wood dreamed big and envisioned starting twenty theme parks throughout the country. In fact, he did build Boston's Pleasure Island and Colorado's Magic Mountain in addition to New York's Freedomland.[6] Pleasure Island, comparable in size to Freedomland, offered a less defined historical narrative, although it relied on similar tropes like staged cowboy gunfights and an old railway line. Magic Mountain, which lasted only a couple years, closing just as Freedomland opened, was loosely based on Colorado history and included a cavalry post, a fur trapping ride, a mine ride, and storylines about American railroads and industrialization.[7] But in the end all his parks had financial problems and were short-lived.[8]

Wood enthusiastically pitched his idea for a historical theme park to William Zeckendorf, who ran one of the city's, if not the nation's, largest real estate companies, Webb & Knapp. He also owned large parcels of land throughout the city, including the land on which the United Nations and hotels around Rockefeller Center were built. Zeckendorf had purchased from the state the land on which Freedomland would sit.[9] He was obviously taken with Wood's enthusiastic pitch. In his autobiography Zeckendorf wrote, "Wood put together a masterful presentation of his Freedomland idea. The idea was to create a star-spangled amusement park, America-in-miniature, to which hordes of Easterners would flock. It was a great idea, beautifully presented."[10] While Zeckendorf ultimately downplayed his early enthusiasm for Freedomland, he was sold on the idea in the beginning: "Wood is a promoter's promoter, a terrific, enthusiastic idea man who could sell snow to Eskimos."[11] Considering that Disneyland had succeeded in depicting a similar version of historic events, Freedomland must have seemed like a slam-dunk for investors. Meanwhile, Pleasure Island, opened in 1959, would last ten years while Magic Mountain was already sputtering toward closure.

Freedomland was envisioned not as a small project aimed at hosting local visitors looking for something akin to a county fair, but as a private enterprise with millions of dollars behind it, situated on a large tract of land—land that would prove to be immensely valuable. Although the park was not a municipal project like the 1964 World's Fair that famed city planner Robert Moses would build, its stated educational mission and cultural message easily attracted the support of politicians. On May 25, 1959, at a press conference at the Empire State Building it was announced that Freedomland was coming to New York; construction began and the park opened less than one year later. The opening gala benefitted "the Children's Village, a residential school for troubled boys, located in Dobbs Ferry, N. Y.," although none of those boys were listed as attending.[12] The state of New York paid for draining the land, building roads, and installing services from sewers to highway exits. The endeavor cost sixty-five million dollars, and people believed it would weather the test of time. Although it's hard to fathom now, in 1960, the *New York Times* reported that "its permanent structures have been built to last fifty years."[13]

The park's name reflected the grand vision the developers had for this undertaking and their expectation that the idea of freedom would certainly resonate with visitors. By the mid-1950s, Cold War international politics had fully established "the idea that the love of freedom was the defining characteristic of American society." In fact, Eric Foner writes, "by the end of the 1950s, the idea that the level of freedom was the defining characteristic of American society had become fully incorporated into the popular consciousness."[14] Freedomland physically embodied the mission to equate freedom with America, and brought this idea to the tri-state area. But as tensions with the Soviet Union escalated in the 1950s, "the Cold War subtly reshaped freedom's meaning and practice, identifying it with anti-communism, 'free enterprise,' and the defense of the social and economic status quo."[15] In certain ways, freedom at Freedomland fit this changed meaning; it was essentially about free enterprise and consumerism, the freedom to choose and to buy what one pleased, the freedom to enter a world where the only criteria for citizenship was payment. This Cold War narrative mirrors those of the Landmark and Orange history books, situating free enterprise as fundamental to American identity.

The amusement park was designed to celebrate freedom much as it was defined in the 1950s' "consensus" history of the United States. It would celebrate America's democracy, power, and prominence in the world. It would highlight the same major events that the Orange and Landmark books described for their readers. This period saw the creation of a lot of history content for children that reinforced and solidified each other's messages. The rules were simple—there were good guys and bad guys, cowboys and Indians, sheriffs and outlaws. Freedomland operated on the assumptions of the 1950s, assumptions that came out of the culture and stories of World War II, that all children understood: "who was good and who bad; who the aggressor and who the defender; who could be killed and under what conditions."[16]

Freedomland sought to cram all of the continental United States, from sea to shining sea, into eighty acres of marshy land. To do that the landscape itself had to be physically reconfigured. The park straddled an environmental line, sitting on soggy marshland between a huge metropolis and the growing, sprawling suburbs of Westchester County and southern Connecticut. Construction crews had to adjust the topography of this land to mirror the natural qualities of the United States that its managers deemed desirable. They built a miniature version of the Rocky Mountains. The governors of New York, Michigan, Pennsylvania, Minnesota, Ohio, Indiana, and Wisconsin all "sent along bottles of lake water to be poured in on opening day" to fill the miniature Great Lakes, as though the construction of the park was as significant as the opening of the Erie Canal.[17] While Freedomland celebrated the frontier and re-created the Wild West, it simultaneously—and maybe confusingly—also celebrated urbanization in its re-creation of "Little Old New York" in the style of an idealized Lower East Side of the 1890s.

OPENING DAYS

On opening day, June 19, 1960, throngs of people clogged the two highways in the Bronx that led to the park. A crowd of 61,500 people filled both highways, the parking lot, and the park itself, "with as many as 40,000 on the grounds at one time." The park's popularity "caught the management unprepared and forced the suspension of ticket sales for nearly an hour early Sunday afternoon."[18] Within hours, "the parking lot was also filled to overflowing and caused police to close all roads leading to the park for hours. It also caused congestion on the Hutchinson River Parkway."[19] The *New York Herald Tribune* reported, "Freedomland was dedicated in the Bronx yesterday with all appropriate hoopla and ballyhoo plus cowboys and Indians and pirates."[20] For children in New York for whom the wagon train and the locomotive, even the West itself, were abstractions seen on television or read about in books, Freedomland promised to bring these things alive. There would also be a fantasized future of spacecrafts that served as a convenient continuum from the past to the future: America proudly and justly conquered the frontier just as it would inevitably conquer space, "the final frontier."

Visitors to Freedomland were greeted by an enormous sign with letters that were nine and a half feet tall by four feet wide. They were supported on poles that stood fourteen feet apart and were capped with flags. Visitors entered the park through a reproduction of an imagined mid-nineteenth-century New York City and followed a path that went in a circle, moving west across the Great Plains and Rocky Mountains and then turning south to head back across the Southwest and New Orleans. Although the eighty-five acres and thirty-five attractions make the park sound expansive, visitors might have found it cramped when compared to other recreational spaces like Coney Island's expansive boardwalk. Some newspapers proclaimed, tongue in cheek, that a visitor could walk across the entirety of the United States without ever leaving New York—emphasizing how the park shrank vast territory into a place where a "Tour of U.S. on Foot [is] Easy."[21]

For the opening of Freedomland, New York City issued a proclamation stating that the park's purpose was to "restage 200 years of the American heritage,

Figure 4.3. Large signposts greet visitors at the parking lot at Freedomland U.S.A. Artkraft Strauss records, Manuscripts and Archives Division, New York Public Library, Astor, Lenox, and Tilden Foundations.

from pioneering days to the wonders of the space age."[22] The dedication ceremony featured notable politicians like Mayor Robert F. Wagner, Senator Jacob K. Javits, and Senator Kenneth B. Keating. In his statement during the park's dedication, the park's president, Milton T. Raynor, distinguished Freedomland from the established and more famous Coney Island. He pointed out that unlike Coney Island (but like Disneyland), this park "would have a policy of 'cleanliness and wholesomeness for the whole family.'" Taken in by the fanfare, a reporter from the *New York Herald Tribune* claimed that Freedomland rendered "'obsolete' conventional amusement parks, freak shows and games of chance."[23] The reporter implied that Freedomland, a family-friendly park, was superior to a place like Coney Island, with its gaudy and lurid attractions. In fact, boosters like Bronx borough president James J. Lyons said that beside it, "Disneyland will be a sideshow."[24]

But it was Mayor Wagner who explained Freedomland's broader meaning. "Our millions of residents, and the additional millions of visitors, are living proof of the democracy and freedom enjoyed in our land, which is symbolized by the Statue of Liberty guarding our harbor," the mayor began the day it opened. "And, as the home of the United Nations, New York City is the capital of the world, the host to diplomats and visitors from every corner of the globe."[25] Freedomland "will be entertaining, we know. But more importantly, it will educate our young people and our older citizens, and the newcomers to these shores to the greatness that is America."[26] The hubbub around Freedomland speaks to the power of the nostalgic story it told.

Other city and state officials also got behind C. V. Wood's ambitious park plans—including the governor of Massachusetts, Foster Furcolo, who had supported another project of Wood's, the construction of Pleasure Island in Boston. On the morning of opening day the *New York Times* published a twenty-page ad supplement that included articles and drawings of the park and its attractions, a few actual photographs, and greetings from Nelson Rockefeller, the governor of New York, and Mayor Wagner.[27]

Two years later, Mayor Wagner also contributed an opening letter to the 1962 Freedomland brochure, placing the site on a national and international stage. He wrote, "Visitors from every one of our fifty states and every member country of the United Nations have come to Freedomland for the enjoyment it offers so lavishly." He emphasized its New York location, saying, "We New Yorkers are justly proud of this wonderful park with its authentic replicas of Americans, and its hundreds of shops, exhibits, and rides."[28] The new borough president Joseph F. Periconi also welcomed visitors with a letter in the brochure: "No trip to New York City is complete unless it includes a tour of the exciting panorama of America provided by Freedomland. . . . We in the Borough of The Bronx take pride in the fact that this show place of fun and laughter chose The Bronx as the home for its authentic replicas of The American Scene."[29]

Freedomland's name and the stories it told meant that certain contradictions were built into the park from the beginning. An oft-run advertisement (figure 4.4) signaled who was most welcome at the park—white nuclear families with two parents and two blond kids. The image featured a girl in pigtails and her brother whose pose mirrors his dad's, leaning forward in excitement. This "nuclear family" excluded many residents of the Bronx, who by the 1960s were neither white nor blond. The story of America that was celebrated at Freedomland was of a white America, of men conquering the West, not the story of an increasingly diverse people, particularly those living in a borough that would become infamous for civil strife, poverty, and burning buildings. The designers of Freedomland imagined a very specific, predominantly white audience who had a particular idea of American history that did not include the stories of African Americans, immigrants, or poor people.

Advertisements for the park touted the fact that Freedomland was accessible by public transportation, unrealistically claiming that the trip was only thirty minutes from Times Square. To get there by public transportation, a visitor had to ride forty-five minutes on the IRT subway and then travel another twenty minutes by public buses, hardly an enticing prospect for working people on their day off or for kids with a few dollars to spare. Travel to this site was much easier

Figure 4.4. Freedomland brochure (Federal Concessions, Inc., Western Printing and Lithographing Co., 1962).

for suburbanites coming by car. For this reason, on opening day most visitors came not from the city but from the suburbs.

Despite the fact that suburban families were the target audience for Freedomland, certain days were reserved for poorer city kids. According to the *Amsterdam News*, "The management of Freedomland, U.S.A. and the Locality Mayor's Committee will sponsor a big two-day round of entertainment and excitement on August 26 and 27 for some 15,000 of New York's underprivileged children at the entertainment center. It will be Freedom Day for the youngsters." Harlem's children would be "taken [there] by chartered buses for a round of thrills and pleasure as only the facilities of Freedomland can provide."[30]

ATTRACTIONS AND SPONSORS AT FREEDOMLAND

Freedomland's mission was to retell (and reanimate) the history of the United States geographically. To do this, it combined the conventions of historical exhibits with the entertainment elements of amusement parks. The park comprised seven different areas, each corresponding to a particular place and period of American history—Little Old New York: 1850–1900, Chicago: 1871, the Great Plains: 1803–1900, San Francisco: 1906, the Old Southwest: 1890, New Orleans and Mardi Gras, which was not given a year but served as a catchall site of carrousels, mazes, and other rides (including a Civil War battlefield).[31] In addition, Satellite City, situated where Florida would be, focused on outer space—the next frontier in 1960s America. Once visitors entered through the "port" near Little Old New York, on the eastern edge of the park, they would make their way across to the Great Lakes, to Chicago, and then to the West, conquering and "taming" the wild frontier as they went. A visitor could also travel south to the cotton fields of Alabama and Mississippi or visit America's agricultural past filled with buffalo and cows. In addition, Freedomland offered visitors the chance to survive violent disasters like the Great Chicago Fire of 1871 or the 1906 San Francisco earthquake. Streetcars, steamboats, bull boats, railroad trains, horse-drawn carriages, canoes, and tug boats all crisscrossed the terrain of Freedomland. One reporter stated, "For the history bug with a family that likes amusement parks, Freedomland is the ideal combination. Skip the battlefields for once and take a ride on a stage coach of the Old West or a Great Lakes trip on a stern wheeler."[32] In this way, Freedomland situated itself apart from frivolous amusements as well as more serious (or tedious-sounding) historic sites by actually highlighting its lack of authenticity and emphasizing its fantastical qualities.

At its best, Freedomland sought to "enable parents and teachers to give youngsters an entertaining way to find out about our American heritage," as the president of the company announced at its opening in 1960. "Textbooks and lectures fall short of showing the kind of daring and imagination it took to build our country. Here at Freedomland," he argued, "we're bringing the highlights of our history to life—vividly and excitingly. Every youngster who sees the re-creations we have to offer will look at our history with new eyes."[33] Furthermore, Freedomland would open the eyes of the entire family. One article that reads like an advertisement suggests that Freedomland would be a treat for mothers celebrating Mother's Day. There, a family could experience a cross-country road trip without the "fuss and bother of packing suitcases, making train reservations and checking timetables."[34] Once again it is the lack of realism that is appealing.

To finance the exhibits, Freedomland found corporate sponsors who would lease space for a price per foot. While the park provided the structures and storefronts, individual sponsors designed their particular space and paid for costs like construction, insurance, and other fees. Sponsors were often matched with appropriate attractions where they could either display or actually sell their products. For example, American Express sponsored the travel to the frontier exhibit, and the American Oil Company sponsored a live-action display of replicas of antique cars.[35] The park's Little Old New York section included a replica of Macy's original dry goods store. Freedomland often re-created business establishments rather than the monuments or government buildings that other make-believe towns displayed, a fact that underlines the commercial nature of the exhibits and the emphasis on free enterprise that so many felt distinguished America during the Cold War. Scholars have studied the conflicting motivations inherent in an activity that combines historical presentation and profit making. Christine Boyer explains that at the redesigned South Street Seaport in New York City, "the private sphere of nostalgic desires and imagination is increasingly manipulated by stage sets and city tableaux set up to stimulate our acts of consumption, by the spectacle of history made false."[36] A visit to Little Old New York was particularly fascinating since it re-created the very city where the park was located. The emphasis was less on geographical travel and more on a kind of time travel to the "good old days" when New York was ostensibly a quainter place. Both the 1939 and 1964 World's Fairs also featured a Little Old New York, making this a common trope for attractions that touted both the past and the future—but specifically not the present—as assets.[37] While Freedomland boasted costumed quintets playing music, it also offered attractions that referenced real historical events. Reports of the park from opening day suggested that visitors could "hoot at a New York suffragette parade."[38] Nonetheless, this was a greatly watered-down event. Reports in the paper and photographs of the event show a single activist who was not confrontational in her demand for voting rights but was merely smiling and holding up a sign. What was in reality an arduous fight for women's rights was reduced to frivolous entertainment.[39]

The Old Chicago exhibit included a steam-powered railroad and was sponsored by the Atchison, Topeka and Santa Fe Railway Company. In the Great Plains area the Borden Company sponsored a farm called Elsie's Boudoir and a milk bar. (Freedomland's Elsie was named for another cow who had been featured at the 1939 World's Fair in New York; Freedomland's Elsie moved to the 1964 World's Fair when Freedomland closed.) In the San Francisco area Chun King sponsored a Chinese restaurant. The Old Southwest offered a Mexican restaurant sponsored by the Frito Company (which became Frito-Lay in 1961), and other sections of the park featured displays from Coca-Cola, General American Industries, and Benjamin Moore Paint Company. The New Orleans section offered a plantation restaurant sponsored by J. D. Jewell, a chicken company. Satellite City housed an automated services station sponsored by AMOCO and a space ride sponsored by Braniff International Airways. Hallmark and Eastman Kodak also offered visitors "correspondence centers" and "picture taking stations" throughout the park.[40] The fact that these historical exhibits were sponsored by corporations to promote commercial products is a reminder that while education was the ostensible drawing card for Freedomland, it was not at the core of its mission.

The merchandising at Freedomland was extensive and created a jumbled atmosphere of consumption that combined "historical" items and contemporary brand association. In addition to corporations selling products and services and restaurants selling food, Freedomland offered visitors a range of souvenirs to take home as a reminder of their visit. When C. V. Wood arranged for venders to sell their merchandise, he required them to include the name of the park in their ads and displays. The vendors at the park included "national companies, local retailers and tradesmen." Souvenirs included ashtrays shaped like Freedomland U.S.A., cigarette lighters, bottle openers, bumper stickers, salt and pepper shakers, a Chicago Fire shot glass, binoculars, charms, wallets, hats, scarves, an Indian headdress, a jigsaw puzzle featuring a map of Freedomland, and an "automatic pencil with refillable lead in the shape of a rifle."[41] Many of these souvenirs conjured up clichés of American history—Indians in headdresses, rifles and knives, and wanted posters. The merchandising at Freedomland was formidable; a special Macy's and Freedomland paper bag was produced for people to carry their souvenirs.[42]

THE PROBLEMATIC NATURE AND FAILURE OF FREEDOMLAND'S ATTRACTIONS

A large part of the problem with Freedomland from the beginning was its muddled purpose. When it was announced in 1959 that the park would open just one year later, the mayor and the president of the Board of Education both "emphasized the historical and educational nature of the center." But in fact, ads for Freedomland generally emphasized the amusements it offered in the form of rides and "thrills."[43] Certainly its presentation of history was superficial compared to the historical museums of the time. And although some people truly believed it taught history, many took that promise with a grain of salt. Freedomland's dual purpose would ultimately result in the park neither thrilling nor educating all that well.

Historical museums like Sturbridge Village seemed to have a clarity of purpose that Freedomland lacked. In the summer of 1946 Sturbridge Village was opened in Massachusetts on the site of an old colonial New England village. A full-blown historical reconstruction, it offered blacksmith shops, homes, and grazing land for cows and goats. Employees played the roles of blacksmith, storekeeper, weaver, and common laborer, all dressed in colonial-era garb. Sturbridge Village told the story of a peaceful people who would establish a "commonwealth" and "settle" a wild New World filled with dangers and savages.

Similarly, older historical sites in the South like Colonial Williamsburg—a site endowed by John D. Rockefeller Jr. in 1926 and under construction for decades—were expanded into entire faux "plantations" and touted as family-oriented tourist destinations. Here again the triumphant presentation of American history was told as the story of white men building the country. Originally, Colonial Williamsburg made no attempt to include slavery in its history.[44]

Nonetheless, these historical sites survived while Freedomland didn't for a few crucial reasons. For one thing, Sturbridge Village and Williamsburg were site-specific, built on land where the towns had historically stood, unlike Freedomland, where the ground had been torn up, moved around, and redesigned to feign other geographic areas. For another, Sturbridge Village and Williamsburg were designed to preserve or re-create historical buildings that were meant to last. Freedomland, in contrast, offered flimsy façades that were more like movie sets than historical recreations. The exhibit of the Great Chicago Fire, for example, consisted only of a building façade that "burned" at regularly scheduled intervals.

Designs for Old Sturbridge Village began in 1936, with a very clear understanding of its mission to re-create an old colonial village. Based on A. B. Wells's hobby of collecting, preserving, and re-creating antique objects and buildings, the village is made up of forty buildings, reconstructed and preserved to illustrate life in New England from 1790 to 1840. The mission of this living museum, which is still in operation today, is at its core, educational. "Old Sturbridge Village, a museum and learning resource of New England life, invites each visitor to find meaning, pleasure, relevance, and inspiration through the exploration of history."[45] The village consists of three zones—the center of town, a mill neighborhood, and the countryside—and all focus on life in the 1830s. Craft demonstrations were offered beginning in 1948. While the village hosted family visits, it was explicitly designed to engage student groups.

Sturbridge Village exemplifies some of the changes that historical sites like living museums were making by the 1970s. Like with Freedomland, even today its primary appeal lies in the tactile immersion in the past that visitors experience. Its website proclaims, "Unlike traditional history museums, Old Sturbridge Village encourages guests to put their hands on history—to see, hear, feel, smell, taste, experience and fully immerse themselves in our nation's past." Like most similar attractions, it advertises itself as exciting and engaging in addition to being educational: "By truly making history dynamic, dimensional, immersive, hospitable and inclusive, Old Sturbridge Village makes America's past exciting, relevant and inspiring for today's families, students and individual visitors—ensuring that our nation's vibrant history continues to inform and enrich modern society."[46] Notably, the village suggests that the lessons of the past can valuably inform modern society in ways that Freedomland never considered. In written testimony the director of development and membership at Old Sturbridge Village, William B. Reid, shared that one of their goals was "building knowledge of their heritage and culture" in the service of "developing an understanding of continuity, change, and chronology; and gaining insights into their own lives and contemporary events."[47]

The activities at Sturbridge Village include home visits, crafting, cooking, printing and farming tutorials, and horse-drawn carriage rides. Nowhere will you find earthquakes and fires, battlefields and shootouts, as you might at Disneyland or Freedomland. The demonstrations, in fact, seem to emphasize the

tedium and hardship of life in the past—less-than-glamorous chores are reenacted with exacting detail: "Before Harriet Olmstead can bake her bread . . . in
Old Sturbridge Village, she has to wait two hours for the oven to preheat. . . . During those two hours Harriet will have continuously fed kindling into the old
brick bake oven."[48]

Sturbridge Village and Colonial Williamsburg not only trained their employees in the history they were presenting, but often hired trained historians, a
number of whom honed their teaching and research skills there. While working
at the museum, historian Lizabeth Cohen saw that it "was attracting the best and
the brightest. People who were very interested in bringing history to life, not
only to students in traditional classrooms but also to the general public through
the museum setting." Cohen recalled that her project was to give one of the
buildings, for which there was only a sparsely documented history, a "new
interpretive significance. . . . We gave the house an interpretive rationale that
did not depend on its pedigree as a house, which was very botched and confused."[49] To avoid becoming obsolete in its retelling of history, as Freedomland
did, educators at Sturbridge Village in the 1980s went out of their way to build
social conflict into their historical lessons.[50] Freedomland was not intended to
be a museum, but it approached history as a static story and left little for its visitors to interpret. In its failure, Freedomland foreshadowed the changes that the
public was beginning to look for in their history lessons.

Freedomland, conversely, did not hire historians but placed ads in local papers
to hire men over the age of eighteen, regardless of their interest in history.[51] While
Freedomland employees played the part of historical figures—"three thousand
employes [sic] will be part of the scenery, always dressed in the custom of the
period"[52]–they received little if any historical training.[53] Their role as historical
interpreters was secondary to their costumes and role as promoters of the commercial goals of the amusement park.[54]

Freedomland employed people for their amusement park skills—"buffalo
wrangler, carrousel horse jeweler, totem pole carver, and stagecoach harness-
maker. Other odd occupations at the park included pretzel bending, seal keeping, doughnut rolling, can-can dancing."[55] The park also employed character
actors for roles meant to entertain far more than to educate. John Fortna (Dig-
ger O'Toole) was employed to portray an undertaker who stood ready with his
shovel to measure the pine box for an outlaw who was to be hanged. Bob Oran
(cowboy) was a former boxer and professional wrestler who worked as a stunt-
man in New York City. John Conant was an actor hired as the singing sheriff of
the West.[56]

One could argue that there was less pressure to be "entertaining" and profit-
able at purely historical sites. Although these sites claimed to "bring history to
life" in various ways, their endowments and nonprofit status meant there was
less need to make the exhibits exciting in order to make a profit.[57] Visitors to

Figure 4.5. A group of white Freedomland visitors in 1960s garb hold their hands up as an employee dressed in a Native American costume holds up the covered wagon. *New York Daily News Sunday Color Magazine*, July 16, 1961, 27.

these educational sites expected them to be more didactic in their presentation, and they came specifically to learn about history. Freedomland's visitors, on the other hand, expected both education and excitement.

Just as historical museums had the advantage of clarity of purpose, so too did straight amusement parks. In the late nineteenth century trolley parks created by trolley companies offered rides and attractions at the end of the line to encourage people to ride the system on weekends. Palisades Amusement Park, a trolley park in Fort Lee, New Jersey, not so far from Freedomland, was created in 1898 and remained in operation until 1971. It advertised its vicinity to Manhattan, describing its location in posters as "40 Acres in sight of Broadway."[58]

In the late nineteenth century Coney Island, the famous beachfront that still attracts visitors to the southernmost part of Brooklyn, opened its boardwalk to millions of people who lived in the crowded tenements and apartments of New York. Its parks, with carousels, parachute jumps, roller coasters, and bumper cars, attracted millions of working- and middle-class people who traveled there by trolleys and buses and then by the subway line that reached its shores by 1917. In addition to Luna Park on the Coney Island Boardwalk and the Palisades, Freedomland competed with Rye Playland, just to the north in Westchester. These parks attracted visitors who knew what they were getting—rides and "thrills."

Disneyland was one place that attempted to offer lessons in history along with rides and amusements. And it did so successfully. Disneyland was built around three parallel themes, represented by Frontierland, Tomorrowland, and Fantasyland. A visitor could walk down the anonymous American path of Main Street, U.S.A. to Frontierland, the world of Davy Crockett and other frontiersmen. There, a child learned of the rugged individuals who conquered an unruly nature filled with threats from "wild Indians" and wild bears. Visitors to this area, like at Freedomland, could not participate in the action but could only watch from a guided boat ride that glided by.[59] The narrative of Frontierland was quite similar to that of Freedomland. Frontierland focused primarily on the western frontier—featuring elk and a burning log cabin with a woodsman who had been killed by an oversized Indian arrow. Disneyland's success was proof that the idea of a history-themed park in itself was not doomed to fail. So why did Freedomland flop?

One journalist alluded to the contrasts with Disneyland: "Perhaps the principal difference between Disneyland and Freedomland is that the latter is united on the single, general theme of great action stories of this country."[60] Disneyland, however, offered some additional features. A visitor who finished touring Frontierland could then take a nineteenth-century steam locomotive to Tomorrowland, a future America built around invention and science, medical discoveries, technology, space travel, and gadgets. There, a child could ride in a space capsule that shook as it took off, while he or she gazed out portal windows to see stars speeding by. Finally, the child could stroll over to Fantasyland, a magical world of Disney characters familiar to children from film and television. The variety of activities, especially Disney characters, made for a more satisfying experience than did Freedomland's solitary focus on re-creating an imagined past. Freedomland lacked the exciting inventions of the World's Fair or the fascination of Disney characters to compensate for the irrelevance of the dated exhibits.

Although the attractions in Freedomland were theatrical and intricate, they created a sense of one vague past, with little differentiation or historical grounding. The park shot for authenticity, but tended to fall short. Freedomland promised that the nation's "great action stories of our nation's 'yesterday, today, and tomorrow' come to life in a 205-acre panorama . . . and you will live through the thrills."[61] One reporter described the following scene, noting how all of the senses were enlisted to make the park's story feel real: "Ear-splitting-report of rifles fills the air as fur trappers and Injuns shoot it out on the banks of the river. Farther on, a bear climbs a tree and a skeleton dangles a fishing line into the water." The reporter went on to explain the mechanics of the exhibit. "Sound real? Well it is—or almost. All of the creatures are animated mannikins [sic] triggered by photo electric cells that react as the boat sails by." With enthusiasm, the reporter announced that "the fur trappers ride of the old Northwest . . . is one of 35 rides scheduled to open Sunday at Freedomland in the Bronx . . . the largest amusement center in the country." She emphasized how real the exhibits were: "There are 150 livestock on the grounds and a real blacksmith really shoes them in his shop. Tobacco, tomatoes, lettuce, grapes and corn really grow."[62]

In fact, the exhibits themselves, burdened with the promise of being historical, ended up seeming corny. For example, at the Chicago Fire attraction, actors would select people from the audience to participate in extinguishing the blaze. People who actually saw the exhibit remember how phony it seemed. One person reminisced, "I was selected to help pump one night & so we started pumping and all of a sudden, the pump started moving by itself—it was motorized! As a 12-year old, I was crushed by the fakery."[63]

Another disappointing aspect of Freedomland was that visitors often passively watched rather than actively participated in many of the scenes. Children gazed on as cowboys and Indians shot at each other. They did the same during the Civil War battle reenactment. Nor were they asked to think critically about the actions that were reenacted. Instead, they were often relegated to the role of passive observer. While Disneyland also has many passive rides and experiences, its scale and diversity of attractions compensated for that and minimized the "fakery" that was exposed by glimpses behind the fourth wall.

Many attractions at Freedomland involved transportation but little thrill. A pamphlet and seven-minute video introducing children to Freedomland listed trolleys, steamboats, tugboats, trains, mining cars, horse-drawn carriages, and a moving lake walk as ways to travel around Freedomland. The video begins with children "moving along the lonely road through Indian Country, heading west." It shows visitors "riding shotgun" across the Great Plains, standing at the bow of a steamboat, paddling "an authentic Chippewa canoe," and spotting the Santa Fe Special heading west. The viewer was told, "Travelling along you can get a good idea of how our country looked."[64] This description of different means of transportation provides a glimpse into the way history was being employed. By combining and conflating huge expanses of time to create one generic "past," the park merely created misperceptions. In place of any specificity or even continuous narrative visitors were offered a medley of the greatest hits of consensus history offered for consumption.

The destruction of cities was another big part of the park's narrative, but the damage was controlled and manageable. In Freedomland, the Wild West was free of real danger, just as New York was free of poor people and its streets were free of dirt. Events like the Chicago Fire were free of fatalities. Removing the fear and violence from these scenes of American history left visitors with an experience that felt campy and lacked the adrenaline rush that other parks provided. The complicated history of the country was turned into a staged movie plot. In addition, what Freedomland created was less an authentic reproduction of history or "mundane landscapes" and more what David Lowenthal calls "wishful geographies of the mind."[65] For example, one film promoting Freedomland opened with the image of a group of boys moving along a trail through what looks like arid rocky terrain. According to the narrator, "Up on top you could be anywhere, the trail doesn't have any signposts after you leave Fort Cavalry. You could be anywhere on the Great Plains in the eighteen hundreds when the west was really wild."[66] Yet in this promotional film the children appear visibly bored.

The different historical periods did not follow a clear chronological progression; travelers would find themselves jumping back and forth through time. In fact, many of the areas covered the same period in history, particularly the nineteenth century, indicating again that the park was less focused on history and more interested in entertaining spectacles—the Chicago Fire, the San Francisco earthquake, the battles of the Civil War. Freedomland included an exhibit on space flight at Cape Canaveral, making Florida the only contemporary area represented.

Freedomland relied largely on nostalgia to attract visitors—nostalgia for manageable cities with quaint streets, for the well-worn tropes of the Wild West, for the slow speed of southern plantation life, and simply for a time that felt less threatening, less complicated than the Cold War. It relied on these familiar stories much more than on history as an attraction. But by the 1960s it was becoming clearer that one couldn't turn the clock back, and the past was not so romantic.

In addition, the exhibits representing different eras or places were arranged in a hodgepodge. The Little Old New York exhibit, for example, contained a variety of clichéd shops and amusements that were only vaguely reminiscent of a particular era. The main attractions were the Bank of New York (including a real branch), a brewery, harbor tugboats, a horseless carriage, horse-drawn street cars, a candy shop, and reenactments of women's suffrage rallies and bank robberies.[67] Similarly, the Chicago area included exhibits with little related specifically to the city of Chicago—Chippewa War canoes vaguely related to the wider neighboring territory, a fire house with an antique water pumper, and shops and modes of transportation vaguely associated with the Midwest: sternwheelers, a Hallmark card shop, harbor tugboats, the Santa Fe Railroad to take visitors to San Francisco and back, the Relic house souvenir shop, and the Brass Rail steakhouse. The Great Plains area of Freedomland featured every worn-out cliché about the American frontier—a log replica of a stockade, a frontier trading post, chuck wagons, a working farm, and grazing animals. A Pony Express and the Wells Fargo stagecoach would take visitors on a treacherous ride where gangsters and robbers would greet them at every turn.

One article announcing places to eat in Freedomland reflected the same lack of historical specificity. A steak house, pizzeria, and plantation house were all equally acceptable eateries, with no differentiation between various cuisines and no particular relationship to areas of the country or historical period. "Beer will be served at several restaurants, including the popular Brass Rail Steak House in Chicago, the little Pizzeria in San Francisco's Italian Village and the Chuck Wagon inside the Western Stockade. The Plantation House in the Old South will continue to serve its $1.90 complete dinner with all the trimmings. Both the Steak and Plantation Houses will feature seafood dinners on Fridays."[68]

The Irrelevance of Its History

Making historical stories authentic and entertaining is not as simple as building a roller coaster. The attempt to merge history and commerce at Freedomland resulted in a simplified, idealized history devoid of conflict. Freedomland hoped to enjoy the luxury of straddling that line—reaping the kudos for being "historical" while treating history with the flexibility that accompanied an "amusement park." Despite the fact that Freedomland was a jumble of sometimes silly artificial exhibits loosely referencing history, or at least clichés about history, it might have succeeded at an earlier time. As discussed in the last chapter, the stories it told had made Landmark books a success—cowboys and Indians, the conquest of the West, the growth of cities, the triumph of the "American way of life." When Freedomland was planned, it seemed like an appealing, infallible story, one that was told in schools, churches, movies, and homes nationwide. Simply put, it was the story of progress, of an industrious, freedom-loving people who had come to a primitive, undeveloped nation and settled it, expanding ever westward, bringing with them the spunk, hard work, and values that ultimately made it a prosperous, successful country.

Furthermore, as children, baby boomers were more than happy to watch this story play out in westerns and combat films. The story of good triumphing over evil, not so different from the story of the triumph of democracy over communism, became part of the postwar explanation for the Cold War. The U.S. military was the cavalry defending our homeland and promoting the values of democracy and freedom in the face of oppression and aggression. The very nature of American history as it was told then held a simple, childlike quality that was appealing through World War II. But all this changed in the late fifties and early sixties. The sixties saw the height of the civil rights movement in the South and massive social protests in northern communities as well. The growing antiwar and student movements were also beginning, and the vast changes in science and technology made Freedomland's celebration of a past of pioneers, cowboys, and Indians seem outdated and irrelevant.

It is difficult to find serious reflection on the history lessons Freedomland was trying to teach. It seems likely that the developers simply grasped on to earlier romanticized, iconic stories of the Wild West and southern plantation life, which it was safe to assume would be appealing and familiar to visitors based on the wide array of mass media at the time about these topics. To the extent that native peoples were included in the story, they were either "redskins" who had to be "civilized" by the cavalry or noble, "friendly" Indians who served as scouts or sidekicks, just as they were in the Landmark and Orange book series. Slavery was only peripherally acknowledged through the glorified inclusion of Southern plantations. The attractions revolved around a familiar set of masculine stories. Progress at Freedomland was dependent on violence, physical action, and scientific achievement, all qualities designated male. It was the lone cowboy, technology, and war that moved the narrative along, not a diverse people. Aside from a Young Annie Oakley character actor and the roving suffragist, there is little record of female characters in the park. Women's roles in the story of America were negligible.

CHANGING DEMOGRAPHICS AND SOCIAL AND POLITICAL UPHEAVAL

By the time Freedomland was constructed, the demography of the Bronx—and New York City as a whole—had changed. While Freedomland was appealing to middle-class white families, large numbers of Puerto Ricans and African Americans were moving into older white Jewish, Italian, and Irish enclaves in the South Bronx. An influx of nonwhite groups to the Bronx reflected massive changes in agriculture in the American South and Puerto Rico. The Second Great Migration was taking place at this time and African Americans were moving from the South to northern cities. As the farmlands of Puerto Rico were taken over by sugar companies, small farmers there were displaced and a mass migration of peoples to New York and other cities began. In New York, older, more established African American communities like Harlem were soon overwhelmed by the influx of people who then moved to new neighborhoods in Brooklyn and the Bronx, causing a contemporary reporter to observe, "The story of the lower Bronx in 1955, as it has been for most of its history, is a story of shifting populations."[69] In the seven years from 1950 to 1957, the number of white, non-Hispanic residents of the Bronx dropped by 148,500, while the Puerto Rican population increased by nearly 90,000 and the African American population grew by 33,000. Resistance to this accelerating demographic transformation in the

1950s resulted in housing crises, school conflicts, and climbing delinquency rates. By 1957, African Americans made up 9 percent of the borough, while Puerto Ricans constituted 10.5 percent.[70]

At the same time, many whites, in reaction to the influx of these new immigrants into their neighborhoods and supported by programs like the G.I. Bill and government investments in highways and racially exclusive suburbs, were moving out of the city. In *Popular Culture in the Age of White Flight*, Eric Avila cites the changing urban demographics as one of a number of reasons for the decline in attendance at Coney Island (and other urban amusement parks) in the early 1960s.[71]

Also, in the late fifties and early sixties Americans' sense of freedom and equality was shifting. The idea of the country as one where everyone got along was undermined as news reports showed massive efforts by African Americans in the South to integrate schools, parks, bus stations, public transportation, and swimming pools. Many white Americans were ambivalent about how and whether to integrate. Aside from overt racism, there were those who advocated that integration should "go slow," as Nina Simone invoked in her 1963 song "Mississippi, Goddam." Children played central roles—as symbols, victims, and heroes—in this conflict. Riots erupted when children tried to attend school in Little Rock, Arkansas. Four little girls were killed in the bombing of a church in Birmingham, Alabama, in 1963. Freedom took on an urgent meaning and became a call for mobilization for civil rights. In the first years of the 1960s, in every sector of American life, freedom was invoked in calls for equality. It was a time that saw the founding of the African American journal *Freedomways*, when Martin Luther King Jr. gave his famous speech calling to "let freedom ring," and when Max Roach and Abbey Lincoln recorded *We Insist! The Freedom Now Suite*, which centered around themes from the Emancipation Proclamation and civil rights activism.[72]

As Eric Foner writes, "With their freedom rides, freedom schools, freedom songs, freedom marches . . . black Americans and their white allies reappropriated the central term of Cold War discourse. . . . Together, they restored to freedom the critical edge often lost in Cold War triumphalism, making it once again the rallying cry of the dispossessed."[73] Meanwhile, Freedomland and its name held increasing irony, as it persisted with using the word to convey an apolitical, vague, and falsely universal world.

Given this redefinition of freedom from the Revolutionary War to the civil rights movement, the stories that Freedomland promoted rang dissonant. Bestselling books, too, were questioning the idea of the country as conflict-free: Betty Friedan's *The Feminine Mystique* critiqued women's oppression, James Baldwin's *The Fire Next Time* challenged racism, Joseph Heller's *Catch-22* laughed at the glorification of war, and Rachel Carson's *Silent Spring* revealed the impact of pesticides and the chemical industry. These books all appeared on best-seller lists between 1961 and 1964, signaling cracks in the myth of the American past.

Established folk singers like Pete Seeger and new arrivals like Bob Dylan both identified the ironies and failings of the American history they had been taught in school in the 1950s and appealed to the oldest of the baby boomer generation who were now entering adulthood. In 1963 Seeger sang "What Did You Learn in School Today?," in which he outlines the falsehoods about America that children were taught in classrooms. "I learned that Washington never told a lie / I learned that soldiers seldom die / I learned that everybody's free / and that's what the teacher said to me." And "I learned our country must be strong / It's always right and never wrong / Our leaders are the finest men / And we elect them again and again."[74] Dylan, in his 1964 song "With God on Our Side," included in the appropriately titled album *The Times They Are a-Changin'*, pointed out the hypocrisy of lessons that could have come straight out of Freedomland's depictions of American history. "Oh, the history books tell it / They tell it so well / The cavalries charged / The Indians fell / The cavalries charged / The Indians died / Oh, the country was young / With God on its side."[75]

Not only was Freedomland internally torn over its narrative, it was out of touch with the social and political climate, romanticizing the past while merely acknowledging the future, ignoring the climate of excitement about scientific and technological development. Much like the doll collectors who celebrated the past while the Toy Fair organizers looked to the future, Freedomland re-created the past while Americans were focused on all that was modern and technological. New kitchen appliances, air conditioning, large, fast automobiles, transistor radios, color televisions, and new gadgets were the marks of progress and privilege. Technology and chemistry, the space race, newness, and possibility were the future. "Better Living through Chemistry" was Dupont's slogan, plastered on billboards and advertisements for everything from new floor waxes to new medicines; General Electric's slogan boasted that "progress is our most Important Product." At Disneyland, Monsanto built the House of the Future completely out of plastic and covered in lead paint, thought to be long-lasting and futuristic.[76]

The country itself was focused on massive scientific endeavors. Still smarting from the Soviet Union's successful satellite launch, the young President Kennedy promised to get Americans to the moon before the Russians. The space race was the stuff of daily headlines as the Soviet Union and the United States launched Sputniks, Vanguards, and a host of other satellites into space.[77] Science museums presented an exciting vision of the future not so different from, although far more sophisticated than, that offered by the international Toy Fair in the early part of the century and the Landmark books about great scientists and inventors in the 1950s. These science museums, with their focus on the extraordinary success of America's scientists and inventors like Thomas

Edison and the Wright brothers, were becoming places of great interest at a time when Freedomland was failing.

FINANCIAL DIFFICULTIES

The financial difficulties that are often cited as the reason for the demise of Freedomland stemmed largely from a miscalculation about how popular such a historical amusement park would be in the Bronx at that particular moment in time. The park's decline began early in its short life. Construction costs were enormous, over sixty-five million dollars, and by the end of the first season Freedomland was further in the red than the developers had anticipated. The constant repairs and embellishments taking place in the park meant operating costs significantly exceeded the park's original budget. One article noted, "Spokesmen for the park have said that attendance during the first summer season has been satisfactory, but the construction costs and pre-opening expenses have exceeded the budget."[78]

By the second season, "The historical re-creations of the great areas of America's past that attracted so many tourists last season have been completely refurbished."[79] Yet in its second season Freedomland faced declining attendance. The *Times* reported, "About 8,000 persons went through the turnstiles in the first four hours, compared with 40,000 in the same period on last year's sunny opening day."[80]

After the first season, Freedomland initially didn't renew its advertising contract with Ellington and Co., the firm originally hired to promote the park. In the face of the second season's troubles, Zeckendorf hired a new advertising firm, Cole, Fischer & Rogow, which quickly shifted the advertising strategy away from Freedomland's historical focus.[81] "For the opening season, Ellington had won the account and later based its campaign on selling the park for its historical and educational values. It will not be the tack taken this year."[82] The *Times* reported, "Cole, Fischer & Rogow is aiming at selling fun and excitement with very little emphasis on history and education."[83]

In 1962, the park hired Art K. Moss as general manager, and he orchestrated operations as if on a movie set.[84] For Moss, the park was a little country unto itself. He is quoted as saying "sometimes I just feel like the mayor of a city."[85] As one reporter noted, "Mr. Moss who has done everything but sell heaters to the citizens of the Sahara, sells Freedomland enthusiastically. He sounds, in fact, like a politician on a campaign binge."[86] Moss was an experienced salesman who became the new face of the park. He also had experience in the film industry and emphasized the dramatic qualities of the park.

But the historical "reenactments" of the second year became a jumble of time periods and places. The park added references to historical events far outside the United States but more for the purpose of spectacle than teaching history. Moss's experiences as a film producer began to appear in the park, where it seems he attempted to tap into the potential profitability of Hollywood's historical narratives following the success of *Ben-Hur* (1959), *Spartacus* (1960), *The Ten Commandments* (1956), and *Cleopatra* (1963). This might have allowed the park to maintain its tentative claim to educational value while reorienting toward popular movie narratives. A live action show, "Colossus," merged time periods and geographic locations. As the *New York Herald Tribune* put it, "'Colossus,' a new outdoor spectacle, will present a live reenactment of great scenes of world history as depicted in motion pictures." The reenactments were not of historical battles but were depictions of films adding another layer of fiction to Freedomland's idea of the past. These scenes were all mixed together. "In a new 3,000-seat amphitheater guests will see chariot races from the days of ancient Rome; the Three Musketeers in a sword fight against Richelieu's Guards; jousts and hand-to-hand combat of the Knights of King Arthur; and an exhibition of the greatest horsemen of history, including the Bengal Lancers, gauchos, Cossacks and Tartars. 'Colossus' stars many of the outstanding stuntmen of Hollywood."[87] The creation of such an outlandish spectacle indicated the desperation of Freedomland's promoters. They wanted to make money and clearly would wander far from their mission to make that happen. History was not their concern.

Only one season into its existence, Freedomland had, as the *Amsterdam News* reported, made its narrative into an "historical kaleidoscope. Characters from all history will participate either in scenes that actually occurred or ones requested by individual photographers from a director on the scene." The reporter noted that the show "could result in such odd and offbeat scenes as Japanese samurai warriors charging Mexican bull fighters or Roman charioteers fighting American Revolutionary War soldiers."[88] This big, confused amalgam of "the past" further undermined the accuracy of, or even the affiliation with, the park's historical narrative, the one characteristic that could have distinguished the park from its competitors—Coney Island, Palisades, or Rye Playland. In 1963, adding to the potpourri quality of the park, Mr. Moss was lent the Wax Museum from the Seattle World's Fair, which featured "15 uncanny three-dimensional sculptures of classic paintings, among them a breath-taking portrayal of Leonardo DiVinci's [sic] Last Supper and a life-size Mona Lisa tableau."[89]

Freedomland laid claim to American history when it opened, and then, in attempts to attract customers, reached back to ancient times and forward to the moon. Moss assured people that "Freedomland will maintain its essential character as a panorama of American history and geography," but in fact, the real goal was to broaden "its base to include more thrill rides and fun attractions." Moss noted that they were adding a monorail roller coaster to the Mardi Gras area of the New Orleans section "where one can look for the utmost in hilarity."[90] Write-ups about the second season list the park's historical themes as an afterthought. "A full scale circus, a state fair midway, dozens of thrill rides, all-star big bands, top singing idols, the world-famed dancing waters and exciting spectacles from the colorful American past are only a few of the fabulous attractions on the nonstop fun agenda at Freedomland this summer."[91]

To downplay Freedomland's focus on American history the new advertising firm employed a generic tagline: "A World of Fun for Everyone." One ad from 1961 read, "A galaxy of completely new thrill rides. Freedomland, a glittering array of sparkling live entertainment features. Freedomland, a round-the-clock cavalcade of giant live spectaculars. Freedomland, a breathtaking parade of special gala events!" Newspaper ads targeted adults, and the radio focused more on teenagers, rather than children, hoping this new demographic would help fill the park in the evening. "Take a date to Freedomland! A wonderland of young and gay evening hours. Dance to big name bands. Sit under the stars in a romantic river boat. Enjoy exciting jazz concerts. Hob-nob with stars at celebrity and 'personal appearance' nights featuring famous disc jockeys."[92]

Famous musicians became a main selling point for the park. Duke Ellington and Louis Armstrong performed on the main stage, the Moon Bowl. "A talent budget of 1,200,000 had been set aside for Freedomland when the entertainment center opened its fourth season, April 13. Rcord [sic] talent already booked at the park includes Nat King Cole, Bobby Darin, Patti Page, Paul Anka, Tony Bennett, Xavier Cugat and Abbe Lane, Della Reese and Count Basie. Chubby Checker was the opening attraction."[93]

By 1964, radio jingles promoted Freedomland not as a site for children to learn history while having fun but as a place for teenagers to take dates. Paul Anka sang,

Take a tip from Anka man
Take a date to Freedomland!
The Moon Bowl's free and swinging wild,
Performing night and day,
Great shows night and date,
There's me and Bobby Rydell for you,
Bobby Vinton rocking too and then there's Lesley Gore,
Four Seasons coming to town!
Gloria Lynn!
James Brown!
All summer stars galore
It's just one dollar at the gate
There's rides at Freedomland!
Great rides at Freedomland!
New rides at Freedomland![94]

But all these attempts to save Freedomland were doomed by changes and conflicts taking place around the country, even affecting the very performers who were hired to attract teenagers.

In the summer of 1964, Freedom Summer, the nation was in turmoil and New Yorkers and Americans were encountering real violence in their hometowns. It was that summer that three activists, Andrew Goodman, James Chaney, and Michael Schwerner, were murdered in Mississippi, the Civil Rights Act passed after an arduous fight, the Republican National Convention nominated Barry Goldwater for president, and fifteen-year-old James Powell was shot and killed by an off-duty police officer. This incident sparked a six-night uprising in Harlem and Bedford-Stuyvesant. In 1964 Ronald Wakefield, a famed saxophone player, and his band were staying at the Hotel Theresa in Harlem before they were to play with the Marvin Gaye Revue at Freedomland. They were barricaded in the hotel during the riots and ultimately "they not only have been fined for turning up for engagements late, but they had to duck bullets to get to work."[95] The city's racial turmoil was coming to a head, even infiltrating the miniature "United States in the Bronx."[96]

Freedomland's reorientation toward teenagers and its impending failure prompted some to cut their ties with the park. In 1962, Benjamin Moore Paint Company, whose success depended on selling its products to the growing suburban population of homeowners, sued Freedomland to be released from its contract. The company argued that the park had become a site of "common place and vulgar mass unrestrained teen-age entertainment" and that crime and disorder threatened to undermine the "family" theme that attracted the company in the first place. The company stated that the park had not been maintained "with dignity and propriety" as stipulated in their contract. The suit blamed the shifting age and racial makeup of the visitors for its decline, arguing that the teenage jazz enthusiasts visiting the park wouldn't appreciate the paint's "decoration and protection."[97] There certainly were reports of crime. In 1960 three men "used a stolen motorboat to rob the Freedomland amusement park of $28,827." The robbers all lived in the Bronx and each received between five and eight years in prison despite pleas for leniency.[98] Elsewhere it was reported that displays of Indian mannequins were vandalized by young visitors: "The Pawnees—great and fearless fighters of the plains—are not a match for Bronx kids who invade the project at night and scalp the braves and run off with their loin cloths."[99]

By 1964 Zeckendorf's company, Webb & Knapp, faced an increasingly burdensome amount of debt and was eager to be rid of Freedomland.[100] The *Wall Street Journal* reported that selling the park to Hyman Green relieved "the financially troubled company, controlled by William Zeckendorf, of various obligations." Additionally, "Zeckendorf lined up a $25 million first mortgage loan from a Teamsters Union pension fund and pledged the 407 acres of Bronx land as collateral." Receiving its payout from the Teamsters, Zeckendorf and Webb & Knapp "wrote off completely its $17.9 million of investment from Freedomland, Inc." at the end of 1963.[101] The next year "a number of employees' paychecks bounced." The *New York Times* reported that "Freedomland, the amusement enclave in the northeast Bronx, recently paid some of its employes [sic] with bad checks totaling between $2,000 and $3,000." While "Freedomland officials said 'a mixup in deposits' had caused some checks to be returned for insufficient funds," few believed them. "Numerous employees turned up yesterday. Some said they had been told they would be paid last Friday, then yesterday, then tomorrow." By then it was impossible "to convince the public that Freedomland was financially viable."[102]

Webb & Knapp tried to control the rumors that the park had gone bankrupt by suggesting that the World's Fair would bring visitors to the park, though it's worth noting that Freedomland's entrance fee of $3.50 was more than the larger World's Fair's $2.00 ticket. In 1964 the Washington Post reported that Hyman Green, who purchased the park, said "Freedomland seems well on the way to making money this year because of the visitors who are coming to New York primarily for the World's Fair."[103] It would make sense that those visiting the city to get a slice of Americana would stop by this version of the United States. But Freedomland did not survive the season. The company filed for chapter 11 bankruptcy in 1964, now citing competition with the World's Fair.

COMPETITION WITH THE WORLD'S FAIR

There were discussions in the press about whether Freedomland's financial difficulties were anything at all to do with the World's Fair. It is hard not to conclude that the fair presented a more modern, and altogether more exciting experience than Freedomland. The New York Daily News reported that while the evidence was mixed, "The fair is having some adverse effect on Westchester area amusement centers.... Playland, in Rye, reported that attendance was down about 8 per cent from last year.... One official said that the weather has been nearly perfect, so it must be the World's Fair that was diverting persons who would normally come to Playland."[104] Conversely, another article stated that the World's Fair was aiding all the metropolitan area amusement parks since "people use the Fair as an excuse for visiting New York, but they also visit the other places they've heard about."[105] The article stated that Freedomland "reported attendance off somewhat, but not seriously," and quoted one official who said that "Freedomland was benefitting from its attractions designed for family fun, which, he said, were lacking at the fair."[106] But as we have seen, there was desperation in the manic production of new attractions at Freedomland.

The World's Fair, which opened in 1964, faced a number of challenges similar to Freedomland, but it was a very different undertaking. The fair was international in scope and did not hide associations with fun attractions like Disneyland. As Joseph Lelyveld put it in the New York Times in 1964, "At the pavilion, the United Nations, the United States and Disneyland flags fly side by side."[107] Focused on the future and designed to last little more than two seasons, the World's Fair was hardly the long-term threat to Freedomland that its pro-moters maintained. The audiences for the World's Fair and Freedomland were also very different. Freedomland courted families who lived in the vicinity of the park, while the fair aimed at a national and even international clientele. And while Freedomland was surrounded by highways leading to Westchester and Connecticut, the fair was located out in Queens near New York City's two air-ports and accessible by public transit, so it was easy for foreign and local tour-ists to visit. The sheer scale of the World's Fair, at 650 acres, made Freedomland's 85 acres of attractions seem makeshift. And while all but one of Freedomland's attractions looked to the past, the World's Fair touted space travel and modern technologies.

One very successful part of the World's Fair was the storytelling hour at the U.S. Pavilion. Children would sit on stools while the librarian read them sto-ries, a serious attempt to engage and educate children that was absent from Freedomland. Highlighting just how conservative the World's Fair audience was understood to be, George Lewicky, the assistant director of the American Pavil-ion's library, said there had been no complaints about the books in the library even though "the list of subjects includes such controversial topics as equal rights and the conflict of ideologies."[108] The fair showed resistance, too, to addressing the fight for civil rights happening around it, calling even the topic of equal rights controversial.

Compared to the Fair's exhibits, Freedomland's must have seemed simplistic and corny. Both sites claimed their objectives were educational. However, exhib-its at the World's Fair were much more intricate. According to the *Chicago Tri-bune*, "Of particular interest is a school of the future, showing the scientific equipment being developed to speed and ease teaching." The paper noted that "included are electronic teaching machines, programmed instructions, and a variety of audio-visual devices designed to untangle educational knots."[109] Cen-tral to this and other exhibits was the role of science, technology, and the atom in space exploration and America's military might. The Atomic Energy Com-mission announced they were building an exhibit called "Atomsville, U.S.A. to help youngsters along the paths of atomic science."[110] The World's Fair featured machines that could introduce kids to a vast array of scientific equipment, even related to the harnessing of thermonuclear power. The ride to the moon in the main hall was especially popular for school-age children.

Unlike Freedomland, where kids had to travel with their parents by car or navigate the subway and bus system, young people could easily find their way to the World's Fair by the BMT and IRT subway. A twelve-year-old boy named Dominic Tucci snuck onto the Long Island Rail Road at Thirty-Fourth Street's Penn Station and found that it took no time to reach the Fair's gates: "The next thing I knew the man was announcing World's Fair and Shea Stadium."[111] In a

Figure 4.6. An aerial view of the 1964 World's Fair. Photo credit: Doug Coldwell, 1964 World's Fair, Wikipedia.

story that closely resembles the 1967 fictional book *From the Mixed-Up Files of Mrs. Basil E. Frankweiler*, Dominic managed to live in the park for nine days unsupervised.[112] "Wearing a dirty shirt, dirty pants and dusty shoes, Dominic, a green-eyed youngster with blond hair, sat in the Security Building at the fair later and told how he had slept in various pavilions, lied to inquisitive cops and obtained money to buy food by picking coins out of fountains."[113]

The World's Fair had a very different mission from Freedomland. Wanting to attract international visitors, it had little interest in keeping fees low in order to attract NYC visitors, even children. Soon after the opening of the Fair a very heated public debate erupted between local politicians and Robert Moses, the former parks commissioner and president of the World's Fair, about reducing the price of admission to make it affordable for New York City school groups. In September 1963 the Board of Education asked for a flat admission rate of twenty-five cents for each pupil visiting with a class.[114] Moses fought these price reductions at every turn. The *New York Times* reported, "Robert Moses has rebuffed, with characteristic gruffness, the suggestion that school children should be admitted to the World's Fair at reduced rates." "'The Fair,' argues Mr. Moses, is 'a business enterprise that must meet its obligations,'" a point the *Times* took issue with.[115] What followed was a debate about whether the fair was a private or public institution, with the *Times* asking, "If it is a business enterprise, why are New York City, New York State and the United States all subsidizing it with many millions of dollars?"[116] The *Times* cited the Fair's certificate of incorporation, which "empowers it to organize and operate a fair 'for the exclusively educational purpose of educating the peoples of the world as to the interdependence of nations and the need for international peace.'"[117] While Freedomland had simply erased the line between education and entertainment according to the whims of its owners, the idea about whether or not the Fair was an educational public service or a private business meant to entertain became a heated public debate.

In October 1963, the City Council demanded reduced rates for children, arguing that the city, in addition to providing the site, "was spending about $120,000,000 to build and improve 'a network of express highways and scenic parkways leading to the site from all parts of the city.'" Moses still would not reduce rates, arguing "that the loss of revenue, based on several visits by schoolchildren, would be $9,000,000."[118] The president of the Co-Ordinated Community Service announced that *they* would provide tickets to school children for twenty-five cents but let people know that the Fair was not cooperating in this undertaking: "We may have to purchase blocks of tickets outright from the World's Fair, and then discount them as the school children apply." Or, he suggested, "we will turn over the 25 cents in cash to each person: whichever plan is more feasible. Then we will have to work out a system to avoid duplication, while trying to anticipate most of the little problems which are bound to come up in a program of this size."[119]

Race was clearly at the center of this debate. When Moses offered to reduce the fee on Mondays during the summer, the city saw a ray of hope and continued to lobby for the city's children. Hulan E. Jack, the African American borough president of Manhattan and the highest ranking African American politician in the city at the time, critiqued "the World's Fair Executive Committee and President Robert Moses for their arbitrary stand against reduced rate tickets, which could deny indigent Negro and Puerto Rican children an opportunity to visit the Fair."[120]

When public shaming failed to bring Moses around, the city announced that it was "revoking the World's Fair's exemption from the 5 per cent admissions tax in order to subsidize the children's admission fees." Again, the city argued that the fair was educational in its mission. "The children from our city's lower income families are the ones who most need the intellectual stimulation and motivation which the World's Fair could provide,' he said. 'Yet these are the very children who can lest [*sic*] afford the fair's heavy admission charge.'"[121]

After months of back and forth, Mayor Wagner (playing a very different role than he had for Freedomland's opening) and Robert Moses met in person at the mayor's summer home in Islip, Long Island, and agreed to allow children in school groups from New York and surrounding areas to attend for twenty-five cents.[122] Fifteen thousand students flooded the fair on the first day it was available, May 1, 1964.[123] Moses's indifference to attracting children from the city underscores the fact that the fair not only didn't need children to survive, but viewed them as a financial liability, vastly untrue for Freedomland. Moses saw the world—more specifically, the business world—as his audience and wanted to highlight what America and New York had to offer.

In the end, Zeckendorf understood why the World's Fair was a success and Freedomland failed. American society itself was rapidly changing, and the World's Fair made some sort of sense while Freedomland didn't. Zeckendorf went so far as to compare Webb & Knapp's involvement in Freedomland with America's involvement in Vietnam—the conflict that brought about the end to America's World War II "victory culture." He wrote, "We got into Freedomland the way the United States got into Vietnam, back-sideways, without really intending to, and only to clean up the mess somebody else had left behind."[124] Looking back, Zeckendorf acknowledged that even early on investors weren't totally behind Freedomland. By the time Freedomland closed it had become a bit of a joke. One reporter summed it up like this: "They took the Chicago fire and the San Francisco earthquake, the Wild West and the Civil War. They rolled them into the shape of the U.S. and plunked them on a swamp in the Bronx. And they called it Freedomland, so nobody would dare laugh."[125] The reporter's tone was wildly different from the reverent anticipation in early coverage of Freedomland.

Zeckendorf later claimed that he won in the end. He maintained in his autobiography that his interest all along was to increase the value of the land Freedomland stood on. He said that at the outset "we didn't have a penny in the project. All the publicity and traffic Freedomland generated was bound to increase the value of our real estate. How could we lose? We leased them the land." But when Freedomland began to falter the company "took forty percent of the company's stock and advanced them money to pay off a few million in due bills. This process continued: we ended up owning Freedomland . . . Freedomland, with its enormous fixed costs, never got near the break-even point."[126] Freedomland found itself with both fixed costs and a fixed narrative that could not withstand the changing national atmosphere.

For Zeckendorf there was no love lost with the demise of Freedomland, and he could even see the advantages. Freedomland "attracted attention to our acreage, and we did, after closing Freedomland, sell the lease to the land to Abraham Kazan's United Housing Foundation." For Zeckendorf, what had been empty swampland could now be converted into thousands of middle-income

Figure 4.7. An aerial view of Co-op City, where seventy-five thousand people would reside by 1968. Photo by David Rosner, May 15, 2019.

apartments.[127] Some of the same politicians who spoke at the opening of Freedomland were on hand to announce its demise. "Plans to develop 300-acres of Bronx, N.Y., land with a gigantic middle-income housing project that will receive financial help from New York City and New York State were disclosed at a press conference by Mayor Wagner and Governor Rockefeller."[128] Co-op City would quickly rise from the marshes to dramatically alter this part of the Bronx skyline.

As we have seen, the story Freedomland offered began to unravel in the late 1950s and 1960s as the Bronx and the world changed. New York City mayor John Lindsay ran in 1965 on a platform of halting the decline that had already begun. But as one biography points out, "student radicalism, the counterculture, racial tensions and riots, growing conservatism, and antiwar protests made Lindsay's brand of earnest, idealistic, good-government liberalism seem quaint and ineffective and helped create an aura of chaos and dissension beyond his control."[129] Similarly, Freedomland, with its promise of fun and simplistic narratives, also came to seem quaint and outdated.

Freedomland's historical narrative certainly failed to make sense of troubled race relations in America's past and failed to represent women or marginalized communities in American society. It even failed to include the people in the Bronx whose lives were being reshaped by urban decay. The civil rights, women's, and antiwar movements all brought this home. Just as Freedomland shut down, "areas of the South Bronx and Bushwick, Brooklyn, were leveled by fires and to this day have not fully recovered. Something obviously went awry deep inside the social fabric of the city between 1965 and 1977."[130] Telling the story of America simply as that of conquest and victory would no longer do.

Despite its popularity, massive scale, and big dreams, Freedomland did not survive beyond four years. When people were asked what seemed most remarkable about Freedomland, they would say with shrugged shoulders, "It was fun, I didn't go back" or "I don't really remember" or, most often, "It was far away." One person who attended as a teen noted, "There was no place to make out." Decidedly indifferent were the comments about its history. When asked specifically if they were interested in Freedomland because of the historical narratives

Figure 4.8. Plaque dedicated to Freedomland, U.S.A. that now serves as the only official physical reminder of the park that was razed to make space for Co-op City. Photo by Hugo L. González, Creative Commons CC BY-SA 4.0.

or if they thought it seemed realistic, the response was a resounding "no."[131] Those who do remember Freedomland fondly recall the excitement of the place but almost never remember anything about the history. One fan recalls the Schaefer Brewery and the "group of animated figurines that looked like little elves, which were enchanting." Another recalled riding on the horse-drawn trolley, observing the hand-blown glass shop and getting an autograph from Connie Francis. Another recalled that peeking behind the façade was in itself an appeal. Riding in the Civil War wagons, the visitor got "a kick out of seeing the fallen trees and horses rise magically back into position behind us as they reset for the next group of travelers."[132] Freedomland was an amusement park that used well-worn historical narratives from the Cold War as a drawing card. It fell into a trap of trying to fix the meaning of that history even as the world around it shifted. It created a static and unsustainable landscape with little room for interpretation and weak attempts at providing thrills.

Ironically, the World's Fair, always meant to be temporary, has left more of a mark on the landscape than has Freedomland, with its lofty promise of permanence. The Unisphere, New York State Pavilion, Hall of Science, and Heliport (now Terrace on the Park) all still stand on their original sites in Queens. No prominent structures of Freedomland remain marking its former territory. In part, what makes Freedomland so fascinating is its abrupt and thorough erasure from the New York City landscape. It isn't rusting away and disintegrating before our eyes, sixty years later. When Freedomland closed, the physical site was completely razed and immediately transformed into Co-op City.

Until 2013, no reminder of Freedomland existed on what was arguably the largest single piece of private open land in the city of New York at the time of its development. Instead, Co-op City, the housing development, which was originally part of the Mitchell-Lama Housing Program, looms large on the horizon. Thanks to the efforts of a dedicated group of fans of the park, there is a small plaque embedded on a stone in Co-op City dedicated to Freedomland, an extravagant and ill-conceived homage to American history. Freedomland lives on primarily through the variable memories of those who visited during the four brief years of its existence.

Going forward, didactic amusements for children would need to rely less on the tropes of the American West and Antebellum South and configure new stories that included more room for empathy and interpretation and a more diverse array of voices.

CHAPTER 5

Selling Multicultural Girlhood

THE AMERICAN GIRL DOLL, 1986 TO PRESENT

In the fall of 1986, half a million glossy catalogues landed in the mailboxes of American girls, ages eight to twelve years old. This was the opening salvo of the American Girl Company, originally named the Pleasant Company, which introduced three fictional characters of the past, Kirsten, Samantha, and Molly, to thousands of girls of the present. By the end of that holiday season, American Girl had made $1.7 million in sales and launched a commercial juggernaut.[1] From the pages of the oversized catalogue the doll's faces peered out, half smiling, at millions of young readers who would soon become consumers.

The American Girl doll and book collection represents perhaps the most serious and successful attempt in twentieth-century American culture to use dolls and books to teach children about their history. Whereas Freedomland represented not just a use but an abuse of history to sell tickets to an amusement park, the American Girl Company's claim to being educational had merit. A great deal of research went into decisions about how to present American history, whom to feature, and how to interpret historical events. The dolls represent American girls from diverse backgrounds, and the accompanying books offer a far more nuanced view of the past than other case studies in this book. In offering these stories, the company reflected a shift in education, historiography, and broader society to a more multicultural representation of America.

Diverse social movements of the 1950s and 1960s, while far from producing full equality, drew attention to the need for a more inclusive definition of who was an American. During the civil rights movement African Americans highlighted the continued oppression and racism of American society and the women's movement critiqued patriarchal America. These and other protest movements drew attention to marginalized groups in America and provided the impetus for historians to study those who had been left out of the American story. The 1960s and 1970s witnessed a vast outpouring of serious historical scholarship detailing the exploitation of labor by a growing capitalist class of industrialists, the suppression of women's rights, and the experience of immigrant and working-class groups.[2] By the 1980s, the cohesive narrative so long proffered by "consensus historians, schools and the media came to seem outdated and inaccurate."[3] At the same time the multicultural educational movement, with curricula about more diverse groups of people and traditions, began to take hold. It was time for a more inclusive definition of who was an American.

As Diane Ravitch writes, by the 1980s "multiculturalism became a hotly debated issue . . . largely in connection with states' efforts to revise their history curriculum."[4] As a result of those debates, textbooks came to include descriptions of the traditions and celebrations of a diverse set of Americans. At the same time "once-standard heroes such as Captain John Smith, Daniel Boone, and Wild Bill Hickok had 'all but disappeared'" from American history textbooks.[5] The narrative of American history could no longer be told as one of ever greater progress toward equality; it needed to include acknowledgment of America's misdeeds as well. It was in this context that American Girl entered the scene, becoming part of a more inclusive celebratory view of America and scripting for its characters particular diverse cultural practices.

In keeping with this move toward better representation of all Americans, the Pleasant Company, named for its founder Pleasant Rowland, began offering its American Girl dolls and books to the public. The company identified the young girl as a primary consumer—rather than a secondary consumer to her brother. They also understood that the "American girl" could no longer be presented only as white (although the first dolls were) and middle class but in the America of the 1980s and 1990s must also be Black, brown, and Asian, as well as rich and poor. Early on the company offered dolls representing girls from different backgrounds as well as historical periods—a colonial American girl, an orphaned Victorian girl, an African American girl who escaped slavery, a Swedish immigrant pioneer girl, and a girl living through World War II. In doing so the Pleasant Company acknowledged that America, particularly after the Immigration and Naturalization Act of 1965, was a diverse, multiethnic, multicultural country and simultaneously suggested that there was something distinctly "American" about diversity.

This chapter first examines the historical lessons the American Girl dolls and books offered to girls, lessons that accounted for the wide popularity of the books among parents. While there is no doubt that the American Girl doll offered a well-researched, more complex view of American history than the myths about America replayed so often for children, a deeper consideration of the dolls and books demonstrates that, despite their multicultural orientation, they ultimately—in part accelerated after the company was purchased by Mattel—came to reflect a white, middle-class culture in a way that diminished some of the historical lessons. Second, it analyzes how the uniformity of plots, merchandise, and characters in the books actually undermined the sense of diversity they were meant to convey by suggesting that all the girls have the same problems and the same desires. Third, it demonstrates how the clever use of nostalgia in the company's advertising, catalogues, and stores and the placement of illustrations of products in the margins of the books introduced young contemporary American girls to their role as consumers. Finally, this chapter demonstrates how, in the face of contested notions of American identity and the pressures of a global marketplace, the company shifted its focus away from the historical dolls once it had established itself in the toy market.

Although the first three dolls released in 1986 were white, their stories included discussions of labor practices, Native American displacement, and political revolution. As the company grew, it added more stories that dealt with slavery, immigration, and the impact of world war on families. However, in the late 1990s, and especially after Mattel purchased and renamed the company the American Girl Company in 1998, it began to abandon its historical focus. In what looks like a calculation that a different orientation would reap more profits, the company shifted its focus and expanded its reach to become an omnivorous conglomerate that merchandises dolls, clothes, and accessories that include items like miniature computers, popcorn machines, and even wheelchairs, through catalogues, websites, and giant stores in Chicago, Manhattan, and other major cities.

Precursors to the American Girl Dolls and Books

There is a long history of attempts to define the characteristics that make the ideal American girl and to model her behavior. In 1906 Moffat, Yard and Company published *The American Girl Seen and Portrayed*, a highly embellished, beautifully illustrated book by Howard Chandler Christy, an artist and writer who popularized what became known as "the Christy Girl," an upper-middle-class society type.[6] His book argued that the twentieth century "will see the evolution of the highest type of woman-kind the world has ever produced." "The American girl," he said, "would be a combination of the best qualities of her more sophisticated and cultured Old World relatives." From the Germans, it stated, this American girl "retained the Teuton sobriety of character and power of reasoning analytically." From the British, she "derived that love of her home which remains a distinguished characteristic," and from the French she "derived, either by inheritance or by sympathetic imitation, that grace and lightness that has made the American woman the only competitor of the Parisienne." Even some of the better qualities of the oft-demonized Irish were absorbed into this definition of the new American girl: "from the Celtic have been derived two characteristics not obtainable else-where, the romanticism that gives love of poetry, art, and music that confers the power of appreciating them." In addition, the American Girl has "the saving grace of humor . . . with which comes the wit of tongue and of mind that sweetens the acerbities of life and is to clever women both sword and shield in social life."[7]

In retrospect, Christy's book seems like a quaint depiction of the then prevailing stereotypes of America's early immigrants from northern Europe. The qualities that characterized the more recent southern or eastern European immigrants are not discussed, even though waves of them were arriving on American shores. Although the Pleasant Company also focused on northern and western European ancestry for their original characters, it's notable that they didn't entirely assimilate. One of the original characters, a Swedish immigrant named Kirsten, retained her home country's hairstyle, her distinctive braided hairdo, even on the frontier. Much like the women of the National Doll Collectors' Club would in the late 1930s, Christy viewed these more recent immigrants through a reactionary prism. The American girl, according to Christy, incorporated the best qualities of her northern European peers from Great Britain, Germany, and France, not of the Russians and Jews coming through Ellis Island. "Let us, for instance, compare the American girl who has made her own all the cultivation and advantages brought to her by our civilization," Christy observed, "with the young peasant woman, who, bundle in hand and kerchief on head, makes her awkward, blundering way amid the throng of emigrants that has been landed in one of our great cities, and gazes stupidly upon the wonders of the New World to which she has come."[8] He asked, "What is it that makes the difference?" and answered "race, education, and surroundings."[9] For him the white American girl had the advantages of nature and nurture, race and surroundings, and was therefore superior to newly arrived immigrants.

Another book, published about a decade later in 1915, called *The American Girl: Her Education, Her Responsibility, Her Recreation, Her Future*, was written by Anne Morgan, the daughter of John Pierpont Morgan. Morgan criticized the idea that American girls should model themselves on European girls and instead suggested that the American girl should be a symbol of American independence and isolationism. With the conflict of World War I on the horizon, this American girl, according to Morgan, needed to leave behind her longing for a past European world and look to the work of creating a new American identity. "The American girl who seeks to avoid the inevitable conflict by looking to European sanctuary is indeed deceived." Morgan writes, "She longs for the finish and beauty of the old order, and, in looking far afield to what past generations have accomplished, she fails to realize that it lies in her own hands to bring that same beauty into her own surroundings."[10]

For Morgan, creating a new American character was essential for the country's emergence as a unified society and even as a global power. The American girl had to draw on the best of the Old World yet avoid the stratified, class-bound qualities that limited the horizons of European girls and inhibited society's growth. She had to distinguish herself from her more obedient, and subservient, European counterpart who was hampered by retrograde traditions and practices. She needed to reflect her new, young, dynamic country. The American Girl doll Samantha, whose backstory placed her in 1904—around when Morgan was writing—reflects some of Morgan's notion of the American girl as privileged and feminine but slightly rebellious, scoffing at her grandmother's strict rules of etiquette and showing enthusiasm for bicycles. For Morgan, "From the days of the pioneers our heroes have been those who were most ready to turn their backs on the limitations of their present existence and seek a wider and freer development in some better environment."

Morgan encouraged the American girl to look to the future in which "all physical and industrial developments are rapidly changing. . . ." She argued that "unless the boy and girl develop within themselves those characteristics that alone can create the very freedom which they seek, their search will be an idle search."[11] Continuing to reflect on the nature of American identity, Morgan argued, "Freedom of choice is indeed one of the greatest gifts possessed by mankind, but it must come to a well-trained and spiritually developed character, not to an ignorant and unformed child."[12] What is striking about both Christy's and Morgan's formulations is that the American girl would be different from the immigrant girl, and, in Morgan's case, even different from her northern European peers. She might borrow qualities from girls from other countries, but she must be unique, even superior, in the way she combines those qualities.

Over the years there have been examples of dolls that referenced history. As mentioned in this book's first chapter, the teddy bear, fashioned after Teddy Roosevelt and first produced in 1903, was extremely popular. In 1955, the U.S. government asked America's most popular doll company, Madame Alexander Dolls, to make a Liberty doll and also a Statue of Freedom doll to be given to "a little Latvian girl, Dace Epermanis, who was the 150,000th displaced person to enter the United States after World War II."[13] It was a doll that would teach this little Latvian girl that America was defined by freedom. Dolls of historical characters continued to be popular throughout the twentieth century, including a Scarlett O'Hara doll (a fictional character seen as representative of a plantation mistress) and a Queen Elizabeth doll.[14] In 1959 the *New York Times* advertised an American Girl doll produced by the Madame Alexander Doll Company, which looked remarkably similar to the contemporary American Girl doll. Janie was a white doll dressed in a fluffy pinafore with her hair neatly ribboned.[15] Although there is no backstory for this doll that would suggest particular "American" qualities, it is clear that she was dressed as a white middle-class girl of the 1950s.[16] A 2014 Madame Alexander doll looks virtually the same—with long blond

"Janie," the American girl doll, 36 inches tall and made of unbreakable vinyl. She's dressed in a polished cotton pinafore with patent leather shoes; she wears size 3 dress. Blonde or brunette washable rooted hair. By Mme. Alexander.   24.95

Figure 5.1. 1959 advertisement for "Janie," described as an American Girl and bearing resemblances to the American Girl dolls produced by Mattel. "Display Ad 100," *New York Times*, November 15, 1959, 102.

Figure 5.2. 2014 Madame Alexander doll dressed in clothing similar to dolls from the 1950s but in a more dynamic pose.

hair and bangs, in a pinafore dress, with Mary Jane shoes and white socks and frilly sleeves—albeit positioned in a more dynamic pose.

Over the years attempts to model behavior for girls extended beyond dolls to include other toys. Toy appliances like Easy Bake Ovens reinforced consumer roles and domestic expectations for girls. In the 1990s board games like Mall Madness, Dream Phone, Barbie Queen of the Prom, and Mystery Date prepared girls to shop and find a date with the cutest boy. These games from the 1980s and 1990s suggest stereotypical activities for girls—shopping, dating, and if she were professional she would likely be a teacher. The American Girl dolls and books clearly stood out from these games and toys that featured virtually no people of color in their ads and cover art.

When Pleasant T. Rowland founded the Pleasant Company she was doing something completely new—introducing a line of dolls each of which had a whole backstory as a character in American history. She sold the dolls exclusively through the mail.[17] As the American Girl doll collection grew in size and diversity, the Pleasant Company achieved incredible success selling to white (although not exclusively), middle-class parents and children across the country. Although named after its founder, the designation "pleasant" is quite telling in that all the dolls seem to exhibit pleasantness and provide their owners with pleasant company. In addition, "pleasant" suggests nostalgia for a past American girlhood. When Mattel purchased the Pleasant Company in 1998 (and the company was renamed American Girl), it was valued at $700 million.[18] American Girl dolls and their corresponding books, merchandise, clothing, stores, and films continue to dominate the seven- to twelve-year-old market. In 1999, fourth-quarter sales alone grossed $250 million. In 2015 alone, gross sales of the American Girl brands were $572 million (down 7 percent from the previous year).[19] Since its founding, the American Girl Company has sold over thirty-two million dolls.[20]

THE AMERICAN GIRL DOLLS

The American Girl dolls themselves reflect their nine-year-old customers. The eighteen-inch-tall dolls have soft, square-shaped, prepubescent torsos and are far different from the hard, adultlike Barbie dolls. The dolls' eyes, detailed and lifelike, open when the dolls are upright and close when they are reclining. Altogether, their round features and baby-cheeked faces create a childlike silhouette; these dolls are innocent looking and not intimidating. In more recent years, they have become a status symbol for young girls who carry them around in their arms. They are quite expensive, costing more than a handful of Barbie dolls would.

In its "early days" of the 1980s, the Pleasant Company had no stores or website where the dolls could be purchased. Dolls were ordered through the American

Girl catalogue and delivered by mail. This distribution system harkened back to an earlier era when women ordered luxury items from catalogues, an act that reflected their cosmopolitan tastes. The dolls, well crafted and fairly large, arrived wrapped in tissue paper inside an elegant maroon box wrapped in ribbon. The care given to the packaging of these dolls suggested that they were precious and durable and thus worth their hefty price tags.[21] Although American Girl dolls represent girls from a range of socioeconomic backgrounds, in fact their price is not affordable to many families. Originally $88 in 1986 (about $200 in today's money), in 2020 American Girl offered a doll and book for $98 (down from the previous price of $115). The cost rises significantly when clothing, furniture, and accessories are added on.[22] The dolls came with unspoken promises, offering girls a connection to the past and giving parents the feeling there might arise an opportunity to tell their children about their own childhoods. The dolls felt almost destined to become heirlooms, something that could connect generations for many years.[23]

THE HISTORICAL BOOKS

Each American Girl doll was originally accompanied by a book that told the story of the particular historical period the doll represented and described the challenges for girls in that era. Originally, each American Girl doll stood for a different era in American history. The first three dolls, Kirsten, Samantha, and Molly, represented pioneer days (1854), the Victorian era (1904), and World War II (1944), respectively. Soon after the appearance of this trio, two more dolls were introduced: Felicity (the colonial era, 1774) in 1991 and the first African American doll, Addy (Civil War, 1864), in 1993. The company continued to add dolls to the collection over time, among them the 1997 addition Josefina, a doll living in New Mexico in 1824; Kaya, of the Nez Perce tribe living precontact in the Northwest; Julie, a doll living in San Francisco in 1974; and Rebecca, a Jewish doll living on the Lower East Side in 1914. Additional characters continue to be added to this list, and other characters are retired from circulation, presumably based on their popularity.

American Girl dolls are often compared to the popular Barbie dolls, introduced by Mattel in the 1950s. The differences, however, are noteworthy. Barbie exists in a contemporary, ahistorical space, whereas American Girl dolls inhabit particular historical periods. Barbie is eleven and a half inches of hard plastic with exaggerated features including her infamous and unrealistic bust and waist measurements. Barbie also has had over one hundred careers and a muscular paramour named Ken.[24] The American Girl dolls appear innocent by comparison. They are unambiguously childlike, and romantic relationships do not factor into their stories.[25] Instead, the American Girl goes to school and makes friends. As the American Girl website explains, "These nine-year-old fictional heroines

live during important times in America's past, providing 'girl-sized' views of significant events that helped shape our country, and they bring history alive for
millions of children."[26]

These dolls held a particular appeal in the late 1980s and 1990s when parents
worried about the influences of pop stars like Madonna writhing and dancing
on the new channel MTV and television shows like 90210 with plots addressing
drug use and sex.[27] There was a pervasive concern that children were being
exposed to media that were making them "grow up too fast."[28] American Girl
dolls harkened back to pre-electronic, at times Victorian, forms of play. They
spent their time reading and doing crafts (including flower pressing and silhouette kits).

A large part of the appeal of the dolls, at least for parents in the 1980s, was
their tie to the books that related the history of the era that each doll inhabited.
The original Pleasant Company logo featured a silhouetted girl lying on her
stomach reading next to her doll, who has a similar silhouette, who also faces
the oversized book. It's a dark maroon color, rather than black-and-white, like a
more sophisticated, antique-feeling pink. The logo itself evokes a bygone Victorian time, by its use of the silhouette, a popular pastime. Informative and read-
able for ages seven and up, the books contain an afterword with additional
historical information. Each doll was accompanied by six historical books, which
in total illuminate one year of each doll's life narrative. The six books of historical fiction have the same titles, with only the character's name changing.[29] For
instance, each series opens with a book called *Meet Kirsten* or *Meet Molly*. The
second book's plot is always about schooling and is called *Kirsten* (or Addy or
Samantha) *Learns a Lesson*. The third book, *Kirsten's Surprise*, for example, takes
place during the winter holidays. Then follows *Happy Birthday Kirsten*, *Kirsten
Saves the Day*, and finally *Changes for Kirsten*, which ends the series. The last
book always involves the resolution of the main problem the particular girl faced
in the earlier books. Often the resolution involves a reunion with family
members.

The books are made to appeal to their young readers by offering stories with
situations to which young girls can relate. The plots generally revolve around
social circles in school and the formation and trials of friendships. Often there
are snobby mean girls who act cruelly and must be taught a lesson. The protagonists in the stories must decide whether to join the mean girls or befriend the
underdog. For example, the Victorian girl, Samantha, chooses to befriend a girl
who is the subject of ridicule because she has spent her days working in a factory.
While each story takes place in a different era and is a kind of morality play, each
could be the story of any contemporary girl; there is little to distinguish the protagonist's experiences with friendship from those of girls from another era.

Reading the fictionalized stories, however, the reader does learn about American history—and a more nuanced history than in earlier books of fiction and

even school curricula. The reader learns about the struggles of life on the frontier and about the Revolutionary War. She learns about how churches and former slaves who made it to the North during and after the Civil War often welcomed newly arrived, escaped or freed slaves and helped find them work and a place to stay. She learns about food rationing and material recycling during World War II. At the end of the series about Addy the reader learns about the Emancipation Proclamation. These stories reflect the shift in formal schooling toward a multicultural history. And significantly, the main characters are all female and have agency and points of view, even standing up to male antagonists.

The reader also learns some of the harsher historical facts about what life was like in different eras. This is a dramatic departure from the oversimplified stories in the Landmark series. In Addy's stories, the enslaved family is not a group of stereotypical smiling characters in the background but protagonists with complicated feelings and challenges. There is an acknowledgment of the real horrors of slavery. In one scene the reader learns that Addy was forced to eat worms that she had failed to pick off of a cotton plant.[30] Reading the story of Addy the reader also learns that on a plantation the master might sell slaves to another plantation with no concern about separating family members.

The American Girl Company made an innovative decision to bolster and contextualize their plotlines with archival evidence and explanations about the past. The fictional story in each book is followed by a section called "Peek into the Past," replete with primary documents that describe in greater detail some aspects of the historical era referenced in the story. These sections can be as long as six pages and contain a good deal of material. For example, the historical section at the end of the second book about Addy's experience in school explains how difficult it was for African Americans to get an education. The reader learns that by the 1830s "it was against the law in most southern states to teach African Americans to read and write. Many whites didn't want blacks to read about freedom in the North because they were afraid their slaves would run away. . . . Black people who were caught learning to read and write might be whipped or punished in some other way."[31]

DISTORTIONS OF HISTORY

There is no question that these books, particularly the historical sections, are a serious attempt to present history and that they do reflect an ethnically diverse America. Yet there are ways that certain aspects of the presentation either distort history or flatten the differences between eras. Often the books rely on stereotypes of past eras as expressed in the descriptors and styles that have come to represent different eras. Descriptors like the gay nineties, the roaring twenties, and the radical sixties reduce complex historical periods to simplistic tropes.[32] They do what Fredric Jameson says about period films that "falsely reproduce the past, reducing it to recognizable aesthetic styles and settings" and come to replace deeper historical knowledge.[33] At times the American Girl dolls, designed and styled in ways that link them to a simple and imagined past, are a part of this reductionist phenomenon.

Much of the advertising and design of the American Girl products reflect just such stereotypes of particular eras. For example, Felicity, the doll associated with the Revolutionary War, is described as "independent"; Molly, the doll associated with World War II, is presented as "patriotic"; and Kit, who grew up during the Great Depression, is described as "resourceful."[34] The dolls are also styled with various "time-specific" hairdos. Kit, the doll from the Depression, wears a "smart chin length bob," while Julie, the doll from the seventies, has long straight hair with a single braid hanging down in front in a style associated with hippies. Julie also wears bell-bottom pants, while Molly arrives in "authentic styles from 1944."[35] Ultimately, the consumer comes to identify historical periods not with events so much as with hairstyles and other signifiers like clothing and accessories.[36]

The American Girl Company, understanding how important details are in getting girls to connect emotionally with the dolls, needed to find details that would make the dolls universally loved but would maintain specific ethnic characteristics. In choosing a hair color for Rebecca Rubin, the first Jewish doll, there were extensive debates about "typical" Jewish traits. The *New York Times* covered Rebecca's release: "Hair color was a big issue, debated for years. At first it was a dark auburn, but it was thought that might be too untypical.... Then dark brown, the most common hair color for Russian-Jewish immigrants." The designers then worried "that would be too typical, too predictable, failing to show girls there is not one color that represents all Jewish immigrants. In the end ... we created what we felt was an optimum combination." Ultimately, the goal was to not offend anyone: "Historical matters were of less concern than ones which would trigger a reaction in modern Jews."[37] The company settled on "hazel eyes ... and honey-brown curls."[38]

Suggesting certain experiences as universal for an entire race is also problematic. Addy, the first African American doll, is defined by her escape from slavery. In an episode of the TV show *Black-ish*, titled "ToysRn'tUs," the young Black girl character is given a white doll (which bears resemblance to an American Girl doll) as a gift. When her mother tries to exchange it for a Black doll, she is unhappy to discover that the only Black doll available is the one related to slavery which comes with less desirable accessories. The very thing often praised about the American Girl book about Addy—its acknowledgment of slavery—can also pose a problem when slavery is seen to define the experience of Black girls to the exclusion of other experiences.[39] The repeated association between slavery and African Americans then becomes a kind of stereotyping.

Emilie Zaslow addresses the mixed reactions to the Addy doll in *Playing with America's Doll*. She explains that the company explored other time periods for their first Black doll but felt the transition from slavery to freedom was the most sweeping. There was pushback; an article by Brit Bennett in the *Paris Review* reads, "If you were a black girl you could only picture yourself as a runaway slave" whereas white girls had multiple choices of characters with which they identified.[40] Zaslow cites other consumers who felt differently: "I loved that she had skin and hair like mine and her books were so interesting to me as a child. . . . Addy served as a great tool for me to learn about [prejudice and racism]."[41] Until 2017, when a doll named Melody, who lived in 1963 Detroit, was released, Addy remained the only Black protagonist doll in the historical collection (there was another historical Black doll, Cecile, but she was a "best friend" character to a white doll).

The placement of the American Girl dolls in overtly separate time periods also confuses the history. Although the dolls may be only ten years apart in age (Kit is nine years old in 1934 and Molly is that age in 1944), their stories exist in such different worlds that they would never overlap. No connections are drawn between the time of the Great Depression and the economic recovery brought on by World War II. The dolls born ten years apart may as well be separated by the one hundred years that separate other doll characters. Because the same formula shapes each of the stories, for a child who hasn't been alive more than a decade, the historical distance between Addy (1864) and the present is, for all intents and purposes, the same as the distance between Julie, a character from 1974, and the present. Both Addy and Julie lived in the "past," one vast category that no longer exists and does not impact the present. The doll characters (even the ones who could still be alive today if they were nine in 1944, or especially in 1974) are creations of a past that is seen as distinct and disconnected from the present. By breaking history into discrete eras, the company suggests the characters' conflicts are resolved, over, and quite literally things of the past.

Creating a line of dolls that are multicultural yet speak to the universal experiences of girls is well meaning but ultimately ahistorical. This is a perpetual challenge in presenting history to adults and children alike. Authors need to find a way for the reader to relate to people in the past while still communicating that people in different historical moments might have thought, interpreted, and even felt differently than a modern reader. The very format of the American Girl books homogenizes not only the eras but also the characters in ways that sometimes erase differences between historical eras. While representing very different periods in American history, the dolls end up being more like each other than different. All the books place the girls in the same six situations. They all go to school, learn a lesson, have a surprise, celebrate their birthday, save the day, and go through changes. Differences among them are largely erased. The story about Addy in school in 1864 reads much like the story about Samantha in school in

1904. Each new girl faces her first day of class, makes a friend who helps her, meets a challenge, and solidifies her relationship with her friend. The homogeneity of experience across the stories is not without merit, but also causes the historical details to recede.

The uniform nature of the American Girl merchandise also undermines the historical variation between eras. Each doll comes with a similar set of accessories, including a hat, purse, handkerchief, and necklace, though they take on different specific qualities. The difference in merchandise between 1774 and 1864 is as slight as it is between 1934 and 1944. For example, all of the dolls have a bed: Samantha's (in the Victorian era) is brass with a fluffy lace quilt, while Molly's (during World War II) is stark and simple with a thin red cover.[42] One notable result of many dolls having similar furniture and the same size clothing is that in a child's room Addy, the character from the Civil War era, could "sleep" in Samantha's (the Victorian era doll) bed despite the characters' backstories taking place in different eras.[43] While the ways children mix up the chronology and play out alternative histories of the stories can tell us a lot, and, in fact, doing so gives the child agency, it runs counter to the original intention of these historically researched dolls.

Lisa Mae Schlosser explains that while the details of the American Girl dolls' accessories may be historically specific, the variations are minor and "the conformity of the merchandise suggests that all girls like, need, and own the same things."[44] By creating uniform needs through homogenous merchandising, American Girl accomplishes what John Berger argues capitalism more generally achieves through advertising: "All hopes are gathered together, made homogeneous, simplified, that they become the intense yet vague, magical yet repeatable promise offered in every purchase."[45]

Schlosser, in addition, notes that gender roles and the rights of women are not seen to fluctuate over the almost two hundred years of history covered in the books.[46] Although the stories appear to offer a realistic portrait of the past, modern notions of girlhood permeate and thus distort history in the books. Overall, Pleasant Rowland's ideal girl is very modern—clever, educated, and self-reliant—and has "few limitations on her future," a fact that would be less true in some earlier eras. Fred Nielsen points out that "Felicity . . . is altogether too feisty for a girl of the eighteenth century."[47] While it is praiseworthy that girls are not depicted as passive and subservient, the clever and assertive American Girl is really a modern girl, not a colonial or Victorian girl.

Keeping in mind that stories written for girls as young as seven years old must make some nuanced issues more accessible, there are still many instances when the books unnecessarily downplay the painful aspects of American history. In many cases the distortion results from misplaced emphasis. In the Addy stories the reality of slavery seems to fade into the background.[48] While the first book of the Addy series presents a powerfully vivid and emotional picture of the horrors of slavery—beatings, the breakup of families, the terrifying escape—the later books suggest that such suffering is in the past and the story will end as happily as Addy imagined it, through a reunion with the father, brother, and sister who had been left behind. The book's nostalgic and sentimentalized ending leaves the reader with little sense of the enduring racism, the legacy of slavery, that still haunts America today.

In other instances the distortion of history results from omissions. In her story, Felicity, the character from 1774, visits the plantation of her grandfather who was a slave owner. But Felicity never sees the cruelty that is at the heart of her family's prosperity. Nor does the reader. However, the background scenery— the weather, flowers, fruit, and natural setting—is described in great detail.[49] The mild and brief mention of enslaved people in the Felicity books bears resemblance to the Landmark and Orange books of the 1950s and seems a glaring disjuncture when confronted with the Addy character within the same collection.

In 2014 the historical doll collection was rebranded and renamed the BeForever collection, thus emphasizing the homogeneity of the dolls over time rather than the distinctiveness of American girls from different time periods. BeForever suggests timelessness and removes the dolls from any particular historical situations. The name locates the beginning of history with the young consumer and going forward, rather than focusing on heritage and the past. She can achieve immortality, rather than being the product and continuation of history. The deemphasis on and simplification of history leave the reader feeling that these dolls are just like them—picking out clothes, receiving presents, talking with friends. A girl reading the book can identify with the characters in an emotional way without being excessively aware of the differences between them. In the process, however, the historical and cultural differences between the doll and the girl owner recede, as do some important lessons about history.

Teaching Consumerism

With roots in the industrial revolution of the late nineteenth century, modern consumerism came to define American culture over the early decades of the twentieth century and took on increasing significance in its connection to democracy in the postwar era.[50] Over the twentieth century, the focus of the economy shifted from the production of goods to their consumption, and by the time the American Girl doll came along a culture of consumerism as akin to civic action was well established.[51] In fact, the American Girl Company has come to embody this emphasis on consumerism as it produces an endless array of American Girl products. Each doll has her own set of accessories—a birthday outfit, a winter outfit, a sleeping outfit, furniture to create a world for her to live in, as well as toys, jewelry, and keepsakes. And the margins of each book feature illustrations of objects described in the story, which are then available for purchase.

If one accepts that by the late twentieth century America had become, by definition, a consumer society, then it's not surprising that the American Girl Company introduces girls to their identity as consumers. In the early twentieth century writers like Morgan and Christy reflected on the personal and moral qualities that defined the American Girl. But even from the start, despite the appeal of its historical orientation, a great deal of the American Girl Company's success has been due to its clever marketing and promotional strategies. Through carefully illustrated product placement in the margins of the books and an appealing and detailed catalogue, the company entices girls to desire more and more American Girl products. Additionally, a major theme in the books revolves around girls longing for and then receiving particular objects like a doll or a dress as a gift. The emphasis on giving and receiving gifts keeps the focus on consuming objects.

Often in the books, the objects illustrated in the margin are connected to particular emotional experiences in the story. In *Samantha Saves the Day*, for example, Samantha and her friends receive authentic gifts the girls feel proud of. The text explains that an Admiral "gave Samantha a genuine bo's'n's whistle made of shiny brass and taught her how to blow signals like the sailors did. And he gave all three girls sailor hats, which they proudly wore."[52] The hat and whistle are illustrated in the margin. Because the objects are connected to a moving, emotional part of the story (in this case a joyful memory of camaraderie), the reader develops an affective attachment to them. The company successfully translates the nostalgic impulse of the reader (nostalgia for their imagined participation in this story) into a consumer impulse.[53]

In one of the Addy books Addy's mother gives her the cowrie shell her grandmother brought from Africa. This object, also illustrated in the margin, takes on emotional significance in that it connects Addy to her grandmother who was a slave and links Addy's escape with her lineage. And finally, when reunited with her baby sister, Addy sees again the rag doll she had left with her sister when she and her mother ran away and had to leave her sister behind. The doll, like the necklace, is particularly precious because it is attached to the emotions of loss and then joy, separation from and then reunion with family.[54]

Nielsen argues that the American Girl books downplay consumerism, citing examples in which the Addy character is contrasted with a richer girl named Harriet. Next to Harriet, "Addy seems simple, poor, and backward. Harriet has several nice dresses, while Addy wears the same homemade garments day after day."[55] But, in fact, the books focus quite explicitly on the joy of ownership. Harriet's many dresses are something to be envied. Addy may wear the same homemade dress every day, but she does so not by choice but by economic circumstance. In fact, Addy would love to own those dresses. Fancy dresses were central to her idea of freedom. "Back on the plantation Addy had dreamed about being in the North. She'd wear fancy dresses." She repeatedly gazes with envy on Harriet's clothes and at one point looks longingly at Harriet's dress, "light yellow and trimmed with lace."[56] When Addy's mother gives Addy a dress she made for her to wear to the spelling bee, she exclaims, "Look at you! You look like a fancy city girl."[57] The primary difference between Harriet's clothes and Addy's is that Addy's mother made hers for her. How could the young girl reading this not come to feel how precious fancy dresses are and how important it is to own them? One major ambiguity of American Girl is that, overall, the characters from the 1980s and early 1990s are not materialistic or vain; they often learn the value of hard work and treasure homemade heirlooms. But for the young reader, the characters' world is commodified and available for purchase, and the longing for the "authentic" brand item is palpable.

Objects and gifts are a major part of the story lines. In one book, Samantha desires an expensive doll she saw in a local shop. In an early scene she is upset to find out that her grandmother's seamstress, Jennie, a kind of parental figure to Samantha, has left unexpectedly. Samantha's grandmother tries to soften the blow by distracting Samantha and praising her impressive progress in sewing. She then sends Samantha upstairs for a surprise gift. On her bed Samantha finds the doll she has coveted. For the reader, the doll has become connected to the feeling of consolation after the loss of Jennie and to the feeling of being rewarded for a job well done.[58]

The objects that become desirable to the young reader—a doll, a nightgown, a necklace, an abacus, even the kerchief that Addy wears as a disguise while escaping slavery with her mother—are often made desirable not only through their importance to the emotional storyline but by virtue of the tantalizing details associated with them. When Samantha returned to her room after her emotional reunion with Jennie, her feeling of being comforted is reflected in the tangible details of her nightgown. "Her nightgown had never felt so soft and warm. Her bed had never smelled so sweet or been so welcome. She held [her doll] Lydia very close and fell asleep."[59] Again, the emotion of the scene—relief that she found Jennie and confidence that Jennie will still be in her life—becomes connected to objects that represent comfort and security—her nightgown, the familiar closet and bed in her room, the doll—all of which the reader can purchase.

Similarly, in the scene in which Addy receives her grandmother's shell necklace, the description of the tangible details of the necklace strengthen its appeal. "Addy rubbed the shell between her fingers. Its rounded top was smooth as soap. The flat underside was also smooth, except for the middle where the shell closed in on itself. There it felt like the teeth of a fine comb." Addy and her mother "sat in silence a long time, looking at the cowrie shell and thinking about someone they had never met."[60] With this description the fact of slavery recedes and the necklace becomes valued as a thing in itself. The young girl reader can participate in this scene (receiving a necklace associated with someone she has never met) by buying her own shell necklace from the catalogue. The description of the physical sensation of handling this shell necklace further enhances its value. In the catalogue photo, the Addy doll wears a miniature necklace just like the one described in the book.

As John Berger points out in *Ways of Seeing*, "The visual desirability of what can be bought lies in its tangibility, in how it will reward the touch, the hand, of the owner."[61] The American Girl catalogue was extremely effective at cultivating a desire for specific items that the brand produced and that the reader had seen in stories and the catalogue for months beforehand. This accomplished a remarkable feat of creating a desire for a mass-produced heirloom that belonged to a character, not a unique heirloom that a family member might make.

Molly, the doll from World War II, cannot afford to buy many material goods because of rationing and shortages, so her stories suggest that "friendship, family, and simple pleasures" are more valuable than material objects.[62] However, the books actually focus a great deal on the giving and receiving of presents and thereby convey a different message—one that revolves around gift giving and commodity fetishism.[63] Molly's conflict with her English houseguest over what to do for her birthday party is resolved by a gift of pet dogs and matching outfits. Throughout the entire book about Christmas Molly waits for presents from her father. At the story's happy conclusion she receives from her father the doll that she has wanted throughout the book. The description of the doll is lengthy and almost erotic in its detail, and notably the opening of the package mimics the opening of an American Girl doll that comes wrapped in tissue. "Everyone knelt around her as she lifted her gift out of its rustling tissue paper. Molly's gift was a doll—a beautiful doll with dark shiny hair and smiling blue eyes." Molly cherishes its details. "Molly touched the doll's hair with one finger and traced the curve of her pink cheek." The doll is exactly what Molly longed for. "She was dressed in a nurse's uniform and hat like the one Molly had dreamed about. A smart red cape covered her starched dress and tied under her chin. Molly hugged her."[64] Again, these tantalizing details make the doll more desirable. How could any young girl not long for just such a doll? The company does the remarkable act of convincing a young girl to want a doll for her doll.[65]

The suggestion that clothing can provide emotional fulfillment also recurs in the books. In 2011, the American Doll Company offered a new historical doll called Marie-Grace who lived in 1853 New Orleans. Marie-Grace learns about New Orleans and its Mardi Gras and costume balls. She doesn't believe she'll be invited to a ball and doesn't own any costumes were she invited. When her teacher arranges an invitation for her, she also provides a trunk full of costumes. Again, the details—about the materials and the relationships—are tantalizing. "Marie-Grace searched through the cedar-scented costume trunk until she found several sparkling gowns with masks and delicate matching fairy wings."

The dresses brought her happiness. "When she saw her reflection, she breathed a sigh of happiness. The silver shone in the light, and when she spun around, the delicate fairy wings fluttered on her back." The costume reminded her of the past and her mother who had died. "As Marie-Grace looked into the mirror, she remembered the fairy tales her mother used to read to her. For a moment, she could almost imagine her mother standing behind her smiling." In another scene Marie-Grace's friend Cécile and her teacher Mademoiselle Océane help dress her for the Mardi Gras ball. The experience of women dressing and connecting to each other in the process has its own emotional resonance. Other books, including the one about Melody in the 1960s, feature the girl characters twirling in front of mirrors and admiring themselves. This parallels what some consumers do in real life—spend time together selecting clothes. Furthermore, the American Girl Company offers the possibility of reenacting this ritual of intergenerational gift giving—mothers can buy doll clothes for their daughters and little girls and their friends can dress their dolls together.

The Further Abandonment of American History

In 1995 the American Girl Company released a line of contemporary dolls first called by the clunky name American Girl of Today. These dolls signaled a major change in direction for the company—featuring contemporary dolls and downplaying history. American Girl of Today suggests that the dolls, like the original historical characters, belonged to a specific era, although that era is the present. The catalogue read, "She's just like you. You're a part of history too!" Whereas the dolls in the 1980s reflected the nation's preoccupation with multiculturalism, the late 1990s saw the rise of superstars like the Spice Girls, who touted the value of "Girl Power" and shifted focus from structural inequalities toward individual improvement and identity. Emilie Zaslow writes, "Drawing on neoliberalism, girl power encourages girls and women to adopt a paradigm of choice as they construct their feminine and feminist identities."[66] The American Girl of Today lives less in a political, global world and more in the narrower world of home and school. In 2006 the collection was renamed Just Like You, suggesting that the emphasis was now on the doll owner and her traits, rather than on the present era as the commonality among this new line of dolls. Then, in 2010, the collection was changed again to My American Doll, a designation that removes any reference to a specific time and emphasizes personal ownership. These ahistorical "mini-me" American Girl dolls have come to greatly outnumber the historical BeForever collection.

Finally, the further renaming of the collection to Truly Me in 2015 suggests that the dolls are important for being authentic replicas of the girls themselves, with no mention of their time in history or their heritage or even their American identity. Girls can design their own dolls and often choose a doll whose hair

Figure 5.3. Assorted American Girl dolls dressed in various multicultural outfits. Photo by Jane and Kate Buckhurst, May 23, 2020.

and eye and skin color are like their own. This mimicry of physical characteristics results in a doll that is "truly" like her young owner.

This shift clearly represented a calculus on the part of the company that it would be more lucrative to offer dolls that looked more like the girl owner than someone different from them. This shift reflects changes in American culture that Christopher Lasch described in *The Culture of Narcissism*. Lasch notes a shift in American culture from engagement in the world to a focus on the self. Writing in the late 1970s, but rife with parallels to today, he described Americans as focused on "the pursuit of happiness to the dead end of a narcissistic preoccupation with the self."[67] American Girl's narrowed emphasis on the contemporary American Girl doll reflects just such a preoccupation with the self, a phenomenon that would only deepen with the arrival of cell phones, social media, and selfies. The shift in focus toward the contemporary dolls can also be seen as a reaction against the liberal ideology of the company's early years when the dolls celebrated an ethnic, multicultural world. Whereas the original historical books placed the American girl in the context of large social issues like World War II, slavery, and industrialization, the contemporary dolls reside in the world of the contemporary girl.

In the Truly Me collection there are no books to place the dolls in any particular historical context. Ads for the dolls focus on the girl consumer. For example, the Truly Me product line lets every girl "create a truly special doll that's just right for her." In 2001 the American Girl Company introduced a separate line called Girl of the Year that includes a series of limited-release characters set in the present. These dolls do have accompanying books, but their storylines trace the trials of a contemporary girl in her everyday life at school and with her family. These contemporary dolls are modeled primarily on white girls; not until 2017 did the Girl of the Year collection feature a Black doll. Paired with the many dolls that replicate the physical attributes of their owners who are predominantly white, this collection suggests a new kind of investment in whiteness on the part of the company. While the shift away from the historical dolls began in 1995, Mattel's purchase of the company in 1998 greatly accelerated this movement. As the company extended its global reach and envisioned itself as a major corporation rather than a homegrown business, it seems to have taken on the values of the corporate world with its focus on consumption and profit and its emphasis on self-involvement over social participation.

Over time changes to the American Girl catalogue have reflected this shift away from history and toward an emphasis on narcissism and consumerism. As the largest consumer toy catalogue and one of the top thirty consumer catalogues in the country, the American Girl catalogue played a huge role in the company's initial success. With very few exceptions, the covers of the first ten years of catalogues showed a girl with her doll, reading. The following pages displayed the historical dolls in chronological order, referencing their books on each page. Each catalogue opened with a life-sized photo of a particular historical doll. Arjun Appadurai notes that catalogues often "play with many kinds of nostalgia: nostalgia for bygone lifestyles, material assemblages, life stages (such as childhood), landscapes (of the Currier and Ives variety), scenes (of the Norman Rockwell small-town variety), and so on."[68] The early catalogue certainly reflected these themes. Oversized, with thick pages and a brown background, the pages inside featured quiet scenes like those produced when sepia-toned filters are used to create an image that appears taken by an old fashioned low-fi camera. By 2012, the text regularly suggested that these dolls and items would eventually become antiques because they are "exquisitely made and designed to last." They would become part of the child's history and preserve that history long after childhood. The American Girl Company understood that publicity is "in essence, nostalgic. It has to sell the past to the future."[69]

Today, women who were among the first generation of American Girl consumers—now in their thirties—have written nostalgically for the early days of the American Girl dolls and books, conflating their effort to include more diverse stories with the notion that the company was radical. While these expensive dolls are not radical, the liberal ideology backing the company's original mission does appear to have given way to a more conservative ideology today.[70]

For example, the historical narrative about Melody, the doll living through the civil rights movement, conveys a distinctly moderate message of achieving incremental change through nonviolent activism and repeatedly delivers the message to young girls that they should listen to their elders and behave nicely.[71] In this way, far from being radical, the dolls carry on some of the tropes of femininity that earlier collectors themselves cherished.

Originally, each catalogue page displayed one scene, giving the consumer a sense that the doll was unique and special. Each doll was depicted as part of a larger scene from the historical story. The original catalogue was also far less cluttered than today's. It came addressed to the child, not the parent, and suggested to the young girl ways to play with her doll. "Tuck her embroidered hankie in her apron pocket and tie her spoon bag around her waist," giving the consumer an active way to participate in the fantasy world of American Girl and another way to be attached to the objects.

Today's print catalogue usually opens with the contemporary line of Truly Me dolls or the featured Doll of the Year. The Truly Me pages provide instructions for choosing hair and eye and skin color, and giving the doll a style by choosing particular clothes. The focus is essentially on the doll's appearance, and the fact that girls often create a doll who looks like them reinforces that focus. For the most part, the catalogue offers only a sample of the historical dolls displayed within a few cramped pages. The purpose of today's catalogue, smaller in both size and number of pages, seems to be to highlight how special each girl is and to encourage consumerism by offering an endless number of products crammed together. The catalogue repeatedly refers its readers to the website, which includes a shopping section aimed at adults (customers must click a box indicating they are older than eighteen to enter the site), with pages of thumbnail images of products and their prices. Addressing the adults, a cover letter accompanying the catalogue says, "Like you, we believe in the wonder of youth and letting girls be girls a little longer." When the catalogue does address the child, it reminds her how to best use the catalogue: "When you open the pages of this catalogue, you'll open a world of imaginative play through dolls, books, clothing, and more. . . . We encourage you to save this catalogue and return to it often as a reminder that being a girl is something to celebrate and share every day." And the celebration will involve buying products. Many of the objects featured in the contemporary catalogue are not miniature replicas of objects from life in the past, but replicas of everyday items of contemporary life. The number of products in the contemporary catalogue has multiplied enormously, even including a toilet that "makes a flushing sound" and dental braces, which consist of stickers for the doll's two exposed front teeth. In 2017, the *New York Times* applauded the addition of a miniature diabetes testing kit as a sign of the inclusivity of the brand.

THE AMERICAN GIRL STORE: CREATING AND
DOCUMENTING EXPERIENCE

To have the contemporary American Girl experience and to understand the company's move away from teaching history, it is necessary to visit the store, itself a monument to consumerism. In 1998 the first American Girl store opened on the Magnificent Mile in Chicago. Named American Girl Place, as if it were a small town or neighborhood, the flagship store covered thirty-five thousand square feet spread over three stories. Today, there are seventeen stores across the United States. New York's American Girl Place—relocated from Forty-Eighth Street and Fifth Avenue in New York City to Fifty-Second Street near Rockefeller Center—spans nearly forty thousand square feet. Its extravagant entrance has glittering chandeliers that light the foyer.

The store is not simply a place to buy a doll. Rather, it is designed as a miniature world in which a girl can have a variety of experiences with her doll, creating memories that will make her feel even more attached to the brand. Most striking for those who valued American Girl dolls for their representation of history is the fact that there are no historical dolls to be seen on the first floor; they are all relegated to a separate space. Instead there are shelves and shelves of identically dressed contemporary dolls.

The young visitor can choose from an extensive array of activities. Although many customers arrive having already studied an online menu and made reservations for activities and events, there is a directory that points customers to the hair salon, fitting rooms, and café. The young girl can dine with her doll, take it to the hair salon, attend a cooking class or book club, learn a craft like embroidery, or walk through the museum-like displays with her doll. She can have her picture taken with her doll and have the photo framed to take home. Or she can have the photo printed on an "American Girl magazine cover," making her feel like a celebrity. She can also purchase souvenirs, some of which, like T-shirts, are available only on site.

The dolls—contemporary and historical—are posed like museum exhibits. They sit in clean, glass-enclosed cases like those you might find in a museum or in Mrs. Lewis's display of her dolls. Sometimes the displays show dolls sitting together in a bedroom playing cards or games like *Apples to Apples* (clever cross-promotion since the game is also made by Mattel), suggesting that these dolls are special, almost like antiques—and valuable, worth purchasing. Looking at these miniaturized American Girl objects, contemporary artifacts of everyday contemporary girlhood, the imagined lives of these dolls become something to aspire to and to purchase.

The creation of "lived memories" occurs outside the store as well. In 2006 a *New York Times* article described an odd scene in Mount Kisco, New York, a scene that might make second wave feminists' eyes roll. "More than 100 little

Figure 5.4. Display of dolls at the American Girl Place in New York City. Photo by the author, April 17, 2019.

girls were standing up very, very straight, breathing deeply from their rib cages, placing their feet just so, and dropping into a delicate curtsy while saying, 'Good afternoon.'" However seemingly regressive and oppressive, this was "a re-enactment of sorts. The girls were imagining themselves as Felicity, the colonial era doll who would have been wearing stays and been mindful of the proper way a girl should" behave.[72] Here again, it is not Felicity's history that was being remembered so much as the memory of participation—curtseying with a line of girls in Mount Kisco.

AMERICAN GIRL IN SCHOOLS

One place where the American Girl Company still focuses on history is in elementary school classrooms. Problematically, some schools are using lesson plans designed by the American Girl Company and focused on the historical dolls. Each doll has corresponding learning guides based on a working knowledge of the novels. Yet even here the focus is less on history and more on the child herself. Discussion questions, rather than encouraging students to understand the characters' experience in their historical moment, ask that students relate elements of the American Girl–produced plot to their own, modern-day life. For example, "Molly discovers that part of life during wartime is learning to adapt to change and to live with less. . . . Describe a difficult situation in your own life that you have had to adapt to. How did you adapt?"[73]

The incorporation of American Girl books into the formal authoritative setting of school is problematic on many levels. The fictional plots become part of history lessons suggesting that the characters in the books are as real as any figures in American history. Equally problematic is the fact that parents, wanting the full benefit of history class for their child, might feel pressed to buy the dolls and books, or lacking if they cannot. Fully understanding America's past becomes, in this scenario, a consumer activity. As children use these guides they are building an allegiance to the American Girl brand. While theoretically available to all children, history, as presented here, becomes accessible primarily to those who can afford it.

The American Girl Company represents another example of the way private corporations use history and education to sell products. While the company has always been a for-profit organization, it originally made a serious and successful attempt to teach girls about American history. But the shift in focus in the late 1990s from the historical to contemporary dolls suggests to girls that clothes and accessories are as true a representation of identity as are history, family background, and social status. In place of learning about history, contemporary American girls are encouraged to replicate themselves and, quite simply, to consume more objects.

Conclusion

As a child I read fiction that introduced me to many aspects of American history. Scholastic's Dear America series, published in the 1990s, focused on events throughout American history as seen from the perspective of young girls' written diary entries. The 1995 book *The Watsons Go to Birmingham* followed a young African American protagonist who navigates the trauma of the Sixteenth Street Baptist Church bombing in 1963. Katherine Patterson's *Lyddie* taught me about a girl working in a factory in Lowell, Massachusetts. These books all focus on a child (frequently a girl) as protagonist and address issues of race, class, and gender. These books were the product of a long struggle in the twentieth century over American history, one that continues today.

The didactic amusements I consider here were products of the earlier decades of the twentieth century when struggles over the story of America emerged. I began by focusing on the American toy industry at the beginning of the twentieth century. Amid the international conflict of World War I, the industry took its place in the market by linking expressions of patriotism to consumerism and positioning itself to train young people in gendered and racialized roles, with American exceptionalism at its core. I then looked at examples from throughout the twentieth century that use history as their calling card: a Doll Show produced by upper-class female collectors; the popular, consciously historical Landmark and Orange book series that offered children stories about "great" American heroes and events; the short-lived Freedomland amusement park built in 1960, which offered kitschy displays of mythic American history; and finally the American Girl doll and book collection, which offered stories of American girls of different races and cultures. When taken together, these examples demonstrate a variety of approaches to the story of America and the continuing tensions over what that history is. While most of the stories examined here stubbornly adhere to the myths that have historically been told about America, more recently some tell a more honest, nuanced, and inclusive story of America's past that better informs the future.

Consistent across the early examples is the story of unstoppable progress, of white men conquering the West, fighting wars near and far, and setting up the structure for a thriving democracy. It is a story in which, for much of the twentieth century, Native Americans, African Americans, other minority groups, and women were largely absent, underrepresented, or stereotyped. Efforts have been made to dismantle or correct this dominant narrative, for example, when the American Girl Company in the 1990s sought to diversify its doll collection. But these changes are often nominal rather than substantive. When underrepresented characters are offered in the form of a footnote, token, subplot, or afterthought, the story remains a hegemonic one. Most representations of history for children continue to tell a story of America's essential goodness and its steady march of progress rather than a story that acknowledges oppression and notes the fluctuations between progress and regression. The popular story of white male supremacy remains an overarching, even if not the sole, narrative of American history offered to children.

In recent years a secondary literature has emerged that traces the limitations and distortions of this older historical narrative and the efforts to counter it over time. In his comprehensive book *Making Americans,* Gary Schmidt looks at how writers of children's literature struggled to develop a more complete and inclusive view of American democracy in midcentury.[1] Julia Mickenberg's *Learning from the Left* also focuses on the ideals and ideas of midcentury children's literature, particularly the efforts of left-wing writers to offer a more inclusive story of democratic ideals while themselves facing the opprobrium of Cold War critics who sought to temper if not undermine the broad political implications of their vision.[2] More recently, Victoria Grieve's *Little Cold Warriors* looks at how children were shaped by Cold War ideologies through art, advertising, and formal education but also how they participated in actions that either reinforced or undercut that ideology.[3]

Playing with History builds on these efforts to examine historical representations of America while trying to broaden the story to look not only at books but also at dolls, toys, and a theme park because they all work in tandem to inculcate young minds. Who is at the center of the story? Who are the heroes? What does democracy mean as it plays out in everyday lives? How do we acknowledge the mistakes or misdeeds of the country? Because even very young children absorb ideas about their country and who belongs, it is important that adults understand and contextualize what they are being taught. The lessons so ubiquitous in American culture are sometimes mistaken for naturally occurring, impartial truths.

The cultural artifacts examined in this book reflect an ongoing struggle over the nature of our country. As the United States gained international prominence in the twentieth century, particularly after World War II, it has been easy to repeat and build on a story of exceptionalism and heroism. After the war in Vietnam, however, and as the country's demographics have continued to shift away from a majority-white population, some companies, authors, politicians, and other authorities have gone to great lengths to produce a more complicated narrative about American history. Others have doubled down on the myths of America's past and grasped ever more tightly to a historical story based on oppression. Parents' own unconscious ideological beliefs and nostalgic connections to their own toys and stories from childhood may also perpetuate oppressive narratives and stereotypes.

While this study looks at the lessons conveyed to children about American history, it also considers what historically specific conflicts played out around these objects and events. The Doll Show, which displayed individually crafted handmade dolls to the public during the Depression, represented a rejection of the changes brought about by industrialism and reproduced the views of upper-class women who longed for a class-based society more like that of Europe. The doll collectors' vision stood in contrast to that offered at the annual Toy Fair, which displayed mass-produced toys as shining examples of the wonders of a newly emerging, industrial, and democratic nation. The uplifting stories offered by the Landmark and Orange books showcased an effort to establish a unifying narrative after World War II when tensions were simmering and many, particularly women and African Americans, struggled to establish a place for themselves in the American story. Authors and publishers felt pressured, even by J. Edgar Hoover and the FBI, to tell the story of a righteous, patriotic nation while largely ignoring or glossing over practices like slavery, genocide, and imperialism.

A decade later Freedomland offered a simplistic narrative of cowboys and Indians and placid southern plantations that was spectacularly out of place against the backdrop of the early 1960s, when the inequities of the country were front and center. Finally, in the 1980s and 1990s, the American Girl Company did the important work of centering American girls in the narrative of American history and giving them some agency and their own set of values and opinions. The company reflected the country's shift toward both neoliberalism and multiculturalism. Early on they attempted to offer a more inclusive narrative but ultimately yielded to the pressure of an increasingly consumerist and individualized culture. The company also replicated some of the values that the 1938 Doll Show espoused, emphasizing gentility and niceness. Despite being mass produced, the dolls were treated and wrapped like precious handmade products, creating a delicate feminine aura to enhance their perceived value. All of these toys, books, dolls, and spaces tended to romanticize the past in an effort to bolster a specific national story.

Activist movements, often reflecting the national mood, have long paved the way for revising historical narratives. The civil rights movement, by drawing attention to the everyday instances of segregation at lunch counters and on buses and the disenfranchisement of African Americans at the ballot box, called into question the prevailing narrative of a country dedicated to equality. The women's movement drew attention to the fact that women were consistently subjected to oppressive and hostile home and work environments that countered the notion of the empowered American frontier woman, free from the antiquated hierarchies of the Old World. Native Americans demanded that they not be depicted as impediments to the settling of the West but that it be acknowledged that their land was stolen from them, untold numbers of them were killed, and their cultures were decimated.

As an outgrowth of these social and political movements, scholars of children's literature increasingly focused their attention on the question of representation. When my grandmother wrote her PhD dissertation on racism in children's literature in 1975 she was among the few scholars documenting the underrepresentation of minorities and women in children's literature. As Walter Dean Myers noted in his *New York Times* op-ed in 2014 that when he "first entered the world of writing children's literature [in 1969], the field was nearly empty. Children of color were not represented, nor were children from the lower economic class."[4] There had been earlier efforts to change this. For example, every month from 1920 to the end of 1921, the *Brownies Book*, an outgrowth of the NAACP's *The Crisis*, published folktales, articles, games, and photographs by and for African American children, even serving as the first place to publish poetry by Langston Hughes. The magazine "celebrated African American identity, urged racial pride, and encouraged its young readers to aspire to positions of leadership within their communities."[5] In 1927, Associated Publishers, an African American publishing company, began publishing books that placed Black people at the center of their narratives. Although the company's scale did not compare with that of publishing houses like Random House, the effort was important in confronting racism at a time when lynchings were all too common. In 1965 the Council on Interracial Books for Children was founded for the purpose of promoting and developing a "literature for children that better reflects the realities of a multi-cultural society."[6] The council worked to point out "historical inaccuracies, cultural myths, and cultural stereotypes" in children's books, encouraged minority group writers, established a resource center, offered training groups for school systems, and protested blatant racist and sexist representations in other media.[7] There were also significant efforts made on the local level by librarians committed to offering respectful and nuanced books about minority groups.[8] Although the mass market was home to many inaccurate and whitewashed descriptions of America, there were persistent efforts to counter those narratives.

With the women's movement in the 1970s women also accelerated efforts to make demands for representation. The journal *Sex Roles*, founded in 1975 as a place for feminist scholarship, including gender studies, along with other journals like *Signs* and *Feminist Studies*, which followed in its path, made attention to gender stereotyping a serious issue.[9] There have been repeated studies of children's picture books indicating a continuing underrepresentation of women and girls and a continued typing of gender roles. One now-classic study published in 1972 examined the winners and runners-up for the Caldecott Medal from 1967 to 1971 and concluded that these books stereotyped girls and women as "dull."[10] Girls "received attention and praise for their attractiveness while boys are admired for their achievements and cleverness."[11] But there have since been shifts in the girl characters depicted in children's literature. The American Girl books have been successful in depicting girls as clever, interesting, and central to history, even though the newer American Girl stories feel less concerned with breaking down social hierarchies than the early books.

The struggle for adequate inclusion of Native Americans in children's books has also continued over the years. Dr. Debbie Reese of Nambe Pueblo publishes "American Indians in Children's Literature," which provides critical analyses of children's books that feature indigenous people—for example, not recommending a book because "there are some elements that are jarringly inconsistent with actual Navajo life and culture."[12] *The National Geographic Encyclopedia of American Indian History and Culture* is also not recommended because it describes the conquest of the West as if Native Americans "lost their sovereignty," which, according to the reviewer, "makes it sound like the Nations, oops, dropped it somewhere, when in fact the colonizing US government refused or failed to consistently recognize or honor indigenous sovereignty."[13] Although these misrepresentations are not as overt as categorizing entire groups of people as vicious or foolish, they are neither innocuous nor incidental to a child's understanding of the nation. These misguided narratives and descriptions of nonagency have proved deeply embedded in representations of Native Americans across media and continue to serve the cause of white supremacy.

However, there has been a "reorientation of western writing in the last five decades."[14] A 2011 special issue of the *European Journal of American Studies* brings "into focus how post-frontier literature not only has abandoned archetypal male-biased imagery and ethnocentric prejudices associated with the old American West, but also often addresses the problematic nature of western myths."[15] The editors suggest "a flowering or a renaissance of western writing" in the area of adult fiction by authors like Cormac McCarthy, Barbara Kingsolver, Wallace Stegner, and others. Nonetheless, it's not clear how much progress has been made in offering children's books that present a less mythic, more realistic story about the conquest of the West and a less stereotyped portrait of Native Americans. The Cooperative Children's Book Center reports that of the 3,653 children's books the center received in 2018, only about 55 were about Native Americans or First Nations.[16] It is equally important that the myths and lessons provided by childhood leisure activities be the subject of careful consideration.

While the inclusion of underrepresented groups in literature and toys for children is critical, inclusion alone does not adequately suffice as real representation. As Barbie now comes in a broader range of shapes and American Girl dolls represent different races and have varied backstories, it's clear that it is not enough simply to "diversify" product lines, particularly if those characters are represented in stereotypical ways or are limited to only certain experiences— "struggling to overcome either slavery or racism." Such representations will not necessarily teach children about their own experiences of discrimination or the systemic inequalities in the world around them. As Myers points out, as a child he missed representations of ordinary Black people who had a diversity of experiences, replete with their own internal conflicts, or who grew up to be writers, chemists, bankers, or politicians, careers that would have allowed him to see possibilities for himself and opened others to seeing Black people in these roles.[17] Elizabeth Chin makes a similar point when she argues that simply to "diversify" the toy box with "ethnically correct" dolls does not account for differences in experience and cultural practices that exist among heterogeneous young people.[18]

This book is not only about who has been left out of American history for children but also about what events are ignored, glossed over, or misrepresented. Recently there have been considerable efforts in the public sphere to correct misrepresentations of American history. The tendency to offer children uplifting stories, while understandable, underestimates their ability to comprehend a more complex story. Plantation tours now often include—and even focus on— the experiences of enslaved African Americans and describe the lives and work of those on whose backs plantations were built. The newly opened National Museum of African American History is dedicated to telling a more complicated history of the nation. Visiting Monticello years ago, a child would not have known that some of the slaves who worked Jefferson's plantation were the sons and daughters of Jefferson and his enslaved mistress, Sally Hemings, but today children on field trips learn how "the institution of slavery has ramifications in the United States throughout its history to the present day."[19]

The question of how to represent American history has also taken center stage in American culture today. Americans around the country are engaged in heated discussions about whether or not to take down Confederate monuments. The replacement of the image on the twenty-dollar bill of Andrew Jackson, the president infamous for the Trail of Tears, with that of Harriet Tubman, who led untold numbers of enslaved people to freedom, has been delayed due to a decision by the secretary of the treasury Steven Mnuchin.[20] In 2019 "the Library of Congress abandoned plans to feature a mural-size photograph of demonstrators at the 2017 Women's March in Washington because of concerns it would be perceived as critical of President Trump." It had been "envisioned . . . as one of the dominant displays" of an exhibit celebrating the centennial of women's right to vote. In 2020, the president called for instituting "pro-American curriculum" so that "our youth will be taught to love America."[21]

Recent attacks on efforts to include more people in representations of America necessitate even greater vigilance. Reflecting on the role of the Cooperative Children's Book Center, Beryle Banfield points out that "the hard-won Civil Rights gains of African Americans are being steadily eroded through court decisions and legislative actions. Multi-cultural studies are being derided as 'feel good ethnic studies.' The term 'politically correct' has been transformed into a mocking description of vocabulary or actions used to avoid race or gender bias. There is no longer the sense of social concern and social responsibility that existed at the time that the CIBC was established."[22] The struggle over what story to tell has become more heated as the country's political divides deepen.

Political ideologies continue to influence what is taught about American history in formal sites of learning. In January 2020 the *New York Times* printed an extensive article examining high school American history textbooks used in California and Texas. It noted that, on the one hand, publishers have come a long way in their willingness to acknowledge the underside of American history. Both Texas and California textbooks now address "the cruelty of the slave trade, eschewing several myths that were common in textbooks for generations: that some slave owners treated enslaved people kindly and that African-Americans were better off enslaved than free." The textbooks also pay more attention to women and to Latinx and Asian immigrants. Nonetheless, the authors discovered that textbooks in different parts of the country still offered varying banal accounts of American history. For example, "Conservatives have fought for schools to promote patriotism, highlight the influence of Christianity and celebrate the founding fathers." McGraw-Hill reported that a Texas panel asked the press to "point out the number of clergy who signed the Declaration of Independence." On the other hand, "the left has pushed for students to encounter history more from the ground up rather than the top down, with a focus on the experiences of marginalized groups such as enslaved people, women and Native Americans." Like Random House during the Cold War, presses often acquiesce to different ideological pressures, publishing histories with different emphases in different states.[23]

Historical misrepresentations that utilize stereotypes often reflect contemporary prejudices and have real-life consequences. In a *New Yorker* article published in 2019 titled "The Wild West Meets the Southern Border" Valeria Luiselli critiques reenactments of the frontier story, suggesting that they may contribute to the violence played out in the culture in which they are performed. She focuses particularly on Tombstone, Arizona, where half a million tourists a year pay to witness local residents and amateur actors reenact violent scenes from the Wild West and "celebrate hangings and gunfights." Luiselli sees a "connection between these events which glorify and commodify a violent frontier past and the violence that is so frequently directed toward undocumented immigrants in the area." She describes a video produced by vigilantes that shows "civilian militia men in military style uniforms driving down dark roads at night, following and then detaining migrants, and forcing them to sit or kneel on the ground to await the arrival of border patrol agents."[24]

Similarly, a *New Yorker* article published in February 2020 looks at slavery reenactments that are taking place around the country. Some include "an immersive nightly ordeal, complete with horseback-riding paddy rollers and an armed Harriet Tubman." While the events are billed as educational, parents found them offensive and even abusive. In 2013 the parents of a Black student in Connecticut filed a human rights complaint about an Underground Railroad reenactment conducted by Nature's Classroom. Their seventh-grade daughter described "name calling" and "make believe cotton picking." The official script urged leaders to "scare the crap out of the group" and called for "mock slave auctions and pantomimed railroad-gang labor." The parents called it "sanctioned social and emotional abuse."[25]

As children engage with the digital world, it is important to examine the stories about American history that are proliferating online. In the early 1990s the Minnesota Educational Computing Consortium produced *Freedom!*, considered to be the first computer game about slavery. It was distributed around the country until parents reacted to its racist depictions of African American characters. Nonetheless, digital underground railroads are now being produced by Scholastic, National Geographic, and Cincinnati's Freedom Center and are acclaimed by many for grappling with the issue of slavery.

Scholars point out that contemporary video games "play an integral part in the perception of history in everyday life" and "in recent years, have increasingly become integrated in commemorative and historical culture."[26] *BioShock Infinite* is a game that "takes place in the fictional floating city of Columbia at the beginning of the 20th century."[27] The game pits "the nativist and elite Founders that rule Columbia and strive to keep its privileges for White Americans" against "the Vox Populi, underground rebels representing the underclass of the city."[28] The game features a "quasi-religious demagogue called Father Comstock who has turned worship of the Founders (Washington, Jefferson and Franklin) into a twisted political vision stinking of jingoism, white supremacy and extreme xenophobia."[29] As one critic puts it, "It becomes clear that Columbia is dedicated to a conception of U.S. history that not only denies the atrocities Americans have committed in the past [such as the Wounded Knee Massacre] but embraces them and praises the nation for their perpetration."[30] Generally, the digital world does provide children with the opportunity to participate in national conversations and be conversant with other children who are consuming the same media, but it can also propagate stereotypes, myths, and biases about Americans and the country.

Children have never existed in a world apart from politics, and examples of young people making history themselves can be found everywhere—the young girls striking after the Triangle Shirtwaist Factory fire, the activist Greta Thunberg fighting climate change, and the Parkland High School students taking action for gun control. It is not a stretch to see how children incorporate the ideas they learn from their dolls and books into their own civic engagement. During the Women's March of 2017, many people shared images of their children marching or incorporating protest into their own doll play. If children learn that they have agency, that they can be politicians or activists in addition to princesses, it becomes possible to imagine a future filled with fair-minded representatives.

As this book has demonstrated, positivist portrayals of history reflect the culture in which they are offered. Parents, commercial producers, and children themselves all influence what is produced for young people. Eager to offer their children educational toys and books, parents willingly invest in educational products and hand over to companies the decisions about what is educational. Parents' own nostalgia for the stories of their youth sometimes cause them to accept the myths of American history that companies offer. Children themselves have opinions about what is produced. For example, while video games continue to primarily feature boys as characters and consumers, one study notes that girls have taken the initiative and "replaced leading male characters with female characters. . . . These modifications can be understood as critiques of the game design tradition" and highlight the fact that children are not merely passive consumers of media.[31] Additionally, children's preferences do impact what toys are produced. "In 2014 Mattel saw sales drop for their Barbie, Fisher-Price, and American Girl product lines, resulting in a 45 percent decline in net profits for the company. Much of the loss could be attributed to kids, especially girls, choosing 'older' toys at younger ages."[32] More and more often, today, children's play with smart toys is "tracked and monitored to provide behavioral data and market research in real time."[33] While such market research gives children some power to influence what toys are produced, it also raises questions of privacy.[34]

Ultimately, the manufacturers of didactic amusements have an outsized influence when it comes to deciding what lessons children consume. However much they are interested in making educational products, in the end their motives are profit-driven. When it comes to telling the story of America, and creating stories that are palatable to the mass market, they tend to avoid upsetting the status quo by veering toward the simplistic, uncontroversial, and conservative. The orientation toward mass consumption lends itself to simplified and familiar narratives. Another difficulty is, as E. H. Carr pointed out in 1961, that history is not static.[35] The challenge is to create a game, a toy, or even a book that embraces, rather than ignores, the complexity of the past and can convey messages that change as the world around them does.[36]

Over a century ago, when G. Stanley Hall pointed out that dolls educate "the heart and will even more than the intellect," he was underscoring the significance of a child's emotional play in his or her education.[37] In attempting to understand what messages about America children learn from toys, books, and amusements, what has become clear is that children are generally offered oversimplified stories that purposefully avoid the complexity of history. Going forward toy makers and publishers—as much as educators—have the opportunity to offer children a more nuanced interpretation of American history that respects their intelligence and recognizes the agency of all children, past, present, and future.

Acknowledgments

I have been lucky to have a wide network of people support this project and support me. The courses I took at Rutgers allowed me to approach my topics from dramatically different perspectives, leading to a much richer approach to the study of childhood than might have been available to me outside of the field of American Studies.

I am immensely grateful to my mentor, Ruth Feldstein, who has guided and supported me through every stage of this work from my first year of courses through post-graduate school publication. She has pushed my scholarship, shown me how to ask important questions, modeled how to teach, and inspired me with her insightful scholarship.

I am grateful to each of the dedicated and supportive faculty and staff who have taught and guided me: Rob Snyder, Andrew Urban, Susan Carruthers, Tim Raphael, Mary Rizzo, Mark Krasovic, Whit Strub, Lyra Monteiro, James Goodman, Fran Bartkowski, Beryl Satter, and Rachel Devlin. Ann Fabian generously connected me with members of the history faculty at Rutgers–New Brunswick, in a spirit of true collaboration. Janet Golden read a draft of my dissertation and gave me valuable feedback at a crucial moment. Georgia Mellos and Christina Strasburger lent me administrative support and regular morale boosts.

Many thanks to the doctoral students whom it would be impossible to get through graduate school without, each brilliant and inspiring in their scholarship and friendship: Laura Troiano, Katie Singer, Sara Grossman, Naomi Extra, Addie Mahmassani, and Samantha Boardman.

A special thank you to Katie Uva, editor extraordinaire, whose insights and suggestions made this book much stronger and, dare I say, sassier. Thank you to scholars and friends at CUNY and beyond who have inspired me and showed interest in my work, particularly Josh Freeman, David Nasaw, Steve Brier, Betsy Blackmar, Meredith Martin, Jonathan Cobb, Gerald Markowitz,

Andrea Vasquez, and Tom Engelhardt, whose collection of Landmark books was an invaluable resource for me. Thank you to Jim O'Brien for this in-depth index and good humor. My fellow public historians in New York and the CUNY Public History Collective have inspired me and consistently helped me—especially Natalie Milbrodt, Johnathan Thayer, Dominique Jean-Louis, Sarah Litvin, and Benjamin Serby.

I have so much gratitude for the archivists at New York Public Library, the Columbia University Rare Books and Manuscripts Archives, the Smithsonian's National Museum of American History Archives Center, the National Archives and Records Administration in College Park, and the Bronx Historical Society who patiently guided my meandering research journey. Many thanks to Michael Virgintino, for corresponding with me about our mutual fascination with Freedomland.

Thanks to my colleagues at the LaGuardia and Wagner Archives and LaGuardia Community College who allow me to explore public history in new and exciting ways, particularly Richard Lieberman and Stephen Weinstein, who shared their recollections of Freedomland with me. Thank you to my neighbors turned second family, the Buckhursts—especially Jane and Kate, who always let me ask them about their dolls—and my dear friends, Ben Ahles, Matt Alie, Noah Bein, Emily RK Chester, Stephanie Dueño, Georgia Faust, Morgan Day Frank, Amanda Garfunkel, Madeleine Gray, Greg Hill-Ries, Laura Max Holder (and Jayda and Andre), Fielding Hong, Mary-Elaine Jenkins, Kelly Klein, Jacques Lang, Emily Langner, Silvia De Lisi, Nina Macintosh, Sarah Meier-Zimbler, Willy Naess, Neil Padukone, Gitanjali Prasad, Giulia Quintela, Jonah Rowen, Morgan Sykes, Lauren VanDenBerg, Alan Yaspan and the whole Screwballz softball and volleyball team. Thanks to my new family, my Ditta, Bromley/Giannetto, Radke in-laws, and in particular to, Eva Anderson.

Thank you to my husband and teammate in life, Paul Lewis Anderson, who has seen this book go from dissertation draft to book manuscript and kept me (and now our soon-to-be little one!) well-fed the entire way.

I'm so thankful for the support from my brother Zach, sister-in-law Emilie, and my awesome nephew and amazing niece, Owen and Margot—you all light up my life. And to my extended family—too many to name (lucky for me)—who all help give me a sense of my place in the world. I write this in loving memory of Sophie and Alex Rosner, Joan and John Conway, Chris Neaf, David Podell, Adrienne Markowitz, Billy Markowitz, and Anton Vasquez. Finally, there are not enough words in the world to thank my incredible parents, David Rosner and Kathy Conway, who have been my biggest inspiration and supporters, rigorous editors, and emotional pillars.

Notes

INTRODUCTION

1. Carl Becker, "Everyman His Own Historian" (annual address of the president of the American Historical Association, Minneapolis, December 29, 1931), *American Historical Review* 37 (1932): 221–236, https://www.historians.org/about-aha-and-membership /aha-history-and-archives/presidential-addresses/carl-l-becker.

2. Sophie Rosner, "A Descriptive Study to Identify Manifestations of Racist Ideology of Whites toward Blacks in Picture Books Published in the United States: 1959, 1964, 1969" (PhD diss., New York University, 1975), 270.

3. Lizabeth Cohen, *A Consumers' Republic: The Politics of Mass Consumption in Postwar America* (New York: Knopf, 2003).

4. G. Stanley Hall and A. Caswell Ellis, *A Study of Dolls* (New York: E.L. Kellogg, 1897), 53.

5. Hall and Ellis, *Study of Dolls*, 62.

6. Hall and Ellis, *Study of Dolls*, 54.

7. Hall and Ellis, *Study of Dolls*, 53.

8. Hall and Ellis, *Study of Dolls*, 16.

9. Kenneth Clark and Mamie Clark, "The Development of Consciousness of Self and the Emergence of Racial Identification in Negro Preschool Children," *Journal of Social Psychology* 10 (1939): 591–599; Kenneth Clark and Mamie Clark, "Skin Color as a Factor in Racial Identification of Negro Preschool Children," *Journal of Social Psychology* 11 (1940): 159–169; Kenneth Clark and Mamie Clark, "Factors in Racial Identification and Preferences in Negro Children," *Journal of Negro Education* 19 (1950): 341–350.

10. Miriam Forman-Brunell, *Made to Play House: Dolls and the Commercialization of American Girlhood, 1830–1930* (New Haven, CT: Yale University Press, 1993).

11. Tony Schwartz, *New York 19* (Folkways Records, 1970), https://clio.columbia.edu /catalog/8389092?counter=1. The "19" refers to the postal code encompassing parts of Hell's Kitchen. Historically, the neighborhood was known as Lincoln Hill and was traditionally poor and once predominantly African American. Today it is more upscale and known as the home of Lincoln Center.

12. Sarah Banet-Weiser, *Kids Rule! Nickelodeon and Consumer Citizenship* (Durham, NC: Duke University Press, 2007). Some have argued that children's entertainment provides a space for widening the stories of history, broadening or changing concepts of citizenship, and retooling well-worn American myths. For example, in *Kids Rule!* Sarah Banet-Weiser shows how the cable network Nickelodeon approached children as active and engaged citizens and geared news and programming directly to them, refuting the idea that children are only "citizens in training" who "lack of access to political empowerment and engagement," (12). Her book successfully refuses to see the public and private media as inherently good or bad and resists putting them on opposite ends of an ideological spectrum.

13. Robin Bernstein, "Let Black Kids Just Be Kids," *New York Times*, July 26, 2017.

14. Cohen, *Consumers' Republic*, 13.

15. In chapter 3 I refer to this Bobbs-Merrill series as the Orange books.

CHAPTER 1 — MADE IN AMERICA

1. "Scientists Say That Toys Are the Best Teachers for the Little Ones," *Washington Post*, November 12, 1905, SM10.

2. "Notes of Trade and Industry," *New-York Tribune*, February 1, 1915, 11.

3. Richard Longstreth, *The American Department Store Transformed: 1920–1960* (New Haven, CT: Yale University Press, 2010).

4. "Hasbro, Inc. History," in *International Directory of Company Histories*, vol. 16 (Detroit: St. James Press, 1997), http://www.fundinguniverse.com/company-histories /hasbro-inc-history/.

5. H. W. Brands, *American Colossus: The Triumph of Capitalism, 1865–1900* (New York: First Anchor Books, 2011), 23.

6. Gary Cross, *Kids' Stuff: Toys and the Changing World of American Childhood* (Cambridge, MA: Harvard University Press, 1997), 33.

7. Viviana Zelizar, *Pricing the Priceless Child: The Changing Social Value of Children* (Princeton, NJ: Princeton University Press, 1994), 64. Some children continued to work, more often in the factory.

8. Kriste Lindenmeyer, *A Right to Childhood: The U.S. Children's Bureau and Child Welfare, 1912–46* (Urbana: University of Illinois Press, 1997).

9. Zelizar, *Pricing the Priceless Child*, 63. "The child labor conflict is a key to understanding the profound transformation in the economic and sentimental value of children in the early twentieth century" (57).

10. Howard Chudacoff, *Children at Play* (New York: New York University Press, 2007), 54.

11. "Where The Toys Come From: An Industry Which Germany Regards as One of Her Greatest," *Washington Post*, December 15, 1907, E4.

12. "Americans Invent Wonderful Toys," *New York Times*, December 6, 1908, 7.

13. "Americans Invent Wonderful Toys," 7.

14. "Few Simple Toys," *New-York Tribune*, December 23, 1903, 7.

15. FAO Schwarz opened in Baltimore in 1862 before it relocated to New York City in 1870. "News of the Stores: A Fascinating Display of Toys at F.A.O. Schwartz's [*sic*]," *New-York Tribune*, March 11, 1900, B50.

16. "Santa's Stock of Toys," *New-York Tribune*, December 19, 1909, A3.

17. "New and Expensive Toys in the Season's Novelties," *New York Times*, December 21, 1902, 32.

18. Susan Stewart writes in *On Longing*, "We cannot separate the function of the miniature from a nostalgia for preindustrial labor, a nostalgia for craft." Susan Stewart, *On Longing: Narratives of the Miniature, the Gigantic, the Souvenir, the Collection* (Durham, NC: Duke University Press, 1984), 68.

19. Stewart, *On Longing*, 44. Stewart points out that miniature objects were a source of fascination for adults and children alike. Howard Chudacoff notes that early twentieth-century toy manufacturers "fashioned many of the era's mass-produced toys to appeal to parents rather than directly to children themselves" (Chudacoff, *Children At Play*, 78).

20. "Seen in the Shops," *New-York Tribune*, June 24, 1907, 4.

21. "New and Expensive Toys in the Season's Novelties," *New York Times*, December 21, 1902, 32.

22. "Few Simple Toys." *New-York Tribune*, December 23, 1903, 7.

23. "Americans Invent Wonderful Toys," *New York Times*, December 6, 1908, 7.

24. One 2019 description of a toy touted as educational claims it will teach a wide range of skills from motor skills to critical thinking: "Little engineers can create their own rovers, choppers, or crazy rolling contraption with the Gears! Gears! Gears! Rover Gears building kit. . . . It's an engaging way to help kids build STEM skills, motor skills, and practice their critical thinking." https://www.learningresources.com/gears-gears -gears-r-rovergearstm.

25. Cross, *Kids' Stuff*, 94.

26. "History of Steiff Teddy Bears," https://www.steiffteddybears.co.uk/more-things -steiff/history-of-steiff-bears.php.

27. "Union Teddy Bears," *Washington Post*, December 1, 1907, MS1; Cross, *Kids' Stuff*, 94.

28. Cross, *Kids' Stuff*, 95.

29. "Santa's Stock of Toys," A3.

30. "War Toys Popular in Xmas Window," *Atlanta Constitution*, December 17, 1916, C1.

31. "Toys Show Real Class This Year," *Detroit Free Press*, December 5, 1909, 9. See the full quote: "Talking of dolls. The instinct of motherhood is roused throughout small girldom. And here again, the toy-makers meet the demand. . . . Tunnels, railways with terrific curves, and scenic railways are only a few of the mechanical toys warranted to drive boyhood wild with delight."

32. "Americans Invent Wonderful Toys," *New York Times*, December 6, 1908, 7.

33. Cross, *Kids' Stuff*, 72.

34. "Seen in the Shops," *New-York Tribune*, June 24, 1907, 4.

35. "Display Ad 5," *New York Times*, November 27, 1910, 3.

36. Cross, *Kids' Stuff*, 73.

37. Miriam Forman-Brunell, *Made to Play House: Dolls and the Commercialization of American Girlhood, 1830–1930* (Baltimore: Johns Hopkins University Press, 1998); Erica Rand, *Barbie's Queer Accessories* (Durham, NC: Duke University Press, 1995).

38. Cross, *Kids' Stuff*, 27.

39. Longstreth, *American Department Store Transformed*.

40. Alan Trachtenberg, *The Incorporation of America: Culture and Society in the Gilded Age* (New York: Hill & Wang, 1982), 4.

41. William Leach, *The Land of Desire: Merchants, Power and the Rise of New American Culture* (New York: Pantheon, 1993), xiii.

42. "For more than a fortnight thousands and tens of thousands have thronged the streets and packed the stores in their search for articles to be smuggled mysteriously into their homes, which will be brought forth to-day to gladden the heart of young and old alike." "Yule-Tide Cheer," *New-York Tribune*, December 25, 1880, 1; "World Population Review," http://worldpopulationreview.com/us-cities/new-york-city-population.

43. Longstreth, *American Department Store Transformed*, 1.

44. Ralph Merle Hower, *History of Macy's of New York: 1858–1919: Chapters in the Evolution of the Department Store* (Cambridge, MA: Harvard University Press, 1946), table 16, 238–239.

45. Hower, *History of Macy's*, 169.

46. Sears Archives, http://www.searsarchives.com/history/history1890s.htm.

47. Jackson Lears, *Fables of Abundance: A Cultural History of Advertising in America* (New York: Basic Books, 1994), 93.

48. Stephen Nissenbaum, *The Battle for Christmas: A Social and Cultural History of Our Most Cherished Holiday* (New York: Knopf, 1997).

49. "Display Ad 5," *New York Times*, November 27, 1910, 3.

50. "Whole East Side Went Shopping Yesterday," *New York Times*, December 24, 1906, 2.

51. "Whole East Side Went Shopping Yesterday," 2.

52. "How the Children of the Rich and Poor Enjoyed Xmas Trees—But in Different Ways; Babel of Tongues Sing 'Star Spangled Banner'; Immigrants of Ellis Island Gather Around Christmas Tree in Patriotic Service; Newcomers Get Presents; Ritz-Carlton Also Had a Tree, but Only Languid Interest Is Shown by Children of the Rich," *New-York Tribune*, December 24, 1912, 6.

53. Leach, *Land of Desire*, 63.

54. Leach, *Land of Desire*, 61.

55. Leach, *Land of Desire*, 63.

56. "Christmas Toys in Great Array: Atlanta's Shop Windows Are a Delight," *Atlanta Constitution*, December 13, 1897, 9; "Window Trims for Furniture Dealers," *Grand Rapids Furniture Record*, December 1, 1906, 1.

57. "Holiday Shopping Crowd," *New York Times*, December 21, 1902, 19. The term "eye feasts" also equates visual and corporal consumption of nutrition.

58. "Holiday Shopping Crowd," 19. In the twenty-first century, the prevalence of "unboxing videos" seems to replicate and update this desire for looking at, even if not touching and purchasing, consumer goods.

59. "Santa to Flood City with Cheer: New York, Rich and Poor, on Eve of Greatest Yuletide Celebration," *New-York Tribune*, December 24, 1915, 14.

60. "City's Christmas Eve, Final Shopping Rush East and West Side Streets Filled with Happy Throngs," *New-York Tribune*, December 25, 1904, 2.

61. Hower, *History of Macy's*, 280.

62. "City's Christmas Eve," *New-York Tribune*, December 25, 1904, 2.

63. "When Grand Street Shops for Christmas," *New York Times*, December 13, 1908, 9.

64. *Automatic Toy Works Catalog* (New York, 1882), 4, https://archive.org/details/automatictoyworkooauto.

65. Calculated in 2019 through multiple online tools, including http://www.in2013dol lars.com/us/inflation/1882?amount=4 and https://westegg.com/inflation/.

66. *Automatic Toy Works Catalog*, 2.

67. *Automatic Toy Works Catalog*, 3.

68. *Automatic Toy Works Catalog*, 5–6.

69. The mammy character appeared in Harriet Beecher Stowe's *Uncle Tom's Cabin* in 1852 and continued through many iterations in literature and film. For an in-depth look at this characterization, see Ruth Feldstein, *Motherhood in Black and White* (Ithaca, NY: Cornell University Press, 2000).

70. *Automatic Toy Works Catalog*, 6.

71. *Automatic Toy Works Catalog*, 4.

72. "Antique Cast Iron 'Stump Speaker' Mechanical Bank," ca. 1886, "I Always Did 'Spise a Mule Mechanical Bank," ca. 1897, to James Bowen on April 72, 1897, and manufactured by Cromwell, Connecticut's J & E Stevens Company, "Antique Cast Iron Uncle Sam Mechanical Bank," ca. 1886, Shepard Hardware, all at http://zandkantiques.com /antique_toys.html. See also National Museum of African American History and Culture Collection, "Coin Bank in the Form of a Caricatured Boy," object 2007.7.219, Collection of the Smithsonian National Museum of African American History and Culture, Gift of the Collection of James M. Caselli and Jonathan Mark Scharer, https://nmaahc.si .edu/object/nmaahc_2007.7.219?; Barton and Somerville, "Play Things: The Racialized Mechanical Banks and Toys, 1880–1930," *International Journal of Historical Archeology* 19 (2012): 63.

73. Christopher Dingwall, "The Sale of Slavery: Memory, Culture and the Renewal of America, 1876–1920" (PhD diss., University of Chicago, 2015); see also Christopher Dingwall, "Reanimating Slavery: Mechanical Toys, Human Machines and the Play of Race" (paper, Center for Slavery and Justice, Brown University, 2013), https://www.youtube .com/watch?v=SGFbopTJyms.

74. Dingwall, "Reanimating Slavery."

75. "Caricatures of African Americans: The Pickaninny," History on the Net, July 20, 2012, http://www.authentichistory.com/diversity/african/3-coon/2-pickaninny/. See also Robin Bernstein, "Let Black Kids Just Be Kids," *New York Times*, July 26, 2017, A23, where she points out that the "pickaninny" was a "dehumanized black juvenile character . . . comically impervious to pain and [who] never needed protection or tenderness." She argues that these dehumanizing, racist stereotypes served the purpose of making it impossible to feel sympathy for Black children as innocent—or even as children.

76. Diane Roberts, *The Myth of Aunt Jemima: White Women Representing Black Women* (New York: Routledge, 1994), 1; image: https://upload.wikimedia.org/wikipedia /commons/f/f9/New-York_tribune.%2C_November_07%2C_1909%2C_Page_20%2C _Image_44_Aunt_Jemima.jpg; ad for Aunt Jemima pancake flour, *New-York Tribune*, November 1909.

77. "Pan-Cake "Mammy" Is Dead," *Chicago Daily News*, August 31, 1923, 4.

78. Ad, "Aunt Jemima Says," *Good Housekeeping* 76 (January 1923): 147; Maurice Manning, "Aunt Jemima Explained: The Old South, the Absent Mistress, and the Slave in a Box," *Southern Cultures* 2 (1995): 19–44; and Maurice Manning, *Slave in a Box: The Strange Career of Aunt Jemima* (Charlottesville: University of Virginia Press, 1998).

79. See Kimberly Wallace-Sanders, *Mammy: Race, Gender, and Southern Memory* (Ann Arbor: University of Michigan Press, 2009), and Manning, "Aunt Jemima Explained," for broad discussion of the role of the cheerful slave in southern memory.

80. In 2020, Quaker Oats removed the image of Aunt Jemima from their pancake batter boxes amid the Black Lives Matter movement and racial protests demanding moves toward racial justice, such as dismantling Confederate statues. Tiffany Hsu, "Aunt Jemima Brand to Change Name and Image Over 'Racial Stereotype,'" *New York Times,* June 17, 2020, B1.

81. Koba, "Former Slave Creates the First Black Doll Company for His Daughters, Here's Why," *Urban Intellectuals,* http://urbanintellectuals.com/2016/01/17/former-slave -creates-first-black-doll-company-daughters-heres.

82. "Black Dolls," *Pittsburgh Courier,* January 15, 1927, A8.

83. "Holiday Supply of Dolls Is Announced," *Pittsburgh Courier,* November 22, 1930, A7.

84. "Dolls of All Nations," *Baltimore Sun,* December 6, 1908, 19.

85. "The *Constitution* had been counted among the great newspapers of the United States and it came to be regarded as the 'voice of the New South,' thanks to a succession of outstanding editors: Henry W. Grady, Clark Howell, and Ralph McGill." "The Atlanta Journal-Constitution: American Newspaper," *Britannica,* https://www.britannica.com /topic/The-Atlanta-Journal-Constitution.

86. "Negro Dolls for Negro Babies," *Atlanta Constitution,* September 28, 1908, 4.

87. "Negro Dolls for Negro Babies." This notion of having a doll that resembles the owner continues today and can be seen as a different kind of investment in whiteness at the end of the twentieth century with American Girl dolls.

88. "Pretty Negro Dolls for Pickaninnies: Mrs. Foxhall Daingerfield," *Nashville Tennessean,* December 10, 1908, 2.

89. Oscar Wilder Underwood, U.S. Congress, House Committee on Ways and Means, (Washington, DC: GPO, March 4, 1913); E. I. Horsman Jr., "Tariff Letter to the Chairman of the Ways and Means Committee," Congressional Hearing 5211, paragraph 431–Toys, 5216 (Washington, DC: GPO, 1913).

90. U.S. Congress, House of Representatives, "Tariff Schedules," *Hearings Before the Committee on Ways and Means,* v. V, Schedules M and N, (Washington D.C., GPO,1913, 5218). Statement of The Schieble Toy and Novelty Co., W. E. Schieble, President January 27, 1913, Dayton Ohio. https://books.google.com/books?id=EE8-AAAAYAAJ&dq=ways+and +means+committee+toy+manufacturing+1913&source=gbs_navlinks_s 5218.

91. Cross, *Kids' Stuff,* 32.

92. H. C. Ives, Ives Manufacturing Corporation, "Letter to the Chairman of the Ways and Means Committee," Congressional Hearing 5211 (U.S. Congress, January 25, 1913), https://books.google.com/books?id=Ip4qAAAAYAAJ.

93. Cross, *Kids' Stuff,* 32. Cross explains, "When imports vanished during World War I and both patriotism and isolationism were on the rise, the Toy Manufacturers of the U.S.A. won permission from the government to keep producing toys."

94. "Special to the Washington Post," *Washington Post,* August 30, 1914, 12.

95. "Special to the Washington Post," 12.

96. Brent Coates, "The Child Welfare League and the 'Made in Kalamazoo' Exhibit" (Kalamazoo Public Library, July 2010), http://www.kpl.gov/local-history/education/child -welfare-league.aspx.

97. "Toys 'Made in U.S.A.,'" *New-York Tribune*, October 31, 1914, 14.

98. "World Looks to America for Its Toys," *New-York Tribune*, November 26, 1916, B4.

99. "World Looks to America for Its Toys," B4.

100. "American Toy Trade Greatly Helped by War," *New York Times*, March 4, 1917, X7.

101. Elsie Parsons, "War Increases Toy Soldiers Sales," *New York Times*, April 4, 1915, SM13.

102. "Toy Manufacturers Organize," *New York Times*, December 16, 1917, E7; "Toy Makers Organize: National Association Formed to Further Their Interests," *New York Times*, June 10, 1916, 16.

103. "Limerick: *American Toys*," featured in "Shops and Things," *New-York Tribune*, January 5, 1919, D11. See also Cross, *Kids Stuff*, where he also discusses this limerick.

104. "American Toys Are Doing Very Well," *New York Times*, December 19, 1920, E18. Backpaper on this pin reads "I Am an American and I Play with Only American-Made Toys. That is why I am a Member of this Club." https://www.hakes.com/Auction /ItemDetail/4895/AMERICAN-MADE-TOY-BRIGADE-CLUB-BUTTON.

105. "Toy Makers Seek More Protection," *New York Times*, December 18, 1921, 18.

106. "American business relied on whatever stereotypes it could to eliminate German competition." Leach, *Land of Desire*, 85.

107. Henry Ford Archives, "Ford Motor Company Photographic and Film Department," https://www.thehenryford.org/collections-and-research/digital-resources/popular -topics/photo-and-film-department; "A Rare Look at Henry Ford—He Was a Filmmaker Too," *Detroit Free Press*, May 1, 1978, 10B.

108. Phillip W. Stewart, "Henry Ford: Movie Mogul? A Titan of Industry Conquers Filmdom," *Prologue* 104 (Winter 2014), https://www.archives.gov/files/publications /prologue/2014/winter/ford.pdf.

109. Video, *Playthings of Childhood / The Doll's House* (Ford Motor Company, 1920), Library of Congress, FC-FC-2487, https://catalog.archives.gov/id/7419785, https://www .youtube.com/watch?v=LFxtSTl5N5E.

110. *Playthings of Childhood / The Doll's House.*

111. Viviana Zelizer, *Pricing the Priceless Child: The Changing Social Value of Children* (Princeton: Princeton University Press, 1985). Viviana Zelizer points out that childhood was being redefined and sentimentalized in the early twentieth century as children moved from laborers to dependents, from the workplace to schools.

112. Today the fair takes place at the Jacob Javits Center in Midtown Manhattan and showcases more than 1,300 companies in any given year. Angela Moore, "It's Not All Child's Play at Toy Fair," *Los Angeles Times*, February 10, 2003, https://www.latimes .com/archives/la-xpm-2003-feb-10-fi-toyfair10-story.html.

113. "7 Acres of Toys in Yule Preview: 15,000 Playthings," *New York Times*, April 6, 1937, 11. Susan Stewart describes this as a "bourgeois public immersed in the discourse of the 'petite feminine.'" *On Longing*, 62.

114. "Gates of Toyland Crashed by Adults," *New York Times*, April 21, 1936, 25. A portion of the toy show took place at the Hotel McAlpin, on Thirty-Fourth Street and Broadway, near where the doll show examined in the following chapter would be held mere months later.

115. "Trailer Craze Grips Toy Fair: New Types of Playthings Street Streamlines," *New York Sun*, April 5, 1937, 40.

116. "Trailer Craze Grips Toy Fair," 40.

117. "7 Acres of Toys in Yule Preview: 15,000 Playthings," *New York Times*, April 6, 1937, 11.

118. "Trailer Craze Grips Toy Fair: New Types of Playthings Street Streamlines," *New York Sun*, April 5, 1937, 40.

119. I am using the idea of scripted behavior put forth by Robin Bernstein in "Dances with Things: Material Culture and the Performance of Race," *Social Text* 27, no. 4 (2009): 67–94. Bernstein also uses the notion of "scriptive things" in her book *Racial Innocence*, where she explains how human interactions with objects can inform people about roles based on gender, class, age, race, or any number of categories. She points out that certain Black dolls were costumed as servants or included instructions to play "with that doll as a servant." *Racial Innocence: Performing American Childhood from Slavery to Civil Rights* (New York: New York University Press, 2011), 203.

120. David Dunlap, "Memories amid a Makeover at the Toy Center," *New York Times*, April 29, 2008, http://cityroom.blogs.nytimes.com/2008/04/29/memories-amid-a-make over-at-the-toy-center/.

121. Eunice Fuller Barnard, "In Toyland the Child Himself Is the Censor," *New York Times*, December 19, 1937, 114.

122. "Christmas Toys Reach 7-Year Peak," *New York Times*, October 25, 1937, 2.

123. "And Christmas 263 Days Off! Back Yard Swing Dolls More Realistic Games for Adults," *Christian Science Monitor*, April 6, 1937, 4; "More Abundant Life Is Seen in 1937 Toy Fair," *New York Herald Tribune*, April 5, 1937, 17.

124. "7 Acres of Toys in Yule Preview: 15,000 Playthings," *New York Times*, April 6, 1937, 11.

125. "Christmas Toys Reach 7-Year Peak," *New York Times*, October 25, 1937, 21.

126. "And Christmas 263 Days Off! Back Yard Swing Dolls More Realistic Games for Adults," *Christian Science Monitor*, April 6, 1937, 4.

127. Eunice Fuller Barnard, "In Toyland the Child Himself Is the Censor," *New York Times*, December 19, 1937, 114.

CHAPTER 2 — DOLLING UP HISTORY

1. G. Stanley Hall and A. Caswell Ellis, *A Study of Dolls* (New York: E.L. Kellogg, 1897), 3.

2. Warren Susman, *Culture as History: The Transformation of American Society in the Twentieth Century* (New York: Pantheon, 1984), 189–190.

3. Museum of Modern Art, "The Art of the Common Man in America, 1750–1900" https://www.moma.org/calendar/exhibitions/2930.

4. Ira Katznelson, *Fear Itself: The New Deal and the Origins of Our Time* (New York: Liveright, 2014).

5. William E. Leuchtenburg, *Franklin D. Roosevelt and the New Deal: 1932–1940* (New York: Harper & Row, 1965), 2–3; Katznelson, *Fear Itself*.

6. Daughters of the American Revolution, "Our History," https://www.dar.org/national -society/about-dar/dar-history.

7. National Society of Colonial Dames of America, "About Us," http://nscda.org /about-us/.

8. See General Society of Mayflower Descendants, "About Us," https://www.themayflower society.org/our-society/about-us.

9. Alice Hughes, "A Woman's New York," *Washington Post*, November 9, 1938, 14.

10. Lewis Mumford, "The Sky Line: The Golden Age in the West and South," *New Yorker*, April 30, 1938, 68.

11. Mumford, "The Sky Line," 68.

12. "Now Mrs. Lewis Has Time for Family of Dolls: But as a Girl She Played Marbles with Boys-Has 200 in Collection," *Brooklyn Daily Eagle*, April 4, 1937, 3-A.

13. "Now Mrs. Lewis Has Time," 3-A.

14. "Queen's Own Doll in Exhibition Here: Plaything of Victoria, Made in Her Likeness, Only One of 1,800 in Club Show," *New York Times*, June 20, 1939, 16.

15. "Now Mrs. Lewis Has Time," 3-A.

16. David Whisnant, *All That Is Native and Fine* (Chapel Hill: University of North Carolina Press, 1983), 184. As Whisnant has shown, selling "authenticity"—of both foreign or isolated and regional cultural products—became popular in the 1930s.

17. "Doll Show Extended to August 20," *New York Times*, July 31, 1938, 39.

18. "Doll Show Popular with Adult Visitors," *Christian Science Monitor*, July 26, 1938, 5.

19. "Doll Show Popular," 5.

20. "40,000 See Dolls in 2 Weeks of Show Here; 82% of Visitors at Display Are Adults," *New York Times*, July 24, 1938, 28.

21. Leuchtenburg, *Franklin D. Roosevelt and the New Deal*, 2–3.

22. Robert S. McElvaine, *Down & Out in the Great Depression: Letters from the Forgotten Man* (Chapel Hill: University of North Carolina Press, 1983), 21; Katznelson, *Fear Itself*, 99.

23. Susman, *Culture as History*, 157.

24. Leslie Paris, "Small Mercies," in *Acts of Possession*, ed. Leah Dilworth (Chapel Hill: University of North Carolina Press, 2003), 190. See Susan Stewart, *On Longing: Narratives of the Miniature, the Gigantic, the Souvenir, the Collection* (Durham, NC: Duke University Press, 1984), 65.

25. Steven Gelber, *Hobbies: Leisure and the Culture of Work in America* (New York: Columbia University Press, 1999). Gelber points out that between 1928 and the 1940s collecting became an acceptable hobby (outside of fine art collecting): "The identification of hobby with collecting deepened during the great hobby boom of the depression" (66–67).

26. Susman, *Culture as History*, 172.

27. Jane S. Baker, *Selling Tradition: Appalachia and the Construction of an American Folk, 1930–1940* (Chapel Hill: University of North Carolina Press, 1998), 217. Whisnant, *All That Is Native and Fine*, 184.

28. Baker, *Selling Tradition*, 209.

29. Stewart, *On Longing*, 65.

30. Lewis and other women collectors were participating in what Kristin Hoganson has called the global production of American domesticity, wherein middle- and upper-class women like Mrs. Lewis were able to travel vicariously to other countries by importing foreign goods and incorporating them into their homes and social lives, thereby bringing the world to them. Hoganson, *Consumer's Imperium: The Global Production of Domesticity* (Chapel Hill: University of North Carolina Press, 2007).

31. Katherine A. Van Epps, "Doll Collector Collects Data on Wedding Costumes," *Knickerbocker News*, January 23, 1951, B-5.

32. Mary E. Lewis, *The Marriage of Diamonds and Dolls* (New York: Lindquist, 1947).

33. Margaret Mara, "Cradle Rocker Steadies World," *Brooklyn Daily Eagle*, March 1, 1950, 19.

34. Society section, *Brooklyn Daily Eagle*, August 26, 1937, 9.

35. "Adults Give Way to Doll 'Experts,'" *Christian Science Monitor*, July 14, 1938, 5.

36. "Children's Museum Sends Antique Dolls Today to National Show in New York," *Daily Boston Globe,* June 28, 1938, 3.

37. "Boston Doll Delegates Named for National Show in New York: Turning Back Pages of Dolldom History," *Christian Science Monitor*, June 27, 1938, 12.

38. "Boston Doll Delegates," 12.

39. "Children's Museums Urged for All Cities," *Daily Boston Globe*, February 19, 1930, 2.

40. "Women's National Doll Club Plans to Pool Varied Toy Collections in Special Museum," *New York Times*, November 3, 1937, 25. The museum they envisioned would include all kinds of dolls, though not necessarily all kinds of people.

41. "National Museum for Dolls Is on Verge of Realization," *Christian Science Monitor*, March 19, 1938, 3.

42. "Anna Billings Gallup Dies, Headed Children's Museum," *New York Herald Tribune*, October 22, 1956, 10.

43. "Borough Woman Gets Invitation to Royal Tea," *Brooklyn Daily Eagle*, November 17, 1947, 9.

44. Michael Denning, *The Cultural Front: Laboring of American Culture in the Twentieth Century* (New York: Verso, 1997).

45. Marlene Parks and Gerald Markowitz, *Democratic Vistas: Post Office Art during the Great Depression* (Philadelphia: Temple University Press, 1980).

46. Kristen Hatch has identified that Shirley Temple represented the end of an era when girls were central to emerging mass media. Hatch, *Shirley Temple and the Performance of Girlhood,* (New Brunswick: Rutgers University Press, 2014), 2.

47. Stewart, *On Longing*, 61.

48. Lewis, *Marriage of Diamonds and Dolls*, 7.

49. Stewart, *On Longing*, 68.

50. Lewis, *Marriage of Diamonds and Dolls*, 20.

51. Lewis, *Marriage of Diamonds and Dolls*, xiii.

52. Walter Rendell Storey, "Antique Dolls Tell a Story Today," *New York Times,* July 10, 1938, 102.

53. Storey, "Antique Dolls," 102.

54. "Queen's Own Doll in Exhibition Here: Plaything of Victoria, Made in Her Likeness, Only One of 1,800 in Club Show," *New York Times*, June 20, 1939, 16; Storey, "Antique Dolls," 102.

55. In her history of dolls, *Made to Play House*, Miriam Forman-Brunell notes that "unrestricted by clothing and other symbols of the society they criticized, the wise Kewpie boys [were] often mistaken for compliant girls" because "the naked Kewpies" were "without [male] genitalia." Even when sold with clothes, "what little clothing the Kewpies wear is easily mistaken for feminine frocks." See *Made to Play House: Dolls and the Commercialization of American Girlhood, 1830–1930* (New Haven, CT: Yale University Press, 1993), 126.

56. Lewis, *Marriage of Diamonds and Dolls*, 131.

57. Lewis, *Marriage of Diamonds and Dolls*, 133.

58. Lewis, *Marriage of Diamonds and Dolls*, 142.

59. Lewis, *Marriage of Diamonds and Dolls*, 142.

60. Lewis, *Marriage of Diamonds and Dolls*, 142.

61. Jesse Ash Arndt, "Dar Members—143,000 Strong—Celebrate Their Fiftieth Birthday," *Washington Post*, October 6, 1940, B7.

62. "Bar Maintained at Constitution Hall, by DAR," *Afro-American*, January 21, 1939, 2.

63. Ruth Feldstein, *How It Feels to Be Free: Black Women Entertainers and the Civil Rights Movement* (New York: Oxford University Press, 2013), 17.

64. Lewis, *Marriage of Diamonds and Dolls*, 24.

65. Lewis, *Marriage of Diamonds and Dolls*, 27.

66. Lewis, *Marriage of Diamonds and Dolls*, 24.

67. Lewis, *Marriage of Diamonds and Dolls*, 160.

68. Lewis, *Marriage of Diamonds and Dolls*, 160.

69. Myla Perkins, *Black Dolls: An Identification and Value Guide*, bk. 2 (Kentucky: Collector Books, 1995), 25. Perkins herself, as a Black woman, makes clear that doll collecting for her is not just a hobby but a serious way of understanding history. She points out that Black dolls were segregated into two distinct sets of stores and distribution systems.

70. By 1948 Langston Hughes had noted that manufacturers were producing more attractive Black dolls. See Hughes, "Brownskin Cards, Sepia Dolls, All Mean a Merrier Christmas," *Chicago Defender*, December 25, 1948, 6. It wasn't until 1993 that the *Chicago Tribune* reported, "Black Memorabilia Get First Midwest Show and Sale." One collector of Black dolls, Barbara Whiteman, also noted the seriousness of her doll collecting efforts: "I want to make it clear. I am not home playing with dolls. I am collecting for historic purposes."

71. John Dewey, *Human Nature and Conduct: An Introduction of Social Psychology* (New York: Henry Holt, 1922), 16.

72. Ruth E. Horowitz, "The Racial Aspects of Self-Identification in Nursery School Children," *Journal of Psychology* 7 (1939): 91–99.

73. Horowitz, "Racial Aspects."

74. Kenneth B. Clark and Mamie K. Clark, "Skin Color as a Factor in Racial Identification of Negro Preschool Children," *Journal of Social Psychology* 11 (1940): 159–169.

75. Kenneth B. Clark and Mamie Clark, "Emotional Factors in Racial Identification and Preference in Negro Children," *Journal of Negro Education* 19 (1950): 344.

76. Clark and Clark, "Emotional Factors in Racial Identification," 346.

77. See Kenneth Clark and Mamie Clark, "The Development of Consciousness of Self and the Emergence of Racial Identification in Negro Preschool Children," *Journal of Social Psychology* 10 (1939): 591–599; Kenneth Clark and Mamie Clark, "Segregation as a Factor in the Racial Identification of Negro Pre-school Children: A Preliminary Report," *Journal of Experimental Education* 8 (December 1939): 161–163. Reflecting the sexism of the day, Kenneth Clark, then entering graduate school as the first African American doctoral student ever admitted to the Psychology Department at Columbia, was listed as first author, even though these studies were based on Mamie Clark's work. See Gerald Markowitz and David Rosner, *Children, Race, and Power: Kenneth and Mamie Clark's Northside Center* (Charlottesville: University of Virginia Press, 1996).

78. Clark and Clark, "Segregation as a Factor," 161.

79. Clark and Clark, "Emotional Factors in Racial Identification," 348–350.

80. Clark and Clark, "Segregation as a Factor," 163.

81. Ralph Matthews Jr., "Bias That Belies God's Teachings, the Black Doll Is Bad, the White Doll Good," *Baltimore Afro-American*, December 22, 1951, 22.

CHAPTER 3 — "GOSH, IT'S EXCITING TO BE AN AMERICAN"

1. Anne Parrish, "Writing for Children," *Horn Book Magazine* 27 (1951): 85. The quotation used as the title for this chapter is from "Gosh, It's Exciting to Be an American," ad for the first Landmark book, *Chicago Sunday Tribune*, Book Review, November 12, 1950, pt. 4, p. 11.

2. Florrie Binford Kichler, quoted in Nancy Pate, "Return of a Classic Series: Biographies for Kids," *Orlando Sentinel*, October 12, 2003, F1.

3. Katherine B. Shippen, "The Landmark Books," *Horn Book Magazine* 27 (March–April 1951): 95–99. Among the books she wrote for the series are *Andrew Carnegie and the Age of Steel* (New York: Random House, 1958) and *Mr. Bell Invents the Telephone* (New York: Random House, 1952).

4. Shippen, "Landmark Books," 99.

5. See Library Thing, "Childhood of Famous Americans," https://www.librarything .com/series/Childhood+of+Famous+Americans; Gary Schmidt, *Making Americans: Children's Literature from 1930 to 1960* (Iowa City: University of Iowa Press, 2013), 98; Jack O'Bar, "The Origins and History of the Bobbs-Merrill Company" (occasional paper 172, University of Illinois at Urbana-Champaign, Graduate School of Library and Information Science, December 1985), 9.

6. Douglass Adair, "Parson Weems, Streamlined," *New York Times*, November 16, 1952, BR A4, 42. Schmidt, *Making Americans*, 98, confirms these numbers, saying that the Orange series included over 200 titles.

7. Library Thing, "Series: Landmark," https://www.librarything.com/series/Landmark +Books.

8. Nancy Pate, "Return of a Classic Series: Biographies for Kids," *Orlando Sentinel*, October 12, 2003; Shippen, "Landmark Books," 95–96.

9. Marie T. Wright, "Augusta Stevenson and the Bobbs-Merrill Childhood of Famous Americans Biographies," *Indiana Libraries* 12 (1993): 11, http://journals.iupui.edu/index .php/IndianaLibraries/article/view/16712.

10. "Childhoods of Four Famous Americans," *Chicago Daily Tribune*, November 13, 1949, L17.

11. Random House, "Random House. Records, 1925–1992, 702 linear feet (ca. 938,000 items in 1,681 boxes)," Ms Coll\Random House, Columbia University Library, Rare Books and Manuscripts Collection, Finding Aid, https://clio.columbia.edu/catalog/407 9581?counter=2, Hereafter referred to as the Random House Papers.

12. Nancy Wilson Ross, *Heroines of the Early West* (New York: Random House, 1960), 6. Wilson Ross first published a version of this Landmark book aimed at an adult audience in 1944 under the Alfred A. Knopf imprint: Nancy Wilson Ross, *Westward the Women* (New York: Alfred A. Knopf, 1944). Douglass Adair, a contemporary reviewer of the Landmark and other series, maintained that the Landmark books showed "a greater concern for historical accuracy" than earlier series, including the Orange books. See Douglass Adair, "Parson Weems, Streamlined," *New York Times*, November 16, 1952, BR A4, 42.

13. See, for example, Armstrong Sperry, *The Voyages of Christopher Columbus* (New York: Random House, 1950); James Daugherty, *Trappers and Traders of the Far West: The Landing of the Pilgrims* (New York: Random House, 1950). Augusta Stevenson wrote sixteen Orange books and, according to her Wikipedia page, over four hundred children's books. See https://en.wikipedia.org/wiki/Augusta_Stevenson.

14. In a note to senior editor Bob Bernstein, a reviewer of a proposed Landmark book didn't recommend it for publication precisely because "the writing is dull and the reading is heavy going. Both stories are told in a kind of vacuum without any reference—historical or other—that would make it come alive to a child reader. They both give a rather accurate but dry chronological account [but] are not sufficiently relived by an imaginative presentation of the subjects." Letter to Robert Bernstein from Fabio Coen, Subject: Cassell & Co., February 18, 1963, Random House Papers.

15. Two significant exceptions are Schmidt, *Making Americans*, which has a chapter on the Bobbs-Merrill series, and Julia Mickenberg, *Learning from the Left: Children's Literature, the Cold War, and Radical Politics in the United States* (New York: Oxford University Press, 2006). David Spear has also authored a short but informative piece on Landmark: "Generation Past: The Story of the Landmark Books, *Perspectives on History*, October 2016, https://www.historians.org/publications-and-directories /perspectives-on-history/october-2016/generation-past-the-story-of-the-landmark -books.

16. For background on Bobbs-Merrill, the publisher of the Orange books, I rely primarily on Jack O'Bar, "Origins and History," 35, https://catalog.hathitrust.org/Record /000475793.

17. O'Bar, "Origins and History," 1–4, 9.

18. Charity Dye, ed., *Once Upon a Time in Indiana* (Indianapolis: The Bobbs-Merrill Company, 1916).

19. O'Bar, "Origins and History," 7, 27.

20. O'Bar, "Origins and History," 10.

21. O'Bar, "Origins and History," 26–27.

22. "Series: Childhood of Famous Americans," *Library Thing*, https://www.library thing.com/series/Childhood+of+Famous+Americans.

23. George Crane, "Glorifying Our Pioneers," *Spartanburg Herald*, January 3, 1963, 6.

24. Other presses were also focusing, less successfully, on the children's history market, including Signature Books and American Heritage.

25. Adair, "Parson Weems, Streamlined," BR A4.

26. Mannon quoted in O'Bar, "Origins and History," 28.

27. Adair, "Parson Weems, Streamlined," BR A4.

28. See the Random House Papers and specifically the files on Landmark books. Also see the oral history and papers of Bennett Cerf, the editor of Random House: "Notable New Yorkers, Bennett Cerf," Oral History Research Office, Columbia University, http:// www.columbia.edu/cu/lweb/digital/collections/nny/cerfb/transcripts/cerfb_1_4_195 .html.

29. See "Notable New Yorkers, Bennett Cerf," 195.

30. See: Random House Papers, Columbia University Rare Books & Manuscripts Library.

31. It is difficult to convey the breadth of the material available in this collection of nearly 1700 boxes.

32. John Chamberlain, "Books of the Times," *New York Times,* January 25, 1934, 17. See "Notable New Yorkers, Bennett Cerf," 265–268. Cerf's oral history describes the role—intrigue—he and Random House played in challenging the obscenity laws and restrictions that had caused Joyce's work to be banned in the United States.

33. "Notable New Yorkers, Bennett Cerf," 453–455. David Spear also notes this in "Generation Past."

34. Some sources say that the series continued until 1970, but it is clear that the vast majority of the books were published in the period 1953–1963. Following that, reprints with new covers appeared and a few original works, including a 1968 volume called "Landmarks of American History" written by Daniel Boorstin were published. The following year Boorstin would publish an edited collection, *The Decline of Radicalism,* with an essay, "The New Barbarians," that was a clear attack on the New Left and New Left historians, arguing that they were destroying the country. See Boorstin, *The Decline of Radicalism: Reflections on America Today* (New York: Vintage, 1969), which includes the essay titled "The New Barbarians: The Decline of Radicalism."

35. Dorothy Canfield Fisher, *Paul Revere and the Minutemen* (New York: Random House, 1950); Fisher, *Our Independence and the Constitution* (New York: Random House, 1950). See also the listing and summaries of her books on Amazon. They include *The Home-Maker, Understood Betsy, The Bent Wig, The Brimming Cup, Seasoned Timber, The Bedquilt, A Montessori Mother, Mother and Child,* and others. With the exception of *Seasoned Timber,* all were novels built around a young woman protagonist overcoming the biases and strictures of her family and community. See also Elizabeth Wright, "Home Economics: Children, Consumption, and Montessori Education in Dorothy Canfield Fisher's 'Understood Betsy,'" *Children's Literature Association Quarterly* 32 (Fall 2007): 213–230 for a fuller account of her influence.

36. "Notable New Yorkers, Bennett Cerf," 456.

37. See Lawrence Van Gelder, "John Mason Brown, Critic, Is Dead," *New York Times,* March 17, 1969, 39.

38. "Notable New Yorkers, Bennett Cerf," 457.

39. Library Thing, "Series: Landmark," https://www.librarything.com/series/Landmark+Books.

40. In 1944 Bobbs-Merrill published Augusta Stevenson's *George Carver: Boy Scientist,* and in 1953 Landmark published Anne Terry White's *George Washington Carver: The Story of a Great American.*

41. These activities would later become the focus of historical stories about childhood during World War II (the Molly series) produced by the American Girl Company.

42. In Frank Capra's "Why We Fight" series, World War II is depicted as a battle between the "slave world" of fascism and the "free world." See https://www.youtube.com/watch?v=Mm3GsSWKyso. See also John Dower, *War without Mercy: Race and Power in the Pacific War* (New York: Pantheon, 1986), which provides graphic descriptions of the uses of racist propaganda as a motivation for both troops and those on the home front.

43. William Chafe, "America since 1945," in *New American History,* ed. Eric Foner (Philadelphia: Temple University Press, 1990), 145–146.

44. Alice Kessler-Harris, "Social History," in Foner, *New American History,* 163–184. Kessler-Harris argues that the dominant mode of analysis in the years before the war was that history was the "unfolding [of] an ongoing struggle between 'special interests' and

'the people.'" But in the 1940s and 1950s the "consensus" historians held that the country had a "shared set of values that overrode ethnic and class distinctions" (165).

45. Austin McCormick to John D. Rockefeller III, "Statement of New York State Committee on the Youth Correction Authority Plan," March 10, 1944, quoted in Gerald Markowitz and David Rosner, *Children, Race, and Power: Kenneth and Mamie Clark's Northside Center* (Charlottesville: University of Virginia Press, 1996), 7.

46. Bert Kemmerer, "FBI Director Believes Patriotic Appeal Is the Most Effective Now," *Washington Post*, August 22, 1943, B5.

47. A. H. Lass, "Bad Boy: A Portrait and a Prescription," *New York Times*, January 27, 1946, SM7.

48. "U.S. Calls Parley on Juvenile Crime," *New York Times*, July 20, 1946, 15.

49. Richard Hofstadter as quoted in Peter Novick, *That Noble Dream: The "Objectivity Question" and the American Historical Profession* (New York: Cambridge University Press, 1988), 333.

50. Hofstadter's scholarship certainly had a radical tinge. Many of his important works were published by Vintage, first a division of Alfred Knopf, then purchased by Random House in 1960. See such works as *Social Darwinism in American Thought* (Philadelphia: University of Pennsylvania Press, 1944), *The Paranoid Style in American Politics* (New York: Vintage, 1964), and *Anti-intellectualism in American Life* (New York: Vintage, 1962), as examples. Some of these are noted in Susan Baker, *Radical Beginnings: Richard Hofstadter and the 1930s* (Westport, CT: Greenwood, 1985).

51. Novick, a colleague at Chicago, writes about Boorstin's role as a particularly rabid anticommunist. See *That Noble Dream*, 328, 332–333. The efforts to purge academia of leftists and "communist sympathizers" had begun right before the war. The Rapp-Coudert hearings, efforts by New York State to purge the public university system, specifically City College, led to the firing of some noted faculty members and ended the possible recruitment of Bertrand Russell to join its faculty. See Ellen Schrecker, *No Ivory Tower: McCarthyism and the Universities* (New York: Oxford University Press, 1986).

52. Richard Slotkin, *Gunfighter Nation: The Myth of the Frontier in Twentieth-Century America* (Norman: University of Oklahoma Press, 1998), 347.

53. Tom Engelhardt, *The End of Victory Culture: Cold War America and the Disillusioning of a Generation* (New York: Basic Books, 1995), 4–5.

54. Engelhardt, *End of Victory Culture*, 5. See also Mickenberg, *Learning from the Left*, 233. Mickenberg points out that by the late 1940s the study of American history had become a requirement for most high school students. She explains that the narrative generated in textbooks about America's history bolstered the Cold War notion of exceptionalism and white supremacy: "In most cases that study was explicitly intended to further current national imperatives and to naturalize the existing social order."

55. Richard Drinnon, *Facing West—The Metaphysics of Indian-Hating and Empire-Building* (New York: Schocken Books, 1900), 42–43, noted in Engelhardt, *End of Victory Culture*, 16–18.

56. Engelhardt, *End of Victory Culture*, 17.

57. Ruth Miller Elson, *Guardians of Tradition: American Schoolbooks of the Nineteenth Century* (Lincoln: University of Nebraska Press, 1964), 73–74 quoted in Engelhardt, *End of Victory Culture*, 17.

58. Shirley Jackson, *The Witchcraft of Salem Village* (New York: Random House, 1956), 4.

59. Samuel Adams Hopkins, *The Pony Express* (New York: Random House, 1950), 5. This section brings to mind the lyrics to an opening number of *Annie Get Your Gun*, which premiered in 1946.

60. Wilson Ross, *Heroines*, 14.

61. Wilson Ross, *Heroines*, chap. 3, 52–92, titled "First White Woman Across the Rockies."

62. Wilson Ross, *Heroines*, 67. The Indians are generally presented as ignorant, badly mannered, or hostile. Even when depicted as friendly, their manners rarely meet Narcissa's standards: Marcus talks about how he had to maintain the "biblical rules of 'turning the other cheek,'" as if toward a stubborn child, when an Indian "'took hold of my ear and pulled it and struck me on the breast ordering me to hear'" (77).

63. Wilson Ross, *Heroines*, 66–67.

64. Wilson Ross, *Heroines*, 52.

65. Wilson Ross, *Heroines*, 86–88.

66. Wilson Ross, *Heroines*, 91. Bobbs-Merrill had produced an Orange book story about Narcissa Whitman seven years earlier, in 1953: Ann Spence Warner, *Narcissa Whitman: Pioneer Girl* (Indianapolis: Bobbs-Merrill, 1953).

67. Warner, *Narcissa Whitman*, 33–34.

68. Wilson Ross, *Heroines*, 14.

69. Wilson Ross, *Heroines*, 13.

70. Wilson Ross, *Heroines*, 13.

71. Wilson Ross, *Heroines*, 50.

72. See Library Thing, "Series: Childhood of Famous Americans," https://www.librarything.com/series/Childhood+of+Famous+Americans.

73. Library Thing, "Series: Landmark," https://www.librarything.com/series/Landmark+Books. See also Gary Mitchell and Dan Hubbard, *A Collector's Guide and Checklist to American Landmark Books* (privately printed, 2019), n.p.; Exodus Books, "American Landmark Series," http://www.exodusbooks.com/american-landmark-books/5210/?print=true. The series began to fade in popularity by the late 1950s, but not until 1963 did Random House halt production of any Landmark books and then only those that sold fewer than 3,000 copies a year. See letter to Bob Bernstein from Walter Retan, Subject: Landmarks, March 28, 1963, Random House Papers: "As I mentioned some time ago, I think we should not try to keep all of our Landmarks in print. . . . I have had a list made of all Landmark titles selling under 3,000 copies either last year or so far this year. . . . I've indicated the titles which I think . . . are coming almost entirely from schools and libraries. . . . Several of these are not competing—and ineffectually—with more recent books on the same subjects. Others really never should have been put in the series."

74. Wilson Ross, *Heroines*, 9.

75. Wilson Ross, *Heroines*, 9, 17, 19, 83.

76. Sterling North, *Abe Lincoln: Log Cabin to White House* (New York: Random House, 1956), 30-31.

77. Quentin Reynolds, *Custer's Last Stand* (New York: Random House, 1964), 8.

78. Wilson Ross, *Heroines*, 9, 17, 19.

79. Jean Brown Wagoner, *Martha Washington: Girl of Old Virginia* (Indianapolis: Bobbs-Merrill, 1947), 46.

80. Letter from Dorothy Johnson to Robert Loomis, October 30, 1965, Random House Papers.

81. *Mother Takes a Holiday*, Whirlpool, 1950, https://www.youtube.com/watch?v=6ig WGAdFwow.

82. "Mother Takes a Holiday."

83. Wagoner, *Martha Washington*, 15.

84. Wagoner, *Martha Washington*, 113.

85. Wagoner, *Martha Washington*, 139.

86. Wagoner, *Martha Washington*, 139.

87. Wagoner, *Martha Washington*, 17. "Mammy Tuck was a big, fat, comfortable-looking colored woman. She had lived with Mother for a long time. Now she was Mother's cook and ordered all the other servants around." Three times on page 17 the slaves are referred to as servants.

88. Wagoner, *Martha Washington*, 80.

89. Anne Terry White, *George Washington Carver: The Story of a Great American* (New York: Random House, 1953).

90. Augusta Stevenson, *George Carver, Boy Scientist*, 59.

91. Stevenson, *George Carver*, 48.

92. Jonathan Zimmerman, "*Brown*-ing the American Textbook: History, Psychology, and the Origins of Modern Multiculturalism," *History of Education Quarterly* 44 (Spring 2004): 46–69.

93. Marcia Winn, "Bed Time Stories Are a Help," *Washington Post and Times Herald*, September 13, 1956, 55.

94. Zimmerman, "*Brown*-ing the American Textbook," 50, 56–57.

95. Zimmerman, "*Brown*-ing the American Textbook," 55. Textbooks today continue to reflect local political, arguably racist, leanings. See Dana Goldstein, "Two States. Eight Textbooks. Two American Stories. American History Textbooks in Different States Diverge in Ways That Reflect the Nation's Deepest Partisan Divides," *New York Times*, January 12, 2020. Goldstein notes, for example, that while two textbooks teach about the Harlem Renaissance, a textbook in Texas points out that some critics "dismissed the quality of literature produced."

96. Zimmerman, "*Brown*-ing the American Textbook," 55.

97. "Negro Protest Wins at Queens College, Morrison [*sic*] and Commager History Text Dropped," *New York Herald Tribune*, February 14, 1951, 4.

98. Quoted in Cheryl Greenberg, "Civil Rights, Free Speech, and Libel," in *Minority Relations: Intergroup Conflict and Cooperation*, ed. Greg Robinson and Robert Chang (Jackson: University Press of Mississippi, 2016), 72.

99. Elizabeth Myers, *Frederick Douglass* (Indianapolis: Bobbs-Merrill, 1970); Gertrude Hecker Winders, *Harriet Tubman: Freedom Girl* (Indianapolis: Bobbs-Merrill, 1969).

100. Dharathula H. Millender, *Crispus Attucks: Boy of Valor* (Indianapolis: Bobbs-Merrill, 1965). Schmidt argues that the publication of these books was an achievement, even if a limited one: "These are books that do consciously want to show the problematic effects of prejudice, even while they are themselves not always able to emerge out of a cultural consciousness stained by that prejudice." See Schmidt, *Making Americans*, 99, 103–104, 109–111, 118–119.

101. Mark McGuire, "Television in the 1950s Deepened Racial Divides," *Chicago Tribune*, December 28, 2005, http://articles.chicagotribune.com/2005-12-28/features/0512270255_1 _television-black-children-americans.

102. Alan Nadel, *Television in Black-and-White America: Race and National Identity* (Lawrence: University of Kansas Press, 2005), 15–42; Mel Watkins, "What Was It about Amos N Andy?," *New York Times*, July 7, 1991.

103. Wilson Ross, *Heroines*, 47.

104. Robert D. Sutherland, "Hidden Persuaders: Political Ideologies in Literature for Children," *Children's Literature in Education* 3 (1985): 151, 155.

105. The only representation of urban or working-class people, and not Black working-class people, came in sitcoms like *I Love Lucy*, *The Goldbergs*, and *The Honeymooners*. These families were often dysfunctional or decidedly flawed, unlike the sitcoms about middle-class white families. Ralph and Alice, the characters in *The Honeymooners*, lived in a depressing walk-up tenement where their neighbor (who worked in the city's sewers) Norton sometimes entered their drab appliance-less kitchen from a fire escape window that overlooked a bleak gray image of the city. Ralph, a discontented bus driver, planned outrageous schemes to advance in life, while Alice, his very sulky housewife, saw through every one of them. Lucy was zany and kept in tow by a stable Desi, who, while Cuban and an entertainer, a fairly unusual occupation for a 1950s husband, almost always wore a suit and tie.

106. Chafe, "America since 1945," 145–146.

107. This point is examined in Sherrie A. Inness, *The Lesbian Menace: Ideology, Identity, and the Representation of Lesbian Life* (Amherst: University of Massachusetts Press, 1997), 108. See also Mickenberg, *Learning from the Left*, 14–17.

108. Mickenberg, *Learning from the Left*, 125. Mickenberg writes that while the left-leaning authors of children's books were often monitored by the FBI and cited in HUAC hearings, the books themselves "are usually mentioned only incidentally in authors' FBI files, if at all." See Mickenberg, *Learning from the Left*, 139.

109. Augusta Stevenson, "Biographical Notes for Bob-Merrill Questionnaire," quoted in Marie T. Wright, "Augusta Stevenson and the Bobbs-Merrill Childhood of Famous Americans Biographies," *Indiana Libraries* 12 (1993): 21, http://journals.iupui.edu/index .php/IndianaLibraries/article/view/16712.

110. Mickenberg, *Learning from the Left*, 13.

111. See the Random House Papers, in which these questions appear to dominate discussions between the editors at Random House and other presses during the early 1950s. See also Mickenberg, *Learning from the Left*, 13.

112. Richard Hofstadter, "Abraham Lincoln and the Self Made Myth," quoted in Mickenberg, *Learning from the Left*, 243. Hofstadter's most famous student, Eric Foner, wrote his classic book, *Free Soil, Free Labor, Free Men*, as a dissertation under Hofstadter. A strong defender of Hofstadter as a mentor and intellectual, Foner in that and subsequent books traces the importance of slavery as an issue in both the origins of the Civil War and Lincoln's thought. Simply put, that Lincoln's thinking evolved over time does not mean that slavery was not central.

113. Anne Terry White, *George Washington Carver: The Story of a Great American* (New York: Random House, 1953). Some other authors also took chances. In 1948, Arna Bontemps, an African American author, wrote *The Story of the Negro* for Alfred Knopf (and reproduced by Random House decades later), which dealt with the long history of

racism and slavery in the United States. In fact, it was awarded the Newbery Prize in 1949. See Association for Library Service to Children, "Newbery Medal and Honor Books, 1922–Present," http://www.ala.org/alsc/awardsgrants/bookmedia/newberymedal/newbery honors/newberymedal.

114. White, *George Washington Carver*, 163. Schmidt sees this perseverance, a quality in the Orange book about Carver, as a concession to a dominant American narrative during the period—one that avoided confrontation in favor of accommodation. See Schmidt, *Making Americans*, 116–118.

115. Henry Castor, *Teddy Roosevelt and the Rough Riders* (New York: Random House, 1954), 32–35.

116. Castor, *Teddy Roosevelt and the Rough Riders*, 34–35.

117. Wilson Ross, *Heroines*, 4.

118. Shippen, *Andrew Carnegie and the Age of Steel*, 142–143.

119. MacKinlay Kantor, *Gettysburg*, (New York: Random House, 1952), 167.

120. Kantor, *Gettysburg*, 184–185.

121. North, *Abe Lincoln*, 115.

122. North, *Abe Lincoln*, 145.

123. North, *Abe Lincoln*, 148.

124. Hodding Carter, *Robert E. Lee and the Road of Honor* (New York: Random House, 1955), introductory epigraph, n.p.

125. MacKinlay Kantor, *Lee and Grant at Appomattox* (New York: Random House, 1950), xi–xii.

126. White, *George Washington Carver*, 8–11.

127. Random House published a series of Gunther's books on different countries, including *Inside Russia Today, Inside Asia*, and *Inside U.S.A.*

128. These notices in the national press were tracked by Theodore Waller of the American Book Publishers Council: "Memorandum for Conversation with Mr. Black," October 5, 1951, Random House Papers. See also the files of Bennett Cerf at Columbia University Rare Books and Manuscript Collection: Memo to File, "Part 1. Recent Incidents in the Book World Relating to Political Censorship," in Random House Collection, box 15, "Anti-Censorship Committee," 1–6.

129. William Fulton, "Book Company Editor; Branded Red, Quits Job," *Chicago Daily Tribune*, September 18, 1951, 4.

130. This review of attacks on the presses and liberal and left authors is drawn from a memo in the files of Bennett Cerf, Memo to File, "Part 1," 5–6.

131. The statement of principle was itself pretty benign, touting the moral and civic responsibility "to disseminate books which provide information on all sides of controversial issues" and that a "publishers' list of books" should represent the "greatest possible variety of views." Attached to Waller to Klopfer, October 11, 1951, in Random House Collection, box 15, "Anti-Censorship Committee."

132. Theodore Waller, American Book Publishers Council, Inc., "Memorandum for Conversation with Mr. Black," October 5, 1951, in Random House Collection, box 15, "Anti-Censorship Committee."

133. Waller, "Memorandum for Conversation."

134. U.S. Congress, House, Committee on Un-American Activities (HUAC), "100 Things You Should Know about Communism and Education" (Washington, DC, 1948), https://catalog.hathitrust.org/Record/008525217/.

135. HUAC, "100 Things You Should Know," 14.

136. "Notable New Yorkers, Bennett Cerf," 418–419.

137. Quentin Reynolds, *The F.B.I.*, foreword by J. Edgar Hoover (New York: Random House, 1954), 94.

138. Reynolds, *The F.B.I.*, 14.

139. Reynolds, *The F.B.I.*, 91.

140. Reynolds, *The F.B.I.*, ix.

141. Editorial correspondence, Lapolla to Rosenau, 1956, Random House Papers, box 418.

142. Don Whitehead, *The FBI Story: A Report to the People*, foreword by J. Edgar Hoover (New York: Random House, 1956). In fact, the latest reissue came in 2011 from ISHI Press.

143. "How U.S. Jews Unite to Fight Reds," *Chicago Tribune*, November 8, 1949, 10, https://chicagotribune.newspapers.com/image/370385982/?terms=jews%2Bunite%2Bto%2Bfight%2Breds.

144. Editorial correspondence, Paul Lapolla—1954–1965, January 14, 1957, Random House Papers, box 418.

145. Letter from J. Edgar Hoover to Paul Lapolla, July 11, 1957, Random House Papers.

146. Boorstin, *Decline of Radicalism*, 157.

147. Shippen, "Landmark Books," 96.

CHAPTER 4 — FAMILY FUN FOR EVERYONE?

1. "Time Travel: Freedomland," Peteresen Productions, (1963), https://www.youtube.com/watch?v=vpWcFZ-_LqU&feature=emb_logo.

2. Jerry Hulse, "Bronx Cheers (New!) Freedomland," *Los Angeles Times*, August 12, 1962, L9.

3. "Animated History in East Bronx's Freedomland Is Revealed in a Preview," *New York Times*, April 29, 1960, 64.

4. Dorothy Phillips, "Freedomland, the U.S.A. of Fun," *Long Island Star Journal*, June 16, 1960, 23.

5. Based on email correspondence with Michael R. Virgintino on August 12, 2020, author of *Freedomland U.S.A.: The Definitive History* (New York: Theme Park Press, 2018).

6. "Gotham Playland Being Built," *Times Record* (Troy, NY), October 2, 1969, 3. This article mentions the existence of three other parks, including Fiestaland in San Antonio, Gold Rush in Sacramento, and Discoveryland in Miami. A Great Southwest project was supposedly under construction in 1959 in Dallas, but I found scant evidence that it was ever built.

7. Robert McLaughlin, *Magic Mountain*, Images of Modern America Series (Mount Pleasant, SC: Arcadia, 2016); Robert McLaughlin, *Pleasure Island: 1959–1969*, Images of Modern America Series (Mount Pleasant, SC: Arcadia, 2014); "Friends of Pleasure Island Website," http://friendsofpleasureisland.org.

8. Robert McLaughlin and Frank R. Adamo, *Freedomland 1960–1964*, Images of Modern America Series (Mount Pleasant, SC: Arcadia, 2010), 7–8.

9. See William Zeckendorf, *Zeckendorf: An Autobiography of the Man Who Played a Real-Life Game of Monopoly and Won the Largest Real Estate Empire in History* (Chicago: Plaza Press, 2014), 15–16. Interestingly, Zeckendorf begins his autobiography by locating his family on the frontier (rather than beginning his story in New York, where

he became famous, or in Germany, where his family immigrated from). "We New York Zeckendorfs are actually misplaced Westerners. My grandfather, a frontier merchant, lived, traded, and sometimes [was spotted] with the Indians in Arizona territory. Second door wagon trains carried the mail and delivered supplies to the many mining camps ringing Tucson." He goes on to emphasize this American background: "Grandfather had become a deep-dyed frontiersman—he had even scalped an Indian caught rustling cattle. . . . In the war against Geronimo's Apaches, Grandfather served as aid-de-camp to General Nelson Miles. In 1886, after Geronimo's surrender, he was Tucson's parade marshal for a gala honoring the general. I still cherish an old photograph of him, a big, broad-shouldered man, once again in uniform for this occasion."

10. Zeckendorf, *Zeckendorf*, 291–292.

11. Zeckendorf, *Zeckendorf*, 291–292.

12. "Freedomland Fête to Benefit Local Children's Village," *Dobbs Ferry New York Sentinel*, June 17, 1960, 4.

13. Morris Gilbert, "Freedomland in the Bronx: Biggest Disneyland-Type Playground of Them All," *New York Times*, June 12, 1960, 139.

14. Eric Foner, *The Story of American Freedom* (New York: Norton, 1998), 260.

15. Foner, *Story of American Freedom*, 252.

16. Tom Engelhardt, *The End of Victory Culture: Cold War America and the Disillusioning of a Generation* (New York: Basic Books, 1995), 72.

17. William Fulton, "Freedomland, New York Fun Center, Attracts All Ages: No Longer Strictly for the Children," *Chicago Daily Tribune*, June 10, 1962, F7.

18. "Freedom Land Jam Is Eased on 2nd Day," *New York Times*, June 21, 1960, 20.

19. "Freedom Land Jam Is Eased on 2nd Day," 20.

20. David Lyle, "New Freedomland Park Is Dedicated in the Bronx," *New York Herald Tribune*, June 19, 1960, 30.

21. Murray J. Brown, "Tour of U.S. on Foot Easy at Freedomland in Bronx," *Schenectady Gazette*, July 10, 1963, n.p.

22. "Shunpike to Freedomland: An Exciting Journey Back 200 Years in History Erickson," *Boston Globe*, July 10, 1960, 58; "Freedomland—The Biggest Combination of Really Big Shows Ever," *New York Times*, June 19, 1960, ADA13.

23. Thomas Buckley, "25,000 See Freedomland Dedicated in the Bronx: Preview Heralds New Bronx Park," *New York Times*, June 19, 1960, 1.

24. David Lyle, "New Freedomland Park Is Dedicated in the Bronx," *New York Herald Tribune*, June 19, 1960, 30.

25. Text of Speech—Dedication Ceremony of Freedomland, June 18, 1960, Robert F. Wagner Documents Collection, Speeches Series, box 060087w, folder 8, LaGuardia and Wagner Archives, Queens, NY.

26. Text of Speech—Dedication Ceremony of Freedomland.

27. In 2018 Michael R. Virgintino published *Freedomland U.S.A.: The Definitive History*, which includes many of the details about Freedomland that are integrated into this chapter. These details, which paint a clear picture of the park, are not accessible through archival documents alone. The book does not offer citations but includes many photographs, interviews, and almost encyclopedic lists of attractions, souvenirs, and details about the park. I am indebted to Virgintino for this research and refer to his book repeatedly throughout the chapter. Virgintino, *Freedomland U.S.A.: The Definitive History* (New York: Theme Park Press, 2018).

28. "Opening Letter from Mayor Wagner" (Freedomland brochure, Federal Concessions, Inc., Western Printing and Lithographing Co., 1962).

29. "Opening Letter from Joseph Periconi" (Freedomland brochure, Federal Concessions, Inc., Western Printing and Lithographing Co., 1962).

30. "15,000 Kids Will Enjoy Freedom Days," *New York Amsterdam News*, August 12, 1961, 4.

31. Robert McLaughlin, *Freedomland: 1960–1964*, Images of Modern America Series (Charleston, SC: Arcadia, 2015).

32. Robert F. Huber, "Freedomland Is a Blend of History and Pleasure," *Washington Post*, August 19, 1962, B15.

33. "Attorney-Showman Heads Freedomland," *New York Times*, June 19, 1960, 17.

34. "Freedomland Offers Mother an Exciting Vacation Tour," *Schenectady Gazette*, May 10, 1962, 81.

35. "Freedomland Spotlights Free Enterprise Role: Shows Industry Contributions to Nation's Progress," *New York Times*, June 19, 1960, ADA15.

36. M. Christine Boyer, "Cities for Sale: Merchandising at South Street Seaport," in *Variations on a Theme Park: The New American City and the End of Public Space*, ed. Michael Sorkin (New York: HarperCollins, 1992), 204.

37. World's Fair fan website, http://nywf64.com/rheingo1.shtml.

38. "61,500 Jam Freedomland," *Tarrytown New York Daily News*, June 20, 1960, 1.

39. *Mary Poppins* the movie would be released in 1964 and would also have a frivolous and distracted mother comically portraying a suffragette in England.

40. "Freedomland Spotlights Free Enterprise Role: Shows Industry Contributions to Nation's Progress," *New York Times*, June 19, 1960, ADA15.

41. Virgintino, *Freedomland U.S.A.*, 173–179.

42. McLaughlin and Adamo, *Freedomland 1960–1964*, 81.

43. Farnsworth Fowle, "Big Exhibit Park Planned in Bronx," *New York Times*, May 26, 1959, 71.

44. Amy Tyson, *Wages of History: Emotional Labor on Public History's Front Lines* (Amherst: University of Massachusetts Press, 2013), 146.

45. Old Sturbridge Village, "Mission-Narrative," https://www.osv.org/about/mission -narrative/.

46. Old Sturbridge Village, "Historical Buildings, Landscapes, and Gardens," https:// www.osv.org/explore-the-village/historical-buildings-landscapes-and-gardens/.

47. "Prepared Testimony of William B. Reid Director of Development and Membership of Old Sturbridge Village Before the House Appropriations Committee Subcommittee on Labor, Health, and Human Services and Education," Federal News Service, March 21, 2000.

48. "Brick Ovens, Antique Books: Cooking at Sturbridge," *Christian Science Monitor*, January 29, 1981.

49. Lizabeth Cohen and Bruce M. Stave, "Conversation with Lizabeth Cohen: Urban History and the Consumers' Republic," *Journal of Urban History* 30, no. 2 (January 2004): 231–256, doi:10.1177/0096144203258351.

50. Andrew Baker and Warren Leon, "Old Sturbridge Village Introduces Social Conflict into Its Interpretive Story," *History News* 41, no. 2 (1986): 7–11, http://www.jstor.org /stable/42655875.

51. "Immediate Evening Positions Avil. in Our Snack Stands & Restaurants at Freedomland. Applicants Must Be 18 Years of Age and Be Able to Work until 1 A.M.," classified ad, *New York Post*, July 26, 1961.

52. "Animated History in East Bronx's Freedomland Is Revealed in a Preview," *New York Times*, April 29, 1960, 64.

53. Interview with David Rosner, whose brother, David Podell, was among the first teenagers to be hired at Freedomland.

54. This is not to say that modern museums have escaped the pressure to use history and to shape its meaning to a specific narrative. Today, and in the recent past, for example, the Smithsonian has faced enormous pressures from the public and politicians alike. See Scott Boehm, "Privatizing Public Memory: The Price of Patriotic Philanthropy and the Post-9/11 Politics of Display," *American Quarterly* 58 (December 2006): 1147–1166. Boehm notes that the Smithsonian exhibit "The Price of Freedom," about America's military history, "illustrates how the privatization of public space privileges triumphalist interpretive frameworks when militantly patriotic donors demand a say in how their money is spent." In his analysis, "national history museums function as cultural technologies that legitimize state violence when they promote visions of history that reinforce the patriotic mythologies of manifest destiny and historical exceptionalism." He attributes this choice of interpretation to the museum's dependence on more and more private funding: "The casual privatization of the Smithsonian," he warns, "illustrates how private capital can help to preclude productive civic debate" (1150). Also, the struggle over a show about the depiction of the *Enola Gay*, the plane used to bomb Hiroshima during World War II, almost led to the defunding of the Smithsonian in the mid-1990s. See Philip Nobile, ed., *Judgement at the Smithsonian: The Bombing of Hiroshima and Nagasaki* (New York: Marlowe, 1995).

55. Virgintino, *Freedomland U.S.A.*, 101.

56. Virgintino has a section called "Freedomland's Character Actors," 123–140.

57. The home page for Old Sturbridge Village states, "Supporting the Village helps history come alive for more than 250,000 students, families, tourists, and scholars every year" (https://www.osv.org/). The Colonial Williamsburg website states that students can "journey into the past." See http://www.history.org/history/teaching/grouptours /schoolandyouth/index.cfm.

58. "Palisades Amusement Park Restored Vintage Poster Reproduction" (1998),

59. "Across the Street from Disneyland," in *This American Life* (WBEZ), https://www .thisamericanlife.org/radio-archives/episode/259/promised-land?act=1.

60. Morris Gilbert, "Freedomland in the Bronx: Biggest Disneyland-Type Playground of Them All," *New York Times*, June 12, 1960, 139.

61. "Today the Gates to the World's Largest Showplace Swing Open!," *New York Times*, June 19, 1960, ADA3.

62. Dorothy Phillips, "Freedomland the U.S.A. of Fun," *Greenpoint Daily Star*, June 17, 1960, n.p.

63. "Freedomland U.S.A.," in *The Bowery Boys* (podcast, February 27, 2009), http:// www.Boweryboyshistory.Com/2009/02/Podcast-Freedomland-Usa.Html. Still today some adults recall experiencing something real about the past. "The one [memory] that does stand out was the vivid realism of The Chicago Fire. That's the thing about Freedom land [*sic*], you didn't just go to a theme park, you experienced periods of American

history. It was almost like going back in history courtesy of Freedomland's time machine." Jack R., "Freedomland Memories," http://freedomlandusa.net.

64. "Old Freedomland USA Amusement Park Tour, 1963," https://www.youtube.com /watch?v=SNx5fZXu-YM.

65. David Lowenthal, "The Past as a Theme Park," in *Theme Park Landscapes: Antecedents and Variations*, ed. Erence Young and Robert Riley (Washington, DC: Dumbarton Oaks, 2002), 11–12, http://www.doaks.org/resources/publications/doaks-online-publi cations/tparks.

66. Freedomland promotional video (1963), https://www.youtube.com/watch?v=SNx5f ZXu-YM.

67. Virgintino, *Freedomland U.S.A.*, 76–77.

68. Isabel McGovern, "Old Ways and Modern at President Restaurant," *New York Herald Tribune*, June 3, 1961, 9.

69. Sydney Gruson, "Our Changing City," *New York Times*, July 11, 1955, 25.

70. "Negroes 9 Per Cent, Puerto Ricans 10.5 Per Cent of Bronx," *Amsterdam News*, April 11, 1959, 16.

71. Eric Avila, *Popular Culture in the Age of White Flight* (Berkeley: University of California Press, 2004), 2–3.

72. Ruth Feldstein, *How It Feels to Be Free: Black Women Entertainers and the Civil Rights Movement* (New York: Oxford University Press, 2013), 36.

73. Foner, *Story of American Freedom*, 276.

74. Pete Seeger, "What Did You Learn in School Today?," track 5 on *We Shall Overcome* (LP, Columbia Records, 1963).

75. Bob Dylan, "With God on Our Side," track 3 on *The Times They Are A-Changin'* (LP, Columbia Records, 1964).

76. National Lead Company Newsletter, no. 370 (June 21, 1957): 1, http://toxicdocs.org.

77. Nate Haseltine, "Scientists Plot Sputnik's Path," *Washington Post*, October 8, 1957, A3; "Navy to Launch Test Satellite in Near Future," *Daily Boston Globe*, October 9, 1957, 4; "Russia Had 'Moon' First Because of U.S. Policy, GE Official States," *Wall Street Journal*, October 9, 1957, 4.

78. Walter H. Stern, "Zeckendorf May Sell 3 Hotels to the Owners of Freedomland," *New York Times*, September 20, 1960, 78.

79. "Roman Chariot Races at Freedomland Show," *New York Herald Tribune*, June 4, 1961, D8.

80. Nan Robertson, "2d Season Starts at Freedomland: Threatening Sky Cuts into Attendance at Bronx Park," *New York Times*, June 11, 1961, 67.

81. Robert Alden, "Advertising: Freedomland Picks Cole, Fischer & Rogow," *New York Times*, May 8, 1961, 58.

82. Alden, "Advertising," 58.

83. Alden, "Advertising," 58. The new advertising firm was suspected of "running with the mob." The head of the agency, Martin Cole, was to be "convicted of trying to intimidate a federal grand jury witness" who had planned to talk to the FBI. The federal investigation was about the mob's use of the Sands Hotel in Las Vegas for laundering millions of dollars illegally gained in that city's casinos. See "Agency Spy: The List of 10 Diabolical Deeds" *Adweek*, October 19, 2008, http://www.adweek.com/agencyspy/the-list-of-10 -advertising-diabolical-deeds/2989. See also *United States v. Cole*, 329 F.2d 437, 9th Circuit, March 16, 1964, Certiorari Denied June 1, 1964, See 84 S.Ct.1630, http://www.leagle

.com/decision/19711088325FSupp763_1934/UNITED%20STATES%20v.%20COLE and https://law.resource.org/pub/us/case/reporter/F2/329/329.F2d.437.18807_1.html.

84. "Officer at Freedomland Advanced to High Post," *New York Times*, March 21, 1962, 60.

85. Jerry Hulse, "Bronx Cheers (New!) Freedomland," *Los Angeles Times*, August 12, 1962, L9.

86. Hulse, "Bronx Cheers (New!) Freedomland," L9.

87. "Roman Chariot Races at Freedomland Show," *New York Herald Tribune*, June 4, 1961, D8.

88. "Freedomland Opens for Second Year," *New York Amsterdam News*, June 17, 1961, 18.

89. "Freedomland Announces a $6-Million Opening on April 13th," *NY & Brooklyn Daily*, March 29, 1963, 9.

90. "Freedomland Announces a $6-Million Opening," 9.

91. "Accent Is on Non-stop Fun This Year at Freedomland This Summer," *Leader-Observer*, May 3, 1962, 5.

92. "Display Ad 70—No Title," *New York Herald Tribune*, Jun 4, 1961, D5.

93. "Freedomland's Budget Big One," *New Journal and Guide*, April 20, 1963, 14; illustration: "At Freedomland," *New Journal and Guide*, July 18, 1964, 21.

94. 1964 radio ad for Freedomland, https://www.youtube.com/watch?v=2binf-47txu.

95. *Jet Magazine*, "People Are Talking About" section, August 6, 1964, 42; "Ronald Wakefield in Riot Backlash," *New Journal and Guide*, August 8, 1964, C20.

96. "Freedomland Slated for an April 13th Opening," *N.Y. & Brooklyn Daily*, April 9, 1963.

97. "Freedomland Is Sued for 'Changing Character,'" *New York Times*, September 5, 1962, 43.

98. "3 Get Jail in Robbery: Leniency Refused in $28,837 Hold-Up at Freedomland," *New York Times*, August 18, 1961, 49.

99. Bernard Gavzer, "New Amusement Center Combines History, Fun," *Leader-Herald*, June 9, 1960, 1.

100. "Webb & Knapp Official to Head Freedomland," *New York Times*, August 16, 1961, 38.

101. "Webb & Knapp, Inc., Sells Its Interests in Amusement Park," *Wall Street Journal*, July 1, 1964, 11.

102. "Freedomland Aides Get Paychecks Back," *New York Times*, September 9, 1964, 45.

103. "Webb & Knapp Sales Halt Bankruptcy Suit Rumor," *Washington Post*, July 2, 1964, C11.

104. James Hibsch, "World's Fair Attendance Shows Monday Tops Crowds on Weekend," *Tarrytown NY Daily News*, n.d., W9, http://fultonhistory.com.

105. "All Around the Fair World," *Long Island-Star Journal*, May 27, 1964, 6.

106. Hibsch, "World's Fair Attendance."

107. Joseph Lelyveld, "Children at Fair Ride and Shriek: And Some Get Very Weary Sooner or Later," *New York Times*, April 26, 1964, 84.

108. Murray Schumach, "Story Hour Wins Children at Fair: Some Are Even Sidetracked from Big Exhibits," *New York Times*, August 23, 1964, 57.

109. William Fox, "Children Will Thrill to Attractions at Fair: Painless History Lessons Are Interesting," *Chicago Tribune*, April 12, 1964, G17.

110. "Atomic School Planned for Children at Fair," *New York Times*, November 22, 1963, 52.

111. Philip Benjamin, "Where's Dominic Been 9 Days? 12-Year-Old Lived at the Fair," *New York Times*, May 18, 1964, 1.

112. Interestingly, the book *From the Mixed-Up Files of Mrs. Basil E. Frankweiler*, which came out in 1967, traced themes of ennui in the suburbs and the opportunities the city could provide young children. The book in some ways mirrored the mission of the World's Fair in that it helped promote the city as a place for tourism and cultural fulfillment. However, at the World's Fair the suburbs were touted as the most promising place for future generations of (white) Americans to live.

113. Philip Benjamin, "Where's Dominic Been 9 Days? 12-Year-Old Lived at the Fair," *New York Times*, May 18, 1964, 1.

114. Leonard Buder, "Moses Rejects Plea to Cut Rate at Fair for City Students," *New York Times*, September 28, 1963, 1.

115. "The Fair and the Children," *New York Times*, October 5, 1963, 19.

116. "The Fair and the Children," 19.

117. "The Fair and the Children," 19.

118. Charles G. Bennett, "Council to Press Fair on Pupil Fee: Resolution to Seek Reduced Rate . . . ," *New York Times*, October 4, 1963, 1. Eventually Freedomland stopped charging for individual rides and instead charged a flat fee. This change, along with the addition of more performances, seems like an attempt to appeal to teens rather than children.

119. "CCS Offers Plan to Help Poor Kids Attend Fair," *New York Amsterdam News*, October 26, 1963, 8.

120. "Ccs Offers Plan to Help Poor Kids," 8.

121. "Moses Yields a Bit on Fair Admissions: Position on Fees Eased," *New York Times*, October 8, 1963, 28.

122. Charles G. Bennett, "Fair Will Admit Pupils for 25c When They Attend in Groups: 25-Cents," *New York Times*, December 4, 1963, 1.

123. Martin Tolchin, "15,000 Students Take Advantage of First Day of 25c Group Admissions," *New York Times*, May 2, 1964, 13.

124. Zeckendorf, *Zeckendorf*, 291–292.

125. "Freedomland to Become Apartmentland," *Newsday*, February 10, 1965, 5.

126. Zeckendorf, *Zeckendorf*, 291–292.

127. Freedomland was not the only property or investment that Zeckendorf lost money on by the 1960s. The *New York Times* reported that his hotels "lost $6 million in 1962 and 1963." On December 17, 2016, the Facebook page for fans of the amusement park posted a different explanation (or some might say conspiracy theory) for Freedomland's failure: "The public only learned much later (with no internet and social media at the time) that the investors had used the park as a placeholder to speed up the approval process to place high-rise apartment buildings on the land. The property was marshland and the Army Corps of Engineers would not provide immediate approval to build 23 and 30 story apartment buildings that NYC desperately needed to stem the white flight out of the city as the South Bronx was becoming an inner city disaster. The Army Corps stipulated that pilings had to be driven into the ground and monitored every five years for shifting with the currents from Eastchester Bay. Finally, through political pressure from city/state governments, the Teamsters Union and others, the Army Corps

indicated that if buildings three to five stories tall were built on the property and lasted without collapse, foundation issues and wall cracks for five years, then it would grant a variance to begin immediate construction of the apartments. Well, Freedomland as with any theme park had buildings three to five stories and the park lasted exactly five years. When Freedomland filed for bankruptcy, ownership presented the court with the plans for the housing project—Co-op City—that had been developed in the late 1950s. Freedomland, as we learned later, was a 'placeholder' for development of the land." Facebook, December 17, 2016, https://www.facebook.com/permalink.php?story_fbid=1314789965239709&id =246939775358072&comment_id=1316153705103335&reply_comment_id=131769844494 8861&comment_tracking=%7B%22tn%22%3A%22R1%22%7D; Zeckendorf, *Zeckendorf*, 291–292. Further correspondence with Michael Virgintino, author of a book about Freedomland, informed me that this conclusion was reached through interviews and recollections, though they had yet to find the "smoking gun" document to support it. See Nina Wohl, "Co-op City: The Dream and the Reality" (MA thesis, Columbia University, May 2016), https://academiccommons.columbia.edu/catalog/ac:199354, for a history of the housing development built on land where Freedomland had stood.

128. "New York Slates Huge Mid-income Housing Project: State, City to Help," *Wall Street Journal*, February 10, 1965, 5.

129. Vincent Cannato, *Ungovernable City* (New York: Basic Books, 2002), xiii.

130. Cannato, *Ungovernable City*, xii.

131. This impression comes from informal conversations with Peter Ashkenasy and with people who went on to become historians themselves, including Joshua B. Freeman, Richard K. Lieberman, Stephen Weinstein, Lisa Keller, Kenneth Jackson, and others.

132. Virgintino, "Memories of Freedomland," in *Freedomland U.S.A.*, 221–230.

CHAPTER 5 — SELLING MULTICULTURAL GIRLHOOD

1. Meghan Villhauer, "History of American Girl," http://www.agplaythings.com/his toryofag/historyofag.html.

2. Susan Porter Benson, Stephen Brier, and Roy Rosenzweig, eds., *Presenting the Past: Essays on History and The Public* (Philadelphia: Temple University Press, 1986); Thomas Frazier, *The Underside of American History*, 4th ed. (New York: Harcourt Brace Jovanovich, 1982); National Council on Public History, "Where Did Public History Come From?," https://ncph.org/what-is-public-history/about-the-field.

3. Peter Novick, *That Noble Dream: The "Objectivity Question" and the American Historical Profession* (New York: Cambridge University Press, 1988).

4. Diane Ravitch, *Left Behind: A Century of Battles over School Reform* (New York: Simon & Schuster, 2000), 421.

5. Ravitch, *Left Behind*, 421.

6. Wikipedia describes Christy's work as "characterized by . . . a strong sense of values." See https://en.wikipedia.org/wiki/Howard_Chandler_Christy.

7. Howard Chandler Christy, *The American Girl Seen and Portrayed* (New York: Moffat, Yard and Co., 1906), 11, 25–27.

8. Christy, *American Girl Seen and Portrayed*, 20.

9. Christy, *American Girl Seen and Portrayed*, 21.

10. Anne Morgan, *The American Girl: Her Education, Her Responsibility, Her Recreation, Her Future* (New York: Harper & Brothers, 1915), 6.

11. Morgan, *American Girl*, 12.

12. Morgan, *American Girl*, 9.

13. Patricia R. Smith, *Madame Alexander Collector's Doll* (Paducah, KY: Collector Books, 1978), 2.

14. Smith, *Madame Alexander*, 126.

15. "Display Ad 100," *New York Times*, November 15, 1959, 102.

16. See Daniel Thomas Cook, *The Commodification of Childhood: The Children's Clothing Industry and the Rise of the Child Consumer* (Durham, NC: Duke University Press, 2004), for a close study of the origins of the children's clothing industry and consumerism.

17. Pleasant T. Rowland's interest in history extended beyond the Pleasant Company. An alumna of Wells College in Aurora, New York, Rowland spent $40 million to restore the small college town. Although some residents criticized the renovations—filing lawsuits, spitting at, and cursing Rowland—the refurbished historic town drew tourists and faculty alike and contributed to an increase in the college's enrollment. Lisa Foderaro, "Doll's Village: Some See Restoration as Too Cutesy," *New York Times*, December 7, 2007, B1.

18. Foderaro, "Doll's Village," B1.

19. Mattel, "Annual Report" (2014), http://news.mattel.com/news/mattel-reports -fourth-quarter-and-full-year-2015-financial-results-and-declares-quarterly-dividend; Funding Universe, "American Girl, Inc. History," http://www.fundinguniverse.com /company-histories/american-girl-inc-history/.

20. American Girl, "Fast Facts," https://www.americangirl.com/shop/ag/fast-facts.

21. After the company changed to less durable boxes, customers complained of their dolls arriving damaged, and the company had to return to its older, sturdier boxes. Aimée Lutkin, "Those Upset about Not Being Able to Take Off American Girl Doll Underwear Have Been Vindicated," *Jezebel*, May 22, 2017, https://jezebel.com/those -upset-about-not-being-able-to-take-off-american-g-1795434687.

22. See American Girl website homepage, www.americangirl.com, accessed August 28, 2017, which provides the prices of the basic doll.

23. Based on personal recollections and conversations with American Girl doll owners and their parents, particularly Katie Uva on May 18, 2020, and Monica Schadlow on May 20, 2020.

24. Barbie had 108 careers by 2009. Abigail Jones, "Barbie Turns 50: The Ultimate Career Woman," *Forbes*, March 5, 2009, http://www.forbes.com/2009/03/05/barbie-careers -jobs-business_resume.html.

25. Heterosexual romance is not a part of any of the American Girl plots, although there have been a number of tongue-in-cheek articles about the dolls' "gayness." One piece points to the friendships and butch outfits featured in the books as evidence of burgeoning homosexuality. Peyton, "American Girl Dolls Ranked in Order of Gayness," *The Niche*, June 9, 2017, https://the-niche.blog/2017/07/09/american-girl-dolls -ranked-in-order-of-gayness/.

26. American Girl website, www.americangirl.com, accessed 2012.

27. Steven Mintz, *Huck's Raft: A History of American Childhood* (Cambridge, MA: Harvard University Press, 2004), 346.

28. See David Elkind, *The Hurried Child: Growing Up Too Fast Too Soon* (Cambridge, MA: Perseus, 1981).

29. Recently the company began offering the historical doll books with different titles from the original set.

30. Connie Porter, *Meet Addy: An American Girl* (Middleton, WI: Pleasant Company, 1993), 23.

31. Connie Porter, *Addy Learns a Lesson: "A Peek into the Past"* (Middleton, WI: Pleasant Company, 1993), 65.

32. Svetlana Boym, *The Future of Nostalgia* (New York: Basic Books, 2001), 15. Boym points out that such descriptors pose a problem for representing history. She notes that as the nation began to industrialize, certain descriptors came to represent certain eras and create a sense of "discreteness of the past" that was misleading.

33. Fredric Jameson, *Postmodernism, or The Culture of Late Capitalism* (Durham, NC: Duke University Press, 1991), 25. Elsewhere Jameson points out that the problem with these designations is that they "obliterate difference, and . . . project an idea of the historical period as massive homogeneity." In Michael Hardt and Kathi Weeks, eds., *The Jameson Reader* (Malden, MA: Blackwell, 2000), 191; Arjun Appardurai, *Modernity at Large: Cultural Dimensions of Globalization* (Minneapolis: University of Minnesota Press, 1996), 30.

34. American Girl website, www.americangirl.com, accessed July 14, 2016.

35. American Girl website, http://store.americangirl.com/agshop/html/item/id/142141 /uid/70, accessed September 23, 2012.

36. Allen Salkin, "American Girl's Journey to the Lower East Side," *New York Times,* May 24, 2009, ST1.

37. Salkin, "American Girls Journey."

38. American Girl website, "Rebecca Doll & Book," https://www.americangirl.com /shop/p/rebecca-doll-book-gjx51, accessed June 30, 2016.

39. "Toys Rn'tUs," *Black-ish,* March 9, 2017. For a review of this episode, see Sesali Bowen, "*Black-ish* Just Reminded Us Why Black Dolls Matter," *Refinery 29,* http://www .refinery29.com/2017/03/144519/blackish-recap-black-baby-dolls-matter-season-3 -episode-17.

40. Brit Bennet, "Addy Walker, American Girl," *Paris Review,* May 28, 2015, https:// www.theparisreview.org/blog/2015/05/28/addy-walker-american-girl/.

41. Emilie Zaslow, *Playing with America's Doll: A Cultural Analysis of the American Girl Collection* (New York: Palgrave Macmillan, 2017). See also Aisha Harris, "The Making of an American Girl," *Slate,* September 21, 2016, https://slate.com/culture/2016/09 /the-making-of-addy-walker-american-girls-first-black-doll.html.

42. For years, Samantha, the Victorian-era doll, was the most popular character. Perhaps this was because her Victorian-era accessories fit most closely with the princess culture so predominant in the United States. This doll was discontinued and then reintroduced, making two wealthy white characters, Samantha and Felicity, the Revolutionary War doll whose grandfather owns a plantation, the only remaining original historical doll characters available.

43. As Miriam Forman-Brunell points out in *Made to Play House,* girls will often dismiss the prescribed rules of play with dolls and create their own detailed and imaginative worlds and scenarios for their dolls. Forman-Brunell, *Made to Play House: Dolls and the Commercialization of American Girlhood, 1830–1930* (New Haven, CT: Yale University Press, 1993).

44. Lisa Mae Schlosser, "'Second Only to Barbie': Identity, Fiction and Non-fiction in the American Girl Collection," *MP: An Online Feminist Journal* 1 (May 20, 2006): 4, http://academinist.org/popular-culture.

45. John Berger, *Ways of Seeing* (London: Penguin, 1972), 153.

46. Schlosser, "'Second Only to Barbie,'" 5.

47. Fred Nielsen, "American History through the Eyes of the American Girls," *Journal of American & Comparative Cultures* 25 (2002): 87.

48. Nielsen, "American History," 88.

49. Nielsen, "American History," 88.

50. Lizabeth Cohen argues that in the postwar era consumerism was increasingly linked to "more social egalitarianism, more democratic participation, and more political freedom." Cohen, *A Consumers' Republic: The Politics of Mass Consumption in Postwar America* (New York: Knopf, 2003), 403.

51. Meg Jacobs, *Pocketbook Politics: Economic Citizenship in Twentieth-Century America* (Princeton, NJ: Princeton University Press, 2005).

52. Valerie Tripp, *Samantha Saves the Day: A Summer Story* (New York: Scholastic, 1988), 10; Porter, *Meet Addy*, 40.

53. For further exploration of this phenomenon, see Molly Rosner, "The American Girl Company and the Uses of Nostalgia in Children's Consumer Culture," *Jeunesse: Young People, Texts, Cultures* 6, no. 2 (December 2014), http://www.jeunessejournal.ca/index.php/yptc/article/view/223.

54. Porter, *Meet Addy*, 40.

55. Nielsen, "American History," 88–89.

56. Porter, *Addy Learns a Lesson*, 26.

57. Porter, *Addy Learns a Lesson*, 55.

58. Susan Adler, *Meet Samantha: An American Girl* (Middleton, WI: Pleasant Company, 1986), 34.

59. Adler, *Meet Samantha*, 35.

60. Porter, *Meet Addy*, 41.

61. Berger, *Ways of Seeing*, 90.

62. Nielsen, "American History," 90.

63. Karl Marx, *Capital: A Critique of Political Economy*, vol. 1 (1867; Chicago: Charles H. Kerr; reprint Minneola: Dover Publications, 2011).

64. Valerie Tripp, *Molly's Surprise* (Middleton, WI: Pleasant Company, 1986), 172.

65. The characters wanting or valuing a doll of their own is a recurring plot point, and most of the historical dolls have a smaller accompanying doll for sale in the catalogue.

66. Emilie Zaslow, "Moving from Sisterhood to Girl Power," in *APA Handbook on the Psychology of Women*, ed. Travis, Cheryl and Jackie White (Washington, DC: American Psychological Association, 2017), 60.

67. Christopher Lasch, *The Culture of Narcissism: American Life in the Age of Diminishing Expectations* (New York: W.W. Norton & Company, 1979; reprint 1991), 4.

68. Arjun Appadurai, *Modernity at Large: Cultural Dimensions of Globalization* (Minneapolis: University of Minnesota Press, 1996), 76-77.

69. John Berger, *Ways of Seeing* (London: Penguin, 1972), 139.

70. Amy Schiller, "American Girls Aren't Radical Anymore," *The Atlantic*, April 13, 2013; Molly Rosner, "American Girl: How Radical Can a $105 Doll Be?," *Huffington Post*, April 26, 2013.

71. Molly Rosner, "Playing Not-So-Nicely: Respectability Politics, *One Crazy Summer*'s Radical Black Girl Protagonist," *The Public Historian* 30, no. 1 (February 2021).

72. Kate Lombardi, "Each Girl a Felicity and Traveling through Time," *New York Times,* October 29, 2006, O1.

73. *Molly Learning Guide* (American Girl, 2012), 3.

CONCLUSION

1. Gary Schmidt, *Making Americans: Children's Literature from 1930 to 1960* (Iowa City: University of Iowa Press, 2013).

2. Julia Mickenberg, *Learning from the Left: Children's Literature, the Cold War, and Radical Politics in the United States* (New York: Oxford University Press, 2006).

3. Victoria M. Grieve, *Little Cold Warriors: American Childhood in the 1950s* (New York: Oxford University Press, 2018).

4. Walter Dean Myers, "Where Are the People of Color in Children's Books?," *New York Times,* March 16, 2014, SR1.

5. Center for Digital Research in the Humanities at the University of Nebraska—Lincoln, in conjunction with the Center for the Humanities at Washington University in St. Louis, "The Tar Baby and the Tomahawk: Race and Ethnic Images in American Children's Literature, 1880–1939," http://childlit.unl.edu/topics/edi.brownies.html.

6. Beryle Banfield, "Commitment to Change: The Council on Interracial Books for Children and the World of Children's Books," *African American Review* 32 (Spring 1998): 17.

7. Banfield, "Commitment to Change," 18.

8. Nancy Tolson, "The Role of Early Libraries, Librarians, and Booksellers in the Promotion of African American Children's Literature," *African American Review* 32 (Spring 1998): 9–16.

9. Joan Chrisler, "In Honor of *Sex Roles*: Reflections on the history and Development of the Journal," *Sex Roles* 63 (September 2010): 299–310, https://link.springer.com/article/10 .1007/s11199-010-9826-y. See also Roger Clark, Jessica Guilman, Paul Saucier, and Jocelyn Tavarez, "Two Steps Forward, One Step Back: The Presence of Female Characters and Gender Stereotyping in Award-Winning Picture Books between the 1930s and the 1960s," *Sex Roles* 49 (November 2003): 441–449.

10. Lenore Weitzman, Deborah Eiffler, Elizabeth Hokada, and Catherine Ross, "Sex-Role Socialization in Picture Books for Pre-school Children," *American Journal of Sociology* 77 (May 1972): 1125–1150, https://www-jstor-org.ezproxy.cul.columbia.edu/stable /2776222?seq=1#metadata_info_tab_contents.

11. Weitzman et al., "Sex-Role Socialization," 1146.

12. Debbie Reese, ed., "American Indians in Children's Literature," January 18, 2020, http://americanindiansinchildrensliterature.net.

13. Debbie Reese, "National Geographic's *Encyclopedia of American Indian History and Culture*, Not Recommended, Part 2," January 11, 2020, https://americanindiansin childrensliterature.blogspot.com/2020/01/national-geographics-encyclopedia-of .html.

14. David Rio and Øyunn Hestetun, "Introduction: Storytelling the West in Postfrontier Literature," *European Journal of American Studies* 6, no. 3 (2011), https://www.researchgate .net/publication/273183776_Introduction_Storying_the_West_in_Postfrontier_Lite rature.

15. Rio and Hestetun, "Introduction."

16. Cooperative Children's Book Center (CCBC), "Publishing Statistics on Children's/YA Books about People of Color and First/Native Nations Authors and Illustrators," November 21, 2019, https://ccbc.education.wisc.edu/books/pcstats.asp.

17. Walter Dean Myers, "Where Are the People of Color in Children's Books?," *New York Times*, March 16, 2014, SR1.

18. Elizabeth Chin, "Ethnically Correct Dolls: Toying with the Race Industry," *American Anthropologist* 101 (June 1999): 305–321, https://www.jstor.org/stable/683203.

19. Monticello website homepage, http://monticello.org, accessed May 2020..

20. Doreen St. Félix, "The Haunted Image of Harriet Tubman on the Twenty-Dollar Bill," *New Yorker*, June 18, 2019.

21. Michael Crowley, "Trump Calls for 'Patriotic Education' to Defend American History From the Left," *New York Times*, September 17, 2020.

22. Banfield, "Commitment to Change," 17.

23. Dana Goldstein, "Two States. Eight Textbooks. Two American Stories," *New York Times*, January 13, 2020, A14.

24. Valeria Luiselli, "The Wild West Meets the Southern Border," *New Yorker*, June 3, 2019.

25. Julius Lucus, "Can Slavery Reënactments Set Us Free?" *New Yorker*, February 17 and 24, 2020, 40–47.

26. Manuel Franz and Henning Jansen, "A Shining City and the Sodom Below: Historical Guilt and Personal Agency in BioShock Infinite," in *Playing the Field: Video Games and American Studies*, ed. Sascha Pöhlmann (Berlin: Walter de Gruyter, 2019), 221.

27. Óliver Pérez-Latorre and Mercè Oliva, "Video Games, Dystopia, and Neoliberalism: The Case of BioShock Infinite," *Games and Culture* 14, nos. 7–8 (2019): 781–800, 783.

28. Wikipedia, "BioShock Infinite," https://en.wikipedia.org/wiki/BioShock_Infinite.

29. Jason Sheehan, "Reading the Game: Bioshock Infinite," *All Tech Considered*, April 9, 2017, https://www.npr.org/sections/alltechconsidered/2017/04/09/523019414/reading-the-game-bioshock-infinite.

30. Franz and Jansen, "Shining City and the Sodom Below," 227. Along with video games, online consumption in the twenty-first century has changed the market and deserves further scholarly study. It is often unclear to parents how their children are engaging online. On the upside, children can create their own reviews and videos about the products they consume. The internet also provides children with the opportunity to participate in national conversations with other children who are consuming the same media. On the downside, the internet often exposes children to stereotypes, myths, and racist views about Americans and the country.

31. Pekka Mertala and Mikko Meriläinen, "The Best Game in the World: Exploring Young Children's Digital Game–Related Meaning-Making via Design Activity," *Global Studies of Childhood* 9, no. 4 (2019): 287.

32. "Mattel Takes a Hit as Barbie Sales Slump," *Wall Street Journal*, January 13, 2014.

33. Cheryl Williams, "The ROI of Play: Girls' Immaterial Labor, Smart Toys, and the Digital Economy," *Journal of the History of Childhood and Youth* 12, no. 3 (Fall 2019): 474.

34. Williams, "ROI of Play," 471.

35. Edward Hallett Carr, *What Is History?* (New York: Random House, 1961).

36. While adults may give children toys and books thinking they have a certain meaning, children manipulate, interpret, share, and use them in their own ways. In this sense toy makers, writers, and theme park designers cannot dictate, control, or predict what meaning children will derive from their products.

37. G. Stanley Hall, *Aspects of Child Life and Education* (New York: Appleton, 1921), 194.

Index

About the Author

MOLLY ROSNER received her PhD in American studies from Rutgers University–Newark, her MA in Oral History from Columbia University, and her BA from Wesleyan University. She has worked as an educator at cultural institutions and universities in New York City, where she was born and raised. She is at the LaGuardia and Wagner Archives at LaGuardia Community College/CUNY.